Y0-BRN-716

A gutsy, passion-filled, at times hilarious insight into the mind of one of the most creative and influential chefs of our time. It's brave to speak your mind. This book will bring about conversation, new ideas, question habits and points of view that will keep us evolving as an industry.
Jo Barrett

Like all things Shewry, this book is so sharp and timely, so full of purpose, yet somehow leaves you with a warm glow of nostalgia after every chapter. He's yet again perfected the art of perfecting something, and it's frankly infuriating.
Rhys Nicholson

Proof that you can throw away the rule book and live a life with a big heart, endless creativity, a mountain of integrity and, of course, lasagna. In doing just that, Ben has not only offered a blueprint for living, he's reimagined a new, better future for restaurants. Brilliant!
Myf Warhurst

Uses for Obsession is an essential piece of literature. Right next to RZA's *Wu-Tang Manual*.
Adam Briggs

A story of food and kitchens and passionate hope. No holding back, everything is here including the kitchen sink.
Uncle Bruce Pascoe

I fucking loved this book and I can't even poach an egg.
Hugh van Cuylenburg

This is not just about running one of the best restaurants in the world. *Uses for Obsession* could easily be a new handbook in life lessons. It's bold and authentic, enlightening and inspiring. And I now have a spiritual reverence for lasagne.
Jane Kennedy

Ben Shewry writes the way he cooks: with a voice that is disarming, inventive and entirely his own.
Erik Jensen

A raw, unfiltered journey into the heart of culinary passion; a collection of stories full of Ben's wit and introspection, which explore the profound depths of human creativity and connection.
Lennox Hastie

Ben's writing is brave, authentic and earthed. It teaches us the importance of honesty, keeping true to oneself, not being afraid of vulnerability and standing up for what you believe is right.
Jane Tewson

Ben understands the parallels of cooking and skateboarding in a way that is importantly unique; each requires constant practice, commitment, creativity, perseverance, and embracing failure as a lesson instead of a setback. It is obvious to those of us who have experienced the ingenuity of Attica, and it will be obvious to anyone that reads *UFO*. These stories resonate beyond cooking; they can be life lessons for anyone following their passion.
Tony Hawk

USES FOR OBSESSION

A (CHEF'S) MEMOIR

BEN SHEWRY

Published in 2024 by Murdoch Books, an imprint of Allen & Unwin

Copyright © Ben Shewry

All rights reserved. No part of this book may be reproduced or transmitted in any
form or by any means, electronic or mechanical, including photocopying, recording or
by any information storage and retrieval system, without prior permission in writing
from the publisher. The Australian Copyright Act 1968 (the Act) allows a maximum
of one chapter or 10 per cent of this book, whichever is the greater, to be photocopied
by any educational institution for its educational purposes provided that the
educational institution (or body that administers it) has given a remuneration notice
to the Copyright Agency (Australia) under the Act.

Murdoch Books Australia
Cammeraygal Country
83 Alexander Street,
Crows Nest NSW 2065
Phone: +61 (0)2 8425 0100
murdochbooks.com.au
info@murdochbooks.com.au

Murdoch Books UK
Ormond House,
26–27 Boswell Street,
London WC1N 3JZ
Phone: +44 (0) 20 8785 5995
murdochbooks.co.uk
info@murdochbooks.co.uk

A catalogue record for this
book is available from the
National Library of Australia

A catalogue record for this book is available from the British Library

ISBN 9 781 92261 684 5

Cover artwork courtesy of Paul Kremer
Author photo by Julian Kingma
Cover design by Daniel New
Typeset by Midland Typesetters
Printed and bound by CPI Group (UK) Ltd, Croydon CR0 4YY

Certain names and identifying characteristics have been changed to protect the
identities of those involved. Some dialogue and correspondence has been recreated.

Every reasonable effort has been made to trace the owners of copyright materials
in this book, but in some instances this has proven impossible. The author(s)
and publisher will be glad to receive information leading to more complete
acknowledgements in subsequent printings of the book and in the meantime extend
their apologies for any omissions.

We acknowledge that we meet and work on the traditional lands of the Cammeraygal
people of the Eora Nation and pay our respects to their elders past, present and future.

10 9 8 7 6 5 4 3 2

For Kylie, Kobe, Ella and Ruby

CONTENTS

PROLOGUE

It's 3am, and Jason and I are scrubbing. We're attacking the wall of a carbonised extraction hood with fat deposits that have grown like stalactites inside the roof of a cave. We continue, excitedly, in unison, to the rhythm of steel wool on stainless. Scrubbing for twelve hours straight. The joint is filthy. We've filled a bin with rotten food. We do tomorrow's ordering of lamb shoulders and bones, then sleep in the dining room for an hour, then scrub again.

Jason and I met in a different country, a different restaurant, a place we'll call hell. We didn't like each other to start with: he hated the new guy, I thought he was a jerk. Now we're best friends. Hell was a real place, unkempt and wild, unreasonable in workload and violent in nature. After hell, I convinced Jason to join me at my first head chef job, in a restaurant on its knees, a new kind of unrealised hell. Although we were too young to appreciate it, we were the last-ditch effort to redeem this place called Attica.

We start cooking, the hours creeping towards our destination, a solitary table for two at 7pm. A Sunbeam blender screams. We yell things at each other: pass me that; quick chop; fuck, that's not right! Our little engine room is spluttering, lumbering awkwardly towards an uncertain future. Fifty-two continuous hours of work for two, by two. We are nauseous from sleep deprivation. It's a feeling I know well, an unpleasant old friend. Days feel like years. Credit cards are constantly maxed out, calls to suppliers more and more desperate.

The owner wants to give up, not for the first time. I refuse. I can't.

I'm in way too deep. I've given too much of my life already to quit now. I avoid his calls, keep cooking. A melange of fear, relentlessness and depression comes over me. I push away much of it. Five years go by in a blur, then ten. I have no control over anything of importance. Through all of it, I do the only thing I can – I scrub, I cook. I try to polish the Attica stone. It must be better.

With Attica on the brink of bankruptcy, I become the owner in 2015, after a decade as an employee. For hospitality workers like myself, owning your own restaurant is a pipe dream. Our lives are organised in the service of others – owners, investors, customers – and, traditionally, we are some of the most overworked and lowest-paid people in society.

We aren't encouraged to learn how to run a restaurant. Most of us come from working-class backgrounds, and from a young age are warned that the business side is best left to those who understand it. Don't stick your head up, you're not worthy. This keeps us in our place, which is exactly where the owners want us to be, while they may never have done a day's work in a kitchen or on a dining-room floor.

I was a small, strange, bechamel-loving child who worked in kitchens from the age of ten, and whose confidence suffered unimaginably because I was taught that it was never my place to own a restaurant. But now, at 39 years of age, the unthinkable has happened – I've broken through, beaten the system and purchased Attica. This is the pinnacle of my career and the culminative end to a fear of business, to a feeling of unworthiness and self-denial. Although, in reality, it was just the start of a whole new set of challenges, and the beginning of a redesign of every aspect of how we work.

At my 43rd birthday lunch, I eat the most beautiful Cantonese food, a fillet of King George whiting with a fine batter so thin it's ethereal.

Then one of the greatest dishes ever served in Melbourne – a silken, fluffy crab omelette. I stuff these foods in my mouth, hoping that my stomach will hold them.

The most beautiful faces in the world are at the table, smiling at me expectantly. I smile back thinly. In a way I feel dead; the fear has me and I'm spiralling downwards, locked in its grip. I can't see stop signs. I can't reset. I feel utterly powerless. An unimaginable thing is happening and there is no way to change its trajectory.

The Covid storm has been gathering. In Japan, in January, we had heard whispers. It has been building for months, moving across land and sea, and now it's here. My anxiety has been rising; first little twinges like tiny electric shocks, but more recently full-fledged bolts of pain. I'm on the brink, despairing. At times, I'd felt I was able to see ahead of the curve, but now I'm completely and utterly lost. I cannot see a way out of this situation, and there's only one thing I'm certain of: that I will lose the restaurant I've given everything to. I have no safety net, no family wealth. My only asset is the beautiful thing we've built, a place that has made thousands of people happy.

Across my bowl of comforting fried rice, I attempt to fly my mind back to happier memories, like people tooting their cars as they drive past Attica. My infant children playing in the dining room while I prep, letters from guests that convey gratitude for life-changing meals. But there's no lasting comfort to grasp onto, as this darkness descends.

THE SOAP SMELLS NICE

As you walk through Italian customs with thousands of dollars' worth of beef tongues in your luggage, the trick is to appear supremely confident. Chin up, shoulders back, making absolutely no eye contact with anyone in a uniform. If, by unlucky chance, you are stopped and questioned about the contents of your luggage, stay calm and remember you have practised this lie in front of the mirror at home. Keep it as brief as possible. Do not fall into the wordy trap. Customs official: 'What are the contents of your luggage?' You: 'Clothing.' Official: 'Anything to declare?' You: 'Nothing.'

Twenty-four hours earlier, in Melbourne, our sous chef James and I had packed forty tongues into two ice-filled polystyrene boxes. We placed the sealed boxes into plain black suitcases, slim fit, as these seldom attract the interest of customs officials. My name is on both cases, so that if we get busted on entry into Italy, I will only have to pay one fine. It is a nervous wait at the Malpensa luggage carousels for the bags to reappear. My greatest fear is that the duct tape hasn't held and the bag will be soaking wet – a dead giveaway that I'm a chef smuggling food into a country I shouldn't be. This has happened before, my bag leaking a wet trail through the terminal.

Once I brought six large suitcases of food into LAX for an Attica event. As I awkwardly rolled the bags through customs, our team watching on, a particularly diligent customs officer asked me, 'What's in your luggage?' 'Clothing,' I said. The officer gave me a hard stare, then said, 'That's a lot of clothing for two weeks.' I shot an innocent look back, and said, 'I like clothes.' He hesitated for a long moment, his eyes hovering on my bags then said, 'Through you go.' I strolled on, like a supreme being. 'That, my friends, is how it's done.'

James and I unpack the tongues and stuff them into the bar fridges of our luxury hotel rooms in Milan. We are here to cook two dinners for the hotel, a showpiece for a luxury brand. Let's call it The Horrible Hotel. A suite here can cost as much as 33,000 euros a night. The rule of thumb is that the more expensive a hotel, the more avaricious it is. For every little incremental thing you use, there's a charge. The Horrible Hotel isn't horrible yet, but soon it will be. It will reveal itself the way the king-killing belladonna flower does, beautiful at first, but deadly when ingested, as it painfully sucks the life out of you.

Hotels seem purpose-built for screwing over chefs. At every moment of a shift, you are at the beck and call of whatever the hotel needs: breakfast service, lunch service, dinner service, 24-hour room service. Simultaneously, there could also be several private functions, a wedding, a conference. The pressure mounts in quick succession: an order for hot chips comes in from the bar; room service calls, two club sandwiches please, one no mayo with vegan bacon; where are the scones for the front-office afternoon tea? Has the picnic been packed for the guests that requested it? The staff canteen needs the bain-maries refilled. The wedding croquembouche is leaning dangerously to the left. Later it collapses. There are tears from the wedding party. At every hotel, where the work of numerous restaurants is rolled into one kitchen, a succinct word applies more strongly than in any other workplace: clusterfuck.

Knowing all of this intimately, I should have politely refused the invitation when it came, but the words 'Milano' and 'We will pay you' were too lovely to refuse.

Tongues now safely in fridges, James and I are encouraged to join the hotel's executive chef, Francesco, in the hotel bar for aperitivo. For the unversed, aperitivo is like a much better happy hour; instead of cheap drinks and drunks, there are delicious Italian snacks, and, if we are being *legítimo*, lower-alcohol drinks based on bitter liquor to 'open' the stomach before dinner. Walking into the bar, it is hard not to be intimidated. The early evening light paints an evangelical glow over the most beautiful throng of people I have ever seen, the glitterati. The men are in tailored but effortlessly casual silk or cashmere suits, handmade leather loafers showing their impeccably groomed ankles. The women are in ultra-refined and sharply cut dresses, their wet-look hair slicked back. It is a quintessential picture of Milanese sophistication. James and I are amazed.

But, very quickly, our conversation turns away from beauty and glamour. Francesco, in true hotel style, has ordered the fresh ingredients for our dinners a week early. They have perished and he is refusing to re-order them, presumably because the cost will come out of his food budget. James, a great diplomat, has been communicating respectfully, saying we can't use the spoiled produce, that he had asked for the produce to arrive the day before our dinners and it will need to be re-ordered, to which Francesco keeps repeating, *'No, non* lo faro' (No, I won't). At this point, there is only one option left: no new produce – no dinners. I tell Francesco that unless he organises the produce pronto, we are going on strike, and if he would prefer, I could speak to the hotel manager. Rancour flashes in his eyes, but he reluctantly agrees to re-order the produce. I have forced his hand, but there will be repercussions – in hotels, there always are.

We return to our rooms to sleep. I notice the expensive-looking hand soaps in my three Navona-travertine-lined bathrooms. I adore a good bar of hand soap, and these are magnificent, wrapped in delicate tissue. I'm not sure what Eau Parfumée means, but it sounds exclusive. The soaps come in fragrances of green, white and red tea, and I note that they are generously proportioned for a hotel – full-sized, not the usual stingy little round ones.

The following morning is the first day of prep in The Horrible Hotel's kitchen. From the moment we set foot inside the place, it is obvious we are not welcome nor wanted. Francesco has made it clear to his staff that no one is to say hello or help us in any way. James goes to the cool room to collect the beef bones for stock and returns dismayed – they have been stored on the floor. Someone else has ravaged the ingredients we brought with us from Australia – it looks like a break-in, our food thrown about the cool-room shelves. Regardless, we keep a positive attitude and think there must be someone who is nice and will help. I attempt to find a stockpot, but no one knows where they are. Later I find them hidden in a stair-well. I get into an argument when I request to use an empty pot on a chef's section. It's becoming clear that this is going to be difficult. At midday, Francesco begins his shift, and I approach him to ask where the chef assistants are that we'd agreed would help us prep. He gives me a blank look and says, 'We are short-staffed.'

At this point, I do the only thing I can. It's a move I've been keeping in case of emergency. I call God, a mega-famous chef associate who is basically like the Gandalf of Italy. If there's one thing that well-known chefs dislike, it's other chefs having a bad experience in their country. God answers; he is appalled and promises to talk to both the chef and the hotel manager. He says, 'Don't worry, Ben, everything is going to be ok – I will make sure of it. When you are finished, hop on the train and visit me.' I get off the phone feeling smug, as if I have just ordered a hit on a rival gang member.

Before we turn in for the night, James and I have a conference to sketch out how we can exact revenge on The Horrible Hotel for their poor treatment of us. I come up with the idea that we should take the lovely soaps. James thinks this is a bit lame – he'd prefer to put salt in their sugar bins – but, being a very timid anarchist, I convince James to agree to my plan instead. I have noticed that our rooms are serviced three times a day: once in the morning, again in the afternoon and then a final nightly turndown. We calculate that I could steal nine soaps per day from my room and, as James is slumming it with only two bathrooms, he could procure six. Chefs are not known for our high-level maths skills, but we figure we can extract seventy designer soaps during our stay. I am absolutely revelling in the audaciousness of our plan. We agree that when we wake up, we will remove all the soaps from the bathrooms, set a timer for a return soap raid to our rooms at noon, and then again at about 5pm, clearing out the soaps each time they are replaced. It feels amazing to be inflicting such a gruesome wound on The Horrible Hotel!

When we return to the prep area the next morning, a ghost-like Francesco is waiting for us at the kitchen door. Suddenly he is all smiles and pleasantries. It appears there has been a 'misunderstanding'.

He is very sorry for his rotten behaviour and intends to make amends. He says, 'Pleeese, pleeese, just talk to me from now on if there are any *problema*. Today you shall have four chefs to assist you, and tonight I want to take you to a Roman restaurant for dinner.' The hotel manager calls by to apologise; he says he was unaware of the situation but received a call overnight from 'someone' who asked him to straighten things out.

James and I are getting used to Italian traditions, and each night we stop in at the hotel bar for aperitivo. As the golden hour approaches, we decide to return once more. I notice the same group of glamorous Italians who were there the first night and the night after that, the very same suits and ankles, the same wet-look hair and Bottega Veneta dresses. I know something is up, it feels phoney. We bump into Francesco, and I ask him what's going on. He looks a bit uncomfortable, but I persist. He says they are just guests, Ben. I try again and finally he relents: the beautiful people, the little flock of lorikeets, are paid actors. They are hired by the hotel to sit in the bar and drink for free. I can't quite believe it but Francesco insists. The bar is a *teatro*! The hotel's marketing line is 'A meeting place for in-the-know Milanese'. No money for fresh produce or proper assistants, but a day rate for actors to sit in the front booth and put on this performance. The revelation hangs low and sticky, a Milanese smog.

Elsewhere at The Horrible Hotel things improve slightly, although the cooking is still dreadfully hard, as it often is outside of our own kitchen. The chefs don't have the skills required to produce Attica food and are constantly going for a *sigaretta* break, leaving James and I to do most of the work. The kitchen's bank of pasta cookers is not useful for cooking anything but pasta, and the cream – the cream is always an unpredictable stitch-up away from home. We flounder through the two dinners, the first a room full of Italian food media who seem totally mystified by my menu, and the second, paying local guests who find the cooking of two young chefs from Australia perplexing and largely inedible. Soap-stealing aside, there is a single truly good moment in the kitchen of The Horrible Hotel – I get to watch the chefs cooking pasta for room service. They are adding *acqua della pasta* (pasta cooking water) to the pan as they toss their deliberately undercooked pasta and emulsify it with the sauce as they finish cooking the pasta through. I am blown away by this simple, game-changing technique, called *mantecare*, and I use it to finish pasta at home to this day. (I realise this is now a well-known trick, but it wasn't widely known outside of Italy a decade ago. I promise.)

At Milano Centrale station James and I jump on a south-bound train to Emilia-Romagna, past endless views of intensive farms and factories growing, producing, packaging and manufacturing all manner of food, machinery and consumer products; the region accounts for more than half of Italy's exports. Parmigiano Reggiano cheese, Aceto Balsamico Tradizionale di Modena, Modena's incredible vinegar, and salumi, the divine smallgoods of Parma – mortadella and prosciutto – these are the heavenly foods we are most excited to eat. The high-speed train continues through a winter landscape of leafless stick trees and tilled fields on one side, and the pot-holed A1 autostrada on the other.

God stands proudly on the train station platform, wearing a North Face jacket. 'Welcome to Modena, Ben and James.' James is thrilled to meet him, and we have a table at his restaurant that night. Quite often, people who work in high-end restaurants can't afford to eat at them, and God is a chef James really looks up to. Just getting picked up from the train station by him is mind-blowing. Naturally, with all the hype that James has heard about God, his expectations are high, and he anticipates that this dinner will be one of the great meals of his life.

We zoom through the narrow streets of Modena, a small, elegant and affluent city that's home to Pavarotti and Ferrari and various World Heritage sites. In the car, I realise that this experience is much more important for James than it is for me. I've been to places like this before and some of these celestial chefs have become peers. We've cooked together at events around the world where I've eaten their food and I know what to expect from their restaurants. So, as the evening approaches, I become fascinated by how James will experience the restaurant. What does God mean to the uninitiated?

We call by Mercato Albinelli, the famed art nouveau market in the centre of town, for a snack before heading on to God's home. He shares a very large apartment with his family, and their collection of modern art – a riot of colours and styles – is truly flooring. This would be the envy of many international galleries. My art knowledge isn't extensive, but I am taken by God's genuine passion for his collection – he's a walking tornado of art history, dashing about the apartment, waving at this painting, then another, then another, without taking a breath. In his natural habitat, God himself is a work of art.

He is also obsessed with records. He throws a Billie Holiday record onto his mint-vintage Michell Transcriptor turntable and gestures to the huge wheel of Parmigiano Reggiano that sits majestically on its own table in the corner of the dining room. God shows us the way using a *tagliagrana*, a traditional almond-shaped parmesan knife. He breaks off a piece and pops it in James's mouth, then repeats the gesture with me. The flavour of the cheese is subterranean in its depth; it's one of the most wonderful things I've tasted. Hungrily, James and I hack at the wheel, stuffing our faces with lovely cheese, easily the finest parmesan either of us have tasted, barely coming up for a breath. God laughs at us and then says 'Guys, try this...' He whips out a bottle of his best aged balsamic vinegar and drizzles a little onto two golden nuggets of cheese. My God! It is incredible. Hundreds of years of synergy between two exceptional local products.

James and I grin at each other. He looks at his feet and says, quietly, 'How good is this?' But God is not done yet. Like Tigger, he bounces over to a meat slicer and says very seriously, 'Now guys, WAIT, WAIT! – I have the culatello.' 'Cula-what?' we ask. He explains that Culatello di Zibello, a cured ham made from a pig's buttocks, is the finest of all the cured pork products that Italy produces. It can only legally be made during the cooler months, from October to February, and is tied up in a pig's bladder and aged in a cellar. This culatello is the rarest from master maker Massimo Spigaroli, who makes it for Charles III, from the king's own pigs. God explains that, even for him, it's almost impossible to get: he has his name on only a handful of hams hanging in the feted Spigaroli cellar, an hour away in Polesine Parmense. He finely shaves the boneless, pear-shaped ham on the small slicer in his kitchen, rosy slices falling from the blade, and hands us both a piece. It's like looking through a stained-glass window – pure white streaks of fat against cured red meat, translucent and glistening. I place it in my mouth, and it vanishes into a lightly salted pork perfume. I feel immense gratitude; this is truly one of the greatest things I have eaten. He tells us that this particular culatello is so rare he considered not even giving it to us. It is fucking remarkable – not only the best ham I have ever tasted, but ham so good it deserves a category of its own: holy grail ham.

God and I have an over-the-phone business meeting with some other chefs, so James is left to wander about the house for a couple of hours; he is encouraged to continue to eat Parmigiano Reggiano. Our meeting, filled with chef-journalist politics, is about which country we are going to visit next with our chef collective. It's a little strained, as the organisers want to go where the money is, and the chefs want to go where the food is. As I'm young and a junior here, I let God and the others do the impassioned arguing on my behalf.

After a blissful afternoon of fine Emilian foods, God drives us back to our hotel. James and I wander around beautiful old Modena in a culatello afterglow, the soft light of early evening casting shadows from stone buildings in the narrow lanes we explore.

At 8pm, we skip in from the unassuming paved street for our reservation at God's restaurant. Although it does not yet have three Michelin stars, I can sense the formal ambition to attain them. God has made no secret of his ambition either: as an Italian, it means a lot to him to be recognised by the French. The atmosphere is serious, stuffy even. The waiters are stiff, and the small dining room is quiet and music-less. It's in sharp contrast to God's passionate and outgoing personality and taste.

The atmosphere makes James uncomfortable; he has his back up from the get-go – like a cat under attack, the hairs on the back of his neck have risen slightly. He is an exceptionally warm and caring person, which is why he is such a brilliant cook, and this environment doesn't gel with him. His whole heart is in all the food his hands touch, the sparkle in his eyes always showing that his mind is open and welcoming. His instinct is to lead with kindness, but when that is not reciprocated by the waiters – who will not speak to us, because of an archaic set of standards – it is felt as an affront.

God serves us a menu of his most famous dishes from over the years. They fly by, and with each one James becomes more and more disillusioned. Then arrives the most famous historical dish: 'Five ages of Parmigiano Reggiano in different textures and temperatures'.

Part soufflé, part sauce, part wafer, part airy foam, part mousse and, to James, all parts dissatisfaction. 'Ben, this afternoon we ate the most perfect version of this in the form the cheesemaker intended!' he says. 'This should be called "Five crimes against parmesan".'

James has a point. God had already served us the most perfect parmesan in its traditional form; how could he improve on it? Still, James is trying hard to enjoy it, airy foam and all. His way of cooking is founded in realism and deliciousness, and his view of food is in battle with this poet chef. He had hoped for a nice simple bowl of pasta, but instead got a multi-sensory parmesan experiment. We understand the revolution of an Italian chef taking a sacred product and turning it on its head, modernising it – a controversial thing to do back in the day, within a culture allergic to big changes. But, after our experiences today, what is the point of iconoclasm if something doesn't taste as good as the original product? Was it just being different for difference's sake?

I escape the tension at the table with a quick trip to the loo and am shocked by what appears to be a bag of rubbish sitting on the floor in a hallway. I look up to see pigeons sitting above it and laugh as I realise it's art: *Turisti*, a brilliant, hyper-realistic installation of taxidermy pigeons by Maurizio Cattelan, and a Gavin Turk work, cast in bronze and painted black to look like the real thing. I couldn't help wishing the entire restaurant experience was more like these works – looser, more fun and more punk. This is an outrageous move from God: by forcing two unrelated works to talk to each other, he seems to be saying, *Look at the art I have made from this art.*

We start to approach the end and it is announced that God himself will be serving dessert, the intriguingly named 'Camouflage: a Hare in the Woods'. Suddenly, he is at the table and yells, 'BEN, IT'S THE CAMOUFLAGE!' In a flurry, several plates are placed on the table, including 'Camouflage', a flat and thin dish on a rectangular plate that resembles an aerial photograph of an evil forest. God turns to face me. 'AND NOW! EAT THIS!' he says, as he pushes a giant spoonful directly into my mouth. The flavour is absolutely horrendous. I have an immediate gag reflex, but before I can take a breath, he yells, 'AND NOW! NONNA'S SWEET!' He grabs what appears to be a small biscuit and zooms it in after the 'Camouflage' like a parent 'flying' food into an infant's mouth. I am reeling. It is sweet and normal-tasting. 'AND NOW! BEN, ITALIAN COFFEE!' God yells, as he pours a large cup of coffee into my mouth, so strong the spoon could stand up in it. God continues his taste assault on me, completely ignoring James, to whom he has his back turned. James is left to 'enjoy' the dessert by himself, and, through my watery eyes, I can see that he is struggling, seething at the indignity of the dish.

God is not done with me, and another onslaught ensues, as he froths with the excitement only a true believer can conjure. It is extraordinary to see him in full flight, inches from my face, windmilling and gesticulating with such passion. Round after round of 'Camouflage' – a dessert based on hare's liver and blood, burnt ashes of vegetables and other bitter green, brown and black powders – is inflicted on me. I am outside my body by this point. I am floating above it all, watching from afar: a necromancer is feeding me and across the table sits poor, lovely, lonely James, his arms crossed, nostrils flared and eyes dark. Finally, God is done, and he leaves with a final triumphant flourish.

I am left in a deeply disturbed state. What the fuck just happened? I can't work out if I have just been assailed by a deranged megalomaniac, or subjected to one of the greatest works of art of my life. The intense iron funk of 'Camouflage' haunts my mouth. The unlikely combination of rather unpleasant tastes, countered with sweets, then bitter coffee, all served with the most intense energy, had completely redeemed, for me at least, what was otherwise an average meal. I believe in simple principles of interesting deliciousness above all else, but for 'Camouflage' I had to make an exception.

James and I hop on the train back to Milan for our last night, dropping off our bags at The Horrible Hotel and completing one last soap raid. We clock a slick-haired Bottega Veneta woman again at the bar so we bypass the hotel aperitivo and hit the streets of Milan. The next morning, our stay at The Horrible Hotel ends. As we check out, the receptionist hands me an invoice. I wasn't expecting to pay anything, as we were working guests. Scanning it quickly, my heart sinks – there is an 800-euro charge, written in Italian, and I can't decipher what it is for. I panic. 'James, quick, get the soaps out of our bags!' In a mad scramble, James uncovers our huge pillowcase full of soaps. I hold the pillowcase in one hand and attempt to negotiate. Total confusion ensues, as I try to force the soaps onto the receptionist, flapping and pointing at the 800-euro charge on the invoice, crossing my arms in an 'X', like an air traffic controller. Hearing the pandemonium, the office manager appears and asks in English, 'What is the matter?' I blurt out my desperation: 'I don't want to pay for the soaps!' The office manager looks at the invoice and calmly tells me there has been a mistake. Then, flashing a little, soul-crushing look of pity at James and me, he says: 'But you can keep the soaps...'

THE PURSUIT OF NOTHING IN THE PURSUIT OF EVERYTHING

In the beginning, there's always innocence. We stand in crisp white jackets, neckerchiefs and tall hats, a rank of awkward, bright-faced cockatoos. Our Swiss chef-tutor Beat is facing us, his copy of vaunted tome *Le Repertoire de la Cuisine* in hand. In militant French, Beat declaims, 'Even so much as a bubble the size of a pin head, and your crème caramels will be a complete failure.'

He made it clear on day one that we are not yet chefs. Right now we are *merde*, and *if* any of us made it to the end of our two years of full-time training we would still be *merde*. If we were very lucky, though, one day, after thousands of hours of experience, we might be able to call ourselves cooks. Not chefs, cooks. This information had been delivered to us with the subtlety of a car hitting a wall in a frontal crash test.

At this point in my young life, *Le Repertoire* is the smallest but most intimidating cookbook I've held. I am in Hamilton, New Zealand, but for the next two years, every time I set foot in the training kitchen I might as well be in France. In this exaggerated, angry, male-ego-driven faux-French world, controlled by tutors from France, Switzerland, Great Britain and Germany, there is only one language: la cuisine française. Here we pray daily to Auguste Escoffier, the one true culinary god and 'master of modern cookery', to whom *Le Repertoire* is dedicated.

My fondest memory of this time is of an onion that wasn't there. I remember Beat leaning into me and whispering, 'Onions are a vegetable that should never be seen.' I was making a pilaf, carefully guiding my knife through the fleshy leaves of the allium, tiny brunoise spitting out to the right of the blade. In a shallow copper pan I gently, tenderly sweated the onion in butter until translucent, the aroma an aperture to nirvana and nostalgia within this kitchen of fear. I added the rice, chicken stock, bay leaf and salt and brought it to a simmer on the French stovetop. A buttered cartouche was placed over the stock and my pilaf was carefully placed in the oven. Twenty minutes later, Beat inspected the dish. 'Bien,' he said, 'the onion is invisible.'

That phrase could sum up ambitious classical French cookery in its entirety. *The onion is invisible.* This is a cuisine of technique, and immediately I could see vast differences between the home cooking I had grown up with and this new French language of haute cuisine, where the cooking was all about rigorously imposing one's will onto the food through complex technique, often to the individual ingredients' detriment. Even at sixteen years old, it seemed to me that the French were taking the long way to the destination. They'd lay down their Michelin rubber on the *pavé* as they went, and sometimes, when they arrived, it was into a fog – the view obstructed by tradition, weight and stubborn ritual. We learnt that Brillat-Savarin, the early nineteenth-century icon who wrote *Physiologie du goût*, was obsessed with a dish of spinach, cooked across five days, in ten times its weight in butter. The cuisine was suffocated under dairy, eggs, salt, sugar and flour, and seemingly had a severe aversion to acid.

As I learnt the language of 'kitchen French' – the vocabulary of the classical foundations of French cookery: the mirepoix, chiffonnades, blanquettes, veloutés et al – I began to see I was cooking with words that were not mine, to make food that bore no resemblance to my culture, the culture of New Zealand, of Māori cooking culture, which I so admired, and the close-to-the-source cooking and eating rituals of my childhood. I could pronounce the names of recipes and master the technique, but I couldn't connect to their faraway origins, nor to the unobtainable ingredients in these books: caviar, bitter endive, globe artichokes and a cornucopia of unusual fruits. The stereotypical romance of French food wasn't so seductive for me, because when I cooked this cuisine I did not feel like myself. At this stage, I had no idea what my own cooking would be, but as I completed the two years of rigorous formal training, I did have the feeling that it would be the first and last time I would cook any of these dishes.

When everyone learns the same, everyone cooks the same. Today, fine dining is still dominated by French technique, and even when it doesn't appear French, it often is – discreetly hidden, like the onion, its practitioners barely understanding that fact. For me, the absence of self-expression and risk-taking leads to a sameness that underpins the dishes many fine-dining restaurants serve. I would rather pay to see someone really trying to lay themselves out on the plate and fail, than see a safe, well-executed, totally generic dish. Exhibit A: a small slice of perfectly cooked duck breast, a little classical sauce, a dab of puree, a constrained vegetable garnish. Food to fall asleep to. It's ironic that the term avant-garde is a French one.

My search for a style of cooking to love began at Arty Bees, a second-hand bookshop in Wellington. It was 1999 and Thomas Keller's *The French Laundry Cookbook* had just come out. Every young chef I knew had it, but I was looking for something different. I was rifling through the cookbook section when an out-of-print paperback jumped out at me. It was unlike any cookbook I'd seen before, and because it didn't contain a single photo, it seemed to have an internal confidence – a knowledge that it was a document of important recipes waiting to be found. The book appeared to be saying: *I have selected you, not the other way around. I will not beguile you with fancy imagery. Instead, I will reward you with depth and revelation not contained elsewhere.* The book was *Classic Thai Cuisine*, by David Thompson.

As I picked up this modest book, with its old-fashioned fonts, graceful hand drawings and knowing, sensitive words, I didn't know that it would be one of my life's sliding-door moments. I didn't know that within a few years I would invest all my savings to travel to three different countries pursuing its insights. I didn't know that, because of its words, I'd soon leave New Zealand for good.

I darted through the backstreets on my way home, clutching the book like a special gemstone. Soon, in my spare time, I'd cook every recipe it contained, examining each of David's carefully chosen words, striving to translate a cuisine he held in reverence. I'd buy every book on Thai cooking I could find. I'd barely ever met a Thai person, and never eaten at a serious Thai restaurant, but the cuisine was exhilarating, challenging, vigorous – cooking that kept me on my toes, that made me feel alive.

After a year of unsupervised practice, I planned a holiday to Sydney. I ate in fourteen restaurants in seven days, but there was only one real reason for this trip: Sailors Thai, David Thompson's restaurant at The Rocks. Brimming with enthusiasm and unwarranted confidence, I entered the dining room. As I'm prone to do, I ordered the whole menu. My first bite, a *miang* of betel leaf with prawn, galangal, fresh coconut and palm sugar, was a wormhole that instantly transported me to Bangkok. Dish after dish came out, and each one was like a punch in the face. They tasted nothing like the muddled dishes I'd tried to replicate back in Wellington. Their clarity was devastating.

It was one of the most important meals of my life, because it dawned on me that I couldn't learn this food from a book. I'd never eaten a more ruthlessly beautiful meal. The gap between the skill I thought I had and the skill I'd need to acquire was as wide as the Tasman Sea. But I was excited by the feeling of inferiority, a feeling I've always looked for, because it opened up my world, and showed me how much more there was to learn.

Based on that experience, I decided the only reasonable thing to do would be to move from New Zealand to Melbourne. Once I arrived, I realised that the first problem with this plan was that Melbourne was not Sydney. Although it pains me to write this, Sydney has long had a more established Thai restaurant scene than Melbourne. Unperturbed by my own foolishness, and the fact that I was possibly in the wrong city, I noticed that David Thompson had an upcoming class at the Prahran Market cooking school. Frantically, I reserved a spot.

Months later, I arrived at the school with a single ambition: to convince David Thompson to allow me to do work experience in his kitchen. David's second book, *Thai Food*, a hot-pink, silk-wrapped holy writ, had recently come out and had sent me into an absolute tizz. We took our seats, and David appeared and began to cook. I couldn't look away for a second. It was like watching a solar eclipse up close, his aura blinding us all. David cooked a series of dishes with an ease that belied the complexity of what he was doing, rattling off a stir-fried squid dish as black and deep as an M.C. Escher drawing, all while telling some witty, provocative story that had his audience in raptures. I sat at the back, shyly lapping up every word and delicious morsel. In what seemed like seconds, the lesson was over, and everyone was thanking and hugging David, and having their photo taken with him. When it was my turn, all that came out of my mouth was a stuttered, 'Thank you'. My eyes moistened and my courage evaporated. I left without saying anything.

As I walked down Commercial Road, I fumed at myself. What a failure I was, how stupid. I yelled at myself aloud: 'You are fucking weak. Go back in, dammit!' With that, I turned and scurried back to the school. When I found David was still there, I was relieved and terrified. I paused to grab a glass of wine and downed it in one go. Then I went up to him and said, 'Excuse me, Mr Thompson. My name is Ben. I'm a chef, and I wondered if you ever allowed people to do work experience in your kitchens?'

His response surprised me. He told me to call him David, and that of course he took chefs on work experience. 'My best cooking is at Nahm in London now,' he said. 'I'd recommend that you visit me there. Here's my email address. Contact me when you are ready.'

I wanted to hug him tightly, but instead I just stood and beamed. Leaving the school for the second time that day was one of the happiest moments of my life.

Over the next year in Melbourne, I saved and scraped together enough money to fly to London. True to his word, David responded to my emails to organise a start date. I flew into Heathrow on a Sunday and, first thing the following morning, I turned up at the Nahm kitchen door, where I was greeted by confused looks from the kitchen team. They had not been told I was coming, and it took 24 hours of panic on my part for the misunderstanding to be resolved.

I spent six life-changing weeks in the Nahm kitchen, working every hour it was open. On Tuesdays we would unpack the week's produce, all selected by a member of David's family in Bangkok and delivered to Nahm in under 24 hours. Brown coconuts would be cracked, shucked, peeled, grated, soaked, pressed and skimmed for fresh coconut cream. Half would be sent to the pastry section for my all-time favourite dessert, *kao niaw muun* (mango and sticky rice), or the ultra-tricky *kanom krok*, a dish of coconut pancakes that everyone struggled to make except for David's partner, Tanongsak, an accomplished Thai pastry chef. The other half of the coconut cream would be used for soups, or 'cracked' for curries. Live Cornish crabs would be boiled and picked for their sweet meat, which was used in omelettes, relishes, curries and salads. Mountains of aromatic Thai herbs would be picked – *pak chii* (coriander leaf and roots), *bai grapao* (holy basil), *bai horapha* (Thai basil), *bai dtoei horm* (pandan leaf) and *pak chii farang* (sawtooth coriander), among others. Different curries were gently cooked in a row, lined up across the stoves, including my favourite, *geng mussaman*, rich with coconut cream, tender beef shin and waxy potatoes, and with its accompaniment of *kai kem* (salty eggs).

Countless *bai makrut* lime leaves needed to be shredded as finely as strands of hair. In my first week, I was toiling away at it, and finding it very difficult, when David walked by and noticed my chunky slicing: 'That's not to our standard,' he told me. I was crestfallen, but another chef said, 'Mate, you've got the wrong knife. Those French knives are no good, you need a Victorinox.' Later that afternoon, David called by my section again to pass me a snack – a ball of rice coated with fried shallots. I bit into it eagerly as David stood back, watching and smiling. In the centre he had hidden a whole scud, a potent small green chilli, named after the scud missile for good reason. David laughed hysterically as I struggled to calm the fire in my mouth. He popped a small handful of scuds in his mouth as if they were M&M's and walked off chewing, grimacing and shaking his head, like the sick chilli masochist he is. The following day I kicked my Sabatier to the kerb and bought a new rosewood-handled Victorinox cook's knife. Thin blade in hand, my shredding improved, and I was off and running.

The kitchen was short-staffed, and soon they had me running the larder section – something that was unimaginable to me. One day, a film crew came to shoot David cooking, and I had set up the section for him to cook a *pat prik king muu bpaa*, a stir-fried curry of pork with snake beans, green peppercorns and chilli paste. When they arrived, he looked at me, grinning, and said, 'You cook it, chef.' I did as I was told, while David giggled. Like the whole experience of cooking at Nahm, and like the man himself, it was a deeply kind and unexpected thrill that I've never forgotten. Although David is easily one of the most intelligent and gifted chefs I have ever worked with, there was a focused nonchalance to his energy. His food was always exacting, and he was absolutely relentless in his commitment to honour Thai cooking, but he also had a rapscallion sense of humour that could bring real joy to his kitchen. He saw potential in people and, even though he was at the height of his career and had the demands of many full-time staff, he took me – a nothing work-experience kid from New Zealand – under his wing. He treated me as an individual and a friend.

David first learnt to cook Thai food in Thailand, under Sombat Janphetchara, whose mother had trained as a cook at a royal palace. Here he was introduced to Thai memorial books, which are handed out at a person's funeral and document their life, often including ancient ceremonial recipes that were seldom cooked or seen. Across four decades, David has amassed a collection of more than 600 memorial books, and the preservation of the culture surrounding them has become his life's work.

After all the time I'd spent obsessing over Thai cooking, it started to become obvious that I needed to go to the source. So, after six weeks in the Nahm kitchen, I headed to Thailand to stay with the Taengphuak family (friends of my fellow chef Jason), who owned a fish farm an hour out of Bangkok. The farm had several ponds where the family farmed freshwater fish. On the first morning, I helped the other young men as we walked a drag net through a pond. As the tallest, I was placed in the deepest part of the pond. I walked on my toes to keep my head above the water. At first there didn't appear to be many fish in the pond but slowly, as we moved through the water, the fish started to appear ahead of us, and by the last third of the pond there were so many that they were jumping out of the water, back over the net, and slapping me in the face as we hauled the catch in. The live fish were loaded into the back of a small truck and we headed off to market.

It amazed me that even along deserted country roads there were street-food vendors. Our truck pulled up at the family's favourite *khao lam* stall, where an elderly woman grilled sections of bamboo stuffed with sticky rice, palm sugar, black beans and salt. Several deft blows with a cleaver and she cracked one open for each of us. I tore at the sweet, custardy, smoke-perfumed rice, its succulent bamboo flavour beautifully balanced with salt. The use of salt in Thai desserts is ingenious, adding complexity, where many of their European counterparts lack interest through blind devotion to cream and sugar.

At Talaad Thai, the largest wholesale market in Southeast Asia, we began to unload the fish, when an argument broke out.

An unscrupulous fish wholesaler had promised one price before we'd left the farm, but upon arrival he told the family that the price was now half of what he'd offered. They had no choice but to accept it, as the fish were now dead. They told me this happened frequently, and the stress it put them under was obvious.

I spent a morning walking around the sprawling market, chomping on *chomphu* (Thai rose apple), rambutans, mangosteens and other treats. There was a hall of dozens of fragrant curries in brass woks, where I ate, for the equivalent of 25 cents, a plate of green curry with pea eggplants, which was right up in my grill delicious: pungent with krachai, shrimp paste and fistfuls of Thai basil and lime leaves. I was humbled by it because it was so little money, but the quality and intensity of flavour was so immense. It was a lesson to me as a cook, one that I'd learn again and again. When I cook a curry now, I make it count, so I don't insult the purity of this memory.

My host family also took me to the coastal city of Pattaya, where for days I ate everything I saw. I'd mentioned that my favourite dessert was mango and sticky rice, and they sadly informed me that it wasn't mango season – though that didn't stop them looking for it everywhere we went. After a dawn-to-dusk street-food mission, they took me for dinner at the one fancy restaurant in town, where the food wasn't as good as it was on the streets. I ate a really funky relish that had been pounded with fermented fish eggs. The weeks of intense eating finally began to catch up with me, and my *farang* (foreigner) stomach could no longer handle it. I politely said I needed to retire for the evening, but I could feel a tidal wave of nausea approaching from the distance.

I'd been lying down for a short time when I heard animated voices outside my room. My kind-hearted hosts had scootered around Pattaya, looking everywhere for my favourite dessert and had finally found mango and sticky rice. They were feverish with excitement. I opened the door, on the cusp of vomiting, to three expectant faces holding out the plate. I gratefully accepted the food and, forcing a smile, dug a spoon into it. I took one mouthful, then ran for the toilet, where I'd stay for the next twelve hours, hallucinations swirling around the room. At one point I thought I might die, but looking back, that mouthful was totally worth it. Two days later, I was still so sick that I had to cancel a catch-up with David in Bangkok, and instead, I ate Burger King in misery by myself.

When I returned to Melbourne in 2003, for the next few years I intensified my study of Thai cookery. It completely owned me; it drove me wild with its intensity and complexity. I studied it on every day off, as well as before and often after work. Unlike European cuisines that slavishly follow written recipes, it is a cuisine of the mind. I was transfixed by it, mesmerised, addicted. You could say I did my unofficial culinary master's on Thai cuisine, but one can never really master it. There are way too many variables – like staring into a glow-worm cave of thousands of luminescent little stars, each of them with essential meaning and importance. At its highest level, it is without a doubt the most complicated cooking – it's a total brain-fuck, as it makes you submit to the most rigorous level of seasoning. It requires ten thousand lasers to come out of your eyes at the same time, each one of them analysing the details of each tiny glowing light in the constellation, and then you need to make small, precise adjustments to flavour to balance them all at once. Thais call this seasoning *rot chart* – how something tastes. Learning *rot chart* drove me close to the edge of madness.

Much of my study took place in a tiny apartment I was renting on Fitzroy Street, St Kilda. Compared to New Zealand, Australia had a bounty of Thai ingredients available, and I installed a high-powered wok burner on my internal courtyard balcony. Once the wok was fired up, the whole apartment complex would be overcome with the redolent fragrances of toasted spices, garlic, shrimp paste, palm sugar, fish sauce and more. I could hear my neighbours' coughing fits as I emitted waves of capsaicin into the air from woks full of charred dried red chillies. Inside, solid brass woks for coconut cream sat on the stovetop, and my collection of pestle and mortars made from stone, clay and wood were strewn everywhere. A coconut grating stool sat in front of the TV, so I could grate as I watched *The O.C.* Styrofoam chilly bins lined the tiny apartment entrance to hold all the extra ingredients that my bulging fridge couldn't contain.

Rising up the stairwell was the piercing aroma of wok hei ('the breath of the wok'), and fermentations of pork, chilli and glutinous rice. (Before fermentation became a trendy chef thing, then a trendy everybody thing, it was and is a normal everyday part of other people's ancient living cultures; it's just a way of preserving food.) There were also the sounds of constant violence coming from the pounding of my pestle and mortar, competing with the aggressive noise of Fugazi, who blared through my two-channel lounge-room stereo every time I cooked. I attempted, as best I could, to smooth the ruffled feathers of my long-suffering neighbours with curry.

I was not trying to master Thai cuisine; I knew that for a *farang* living outside of Thailand, that was impossible. But I did want to grasp a decent understanding of it, and I'd learnt from David that you could never care too much about its intricacies. Unlike other professions, culinary school is brief, and compared to, say, becoming a doctor, it's completely unstructured. Therefore, further learning needs to be undertaken largely on your own and, if you're lucky, on the job. The level to which you push yourself to learn outside what you know will dictate the level to which you can rise. And the good news is, you can follow what excites you, down any road it takes you.

Less is never more. Cooks and chefs have a centuries-old habit of under-intellectualising what they do, aligning with a centuries-old tradition in which we are kept in our places, within the service economy. Save for a few lucky ones, who by no small miracle break through.

This is where things began to get really wild. I'd always prioritised self-expression over higher-paying jobs, and many people early in my journey saw something in my strangeness and supported it. These fine cooks had provided me with just a little bit of freedom, by allowing me to write recipes for their menus, or carve margarine sculptures for the buffet, or cook strange dishes for governor-generals. They had let me cut buckets of capsicum julienne when I was hired to make nachos for drunk students – and, in doing so, had allowed me to be myself. Every single job I've ever had, I've whittled out a little creativity on the side. When I started at Attica in 2005, I was set free, with no restraints, I wanted to honour the trust all those great people had shown me.

My first menu at Attica had several Thai dishes, including the informally named 'plate of insanity', a dish of seven traditional Thai sweets. This drove Jason nuts because I spent half of each day making this one course, while he laboured on the other seventeen-odd dishes that completed the menu. After six months of working between two cultures, I began to feel that my cooking wasn't evolving. I couldn't bring myself to mash my Thai learnings together with the western dishes on the menu. With western cultures, I felt free to torment recipes, but Thai food had become sacred to me. The rules for Thai food were not imposed by Thai people onto me directly, but they were ones I'd enforce upon myself out of respect. The recipes that make up the Thai pantheon had evolved over many centuries and in my mind were already flawless. I felt I had nothing to add. So rather than insult this majestic cuisine or continue to replicate its classics, I let it enrich my own cooking through a heightened knowledge of seasoning and more intimacy with ingredients. These were vital skills that I didn't receive from my earlier French education, but without them I would not be me.

My fascination with smoke in the Attica kitchen began in late 2005, when I saw an old fridge on the side of the road and dragged it into the backyard. I looked at the fridge and thought it would make a great cold smoker. I would call what followed 'my smoke phase', where I smoked *everything*: butter, cheese, olive oil, water, cream, eggs, fish, meats of all kinds, even flour. If it was food, it went in my smoker. Our menu must have tasted like a bonfire. Within two months the interior of the fridge had melted, so I purchased a second-hand stainless-steel fridge, cut a hole in the side, piped in the smoke via a 44-gallon drum with a burner, and turned the fridge on. *Boom!* I had real cold smoke at 4°C. This took my smoke obsession to new heights, and by 2007 I had inflicted my studies upon a clear broth of trout.

This dish, a holy trinity of smoke, was based on a smoked trout broth, with small slices of smoked trout, pork crackling and sorrel. It arrived at the table encapsulated within a glass dome of fresh smoke that, upon release, filled the personal space of the guest with, well, more smoke. People were mesmerised by this dish. It really seemed to capture the imagination. I didn't conceive of it as a provocation – the smoke was there to deliver the freshest, smokiest experience possible, and, while I'm sure some of our customers felt like they were trying to escape a housefire, it was not there for whimsy but for flavour.

I held back from explaining how I'd been getting the fine smoke in the glass dome, partly because I had been using an electric bong. I used woodchips instead of marijuana, and the bong's fan blew the smoke in a powerful stream that I directed under the dome. The only problem was that the bong wasn't designed for resinous wood, and so the kitchen was burning out a couple of bongs a week. The local bong shop loved us so much they began to offer a discount.

Finding one's own creative rhythm takes patience, dedication to practice, and lots of time. As I began to find it, I realised that creative rhythm could be set into forward motion and, like a snowball, it would build. It's a constant thing, too – nearly anyone can do it for a couple of years, but if you want to innovate continuously, you need to work at it. True innovation requires dead ends, and you have to be willing to walk down them. You'll lose large parts of your life to it: the pursuit of nothing in the pursuit of everything. The craft becomes like a mania. If it's personal and really matters, you will be unable to pull yourself away, gripped by an addiction to the creative practice of it. It can cost you a lot, but to me, this is freedom – the freedom to cook by my own rules, the freedom to be ambitious, the freedom to fail and succeed on my own terms.

Across the years, I learnt to really listen to the ingredients. What did they want to say? What could they tell me? What could I learn from studying them? How could I use that knowledge to cook better? In 2009, as I began to work on the dish that would become our most significant of the decade, I kept coming back to one question: what did the potato want to say? Growing up, I had spent time at the Mōkau marae's wharenui (meeting house). Here I had learnt of the importance of taewa (potato) in hāngī, where food is traditionally cooked in an earth oven. The symbiosis that potatoes have with their home, the soil, was obvious to me. Potatoes taste different if they are grown in sandy coastal loam or rich alluvial plains. As the potatoes grow, the soil provides flavour. The terroir of potatoes! For me, the logical step was returning a potato to the soil that it grew in, to cook and flavour it further. Inspired by the dozens of hāngī of my youth, I began to experiment with every variety of potato I could lay my hands on.

Across four months we tested over thirty varieties, and as many soils, developing our cookery method in Attica's old gas oven, subtly nicknamed 'the flamethrower', with its two temperature settings – incineration or pilot-light warm. We tested backwards and forwards between both until we had time and temperatures locked in and, within two months, we had a major breakthrough – a technique for cooking a potato with an unprecedented, moist, creamy uniformity, end to end. A fortunate side discovery was that soil is a wonderful conductor of heat. The other components – a soft, delicately smoked goat's and cow's milk curd, coconut husk ash, coarsely ground coffee, salty chicken floss, fried saltbush and a single leaf of watercress – were selected to highlight and amplify the potato, and to support memories of the primal act of eating from a charred hole in the earth.

At this point in time, potatoes were considered an accompaniment food, the second or third thought in any dish. There were no courses on menus that made potato the protagonist. More often than not, potatoes were dredged through butter and cream in a gratin, or baked and stuffed with sour cream, cheese and chilli, or braised in a rich curry or stew, or fried and drowned in gravy. All these dishes are absolutely charming, but none of them, not one, lets the potato truly speak.

I named this new dish: 'A simple dish of potato cooked in the earth it was grown'. For the first few months it was not what anyone would call a commercial success. Quite a few of our guests couldn't understand why there was a course comprising a solitary potato on the menu, and they responded with feedback along the lines of 'Where's the meat, mate?' or 'I'd like a side of steak with that.'

Many times at Attica I have held on while we lost customers. This is always income that we need, but more than money, I can't afford to lose sight of who we are. The fight for creative freedom requires you to hold your nerve against the expectations of the market, no matter what your market is. There has been no other way for me, because I am pursuing the thing I love – running an ambitious restaurant. I played the long game, because if I buckled and conceived of a more fashionable menu, I knew this would become a line of work that would slowly kill me. I've rolled the dice on my ability to create a market for my own creative freedom. There have been innumerable moments of self-doubt but, in the end, my feeling of self-belief – the belief that I was the expert on what we were cooking, and that eventually our customers would come around – was stronger. Each night that we open our door to welcome our guests, we earn the right to do so again.

If fine dining is fitting into a neat box of expectations, a commodity that is easy to digest and describe, and requires little thought or engagement to understand, then fuck that. I don't care what fine dining is, because it does not fit what I do, and what I do is the best feeling in the world. It's the pure, can't-mess-with-us, hard-earned feeling of freedom that comes from pursuing your dreams with unconditional love. If I had any advice, it would be this: be brave, don't let anyone tear you down, and fight each day to protect your ability to keep your dreams close. Whether that's in a restaurant or elsewhere, it doesn't matter. Find *your* thrilling inner feeling.

NEW USES FOR POWERPOINT PRESENTATIONS

I was contemplating breaking my own rule. I tried to convince myself that the rule was unreasonable. Inhuman even: indecent, certainly cruel and definitely against natural instincts. But despite my justifications, I still felt severely conflicted. I'd set the rule for good reason, hadn't I? Yes, I had. Written it into our constitution, hadn't I? Yes, I had.

Years before I'd made the rule, we'd had a few sets of couples working in the restaurant, and they'd brought their relationship issues to work – drama-town. They were like a wild bunch of teenagers, fuelled by caffeinated soft drinks, dopamine and Kendrick Lamar. It had affected our ability to do our jobs.

The question was, if I relaxed the rule, would the floodgates open? And if I broke my own rule, what did that say about me?

The rule in question was Attica's awkward no-shagging-the-staff rule.

I walked home and smiled. I thought of our conversation earlier that day: we'd been getting deep on the merits of toothpaste, and the differences between bars of soap and liquid bodywash. I thought to myself that if we could have a fascinating conversation on the most boring things in the world, then we could have a conversation about anything. My stupid heart bounced around like a jester on a pogo stick.

I'd begun to have feelings for Kylie, Attica's operations manager. I'd recently come out of a twenty-year relationship and I had no idea how to act, how to feel or what to do around a potential love interest. The massive dilemma in my mind was this: Kylie, with her strong intellect, creative problem-solving abilities and sense of fairness, had become invaluable to the business, and I had the highest regard for her professionalism. I was acutely aware of my position of power, and the mess I would make if I told Kylie I had feelings for her and she didn't feel the same way.

I tried to push the feelings away as a form of post-separation madness. I tried to tell myself that my feelings for her were ridiculous, that we seemed so different. But no matter how I attempted to talk myself down from this love-ledge, I couldn't get away from the undeniable feeling. I am aware that I am perhaps the most awkward romantic prospect, incapable of identifying if someone is interested in me, totally oblivious when someone is flirting, completely and utterly useless at recognising the intimate feelings of another. Part of that is my dislike for sleazy men, and part of it is my inexperience and lack of confidence with potential partners.

So, for weeks and months I worried constantly about what I should do, given the shitstorm I could create if I didn't handle it delicately. I knew that there was a decent chance Kylie might feel she had to leave a job she loved. I knew the power imbalance between us at work, with myself as the owner of the business. Then one day it came to me, the answer to all my problems, the way out of this tricky situation.

Now, for every good idea of mine that is shared, there are at least fifty other explosively ridiculous ones that should never, ever see the light of day, such is their high-voltage cringe-worthiness. This is one of the fifty. The idea was simple enough: I would make a PowerPoint presentation to win Kylie's heart.

My reasoning was this: when the scary moment finally came and I was forced to tell her to her face that I thought that she was the most awesome person I had ever met, I would be prepared – albeit like a business exec who has put in the strategic groundwork for a company takeover. If it looked like her decision was going down to the wire, then I could whip out my PowerPoint and lay down a *BUT...HAVE YOU CONSIDERED ALL OF THIS?*

Like the most clumsy, awkward, love-struck business-school graduate, I would flash my 112(!) digital slides, detailing all of the merits, reasons, benefits and delights of my proposal. My presentation was titled 'So here's the thing, Kylie Staddon'. It started with the opening slide, 'When I began to write these, I wanted to convince you that I was worthy of your affection' and included the arrow-straight-to-the-heart winning declaration, 'I'll build Ikea furniture for you'. There was the more serious 'Even the quiets are comfortable with you' and the intentionally corny 'You are a magnet and I'm a piece of steel'.

I intended to bring it home with a series of irrefutably charming slides: 'And so even if you don't feel anything for me, I'd want you to see and hear this' (real big of me), 'Because just maybe you'd realise this once how truly special you are' (because that's a new one), 'And I'd want you to know this moving forward' (so unselfish), 'It's been said (by Death Cab for Cutie) that fear is the heart of love'(!!!), wrapping it up with 'But I'm not scared (well, maybe a little of your uppercut)', and finally, 'But whatever you decide, I'll respect your decision and not act like a dick if you aren't interested'.

Mercifully, over the natural course of time, it became obvious, even to this romantically blind goofball, that we'd both fallen in love. The realisation that Kylie felt the same way about me was a wonder. We went shopping for laptops together and spent the whole time smiling at each other. Must have been hell for the Apple Genius. Although I didn't need to book a function room, set up an AV screen, lay out finger sandwiches and muffins, flick the switch on the tea urn and make sure the clicker had fresh batteries, the PowerPoint did come in handy as comic relief a week after we'd gotten together, when I told Kylie about it. She was keen to see it but a little bit nervous, and afterwards she said she found it 'surprising', 'kind of funny' and 'sweet'.

Four years later, I proposed while we were on holiday in France. In a continuation of my smooth moves, I nearly dropped the ring in Lake Annecy before blundering the proposal by beginning, in a serious tone, 'I need to talk to you about something important.' Once I clarified that I wasn't terminally ill, Kylie said yes.

So a rule was ditched and we got hitched. We were really worried about telling everyone, but they were so happy for us. It was lovely. If I look back now and try to understand why she went for me, I'd have to attribute it to the lasting and foundational power of my PowerPoint.

IN DEFENCE
OF WAITERS

On a quiet autumn evening in 2006, a doctor and his wife arrived at the restaurant for dinner. They celebrated with champagne on arrival, as it was a happy occasion: the doctor's birthday. Dinner commenced, and all was well because the couple were being looked after by one of the kindest people I have ever worked with, a young woman we'll call Amy.

Amy is the child of immigrant parents who had fled persecution to move to Australia to build a better life for their daughter. She had started as a part-time food runner in restaurants when she was a law student but, like a moth to a light, she found the hospitality life captivating. To the great despair of her family, Amy dropped out of university to pursue work as a full-time waiter. (In the country where her parents are from, cooking and serving aren't always a privilege of choice, and waiting is viewed as one of the lowest-class occupations.) Many years had passed, and Amy had travelled the world, gaining experience in some of the best dining rooms – this had become her life's work. Amy loved to make other people happy, and her customers loved her back. Her quick smile, warm personality and ability to remember the names of repeat guests were just some of the many reasons. Chefs adored Amy for her humility and sharp wit, but also because she seldom made mistakes. Amy was killing it. She had become a great waiter.

The doctor and his wife were enjoying their main course: lamb shoulder gently simmered in olive oil for hours until meltingly tender and pressed into a salty slab, before being cut into a brick shape. Crusted with coriander seeds and black pepper, the lamb was fried until golden and crispy. Together with its loving friends – parsnip puree, buttered silverbeet, currants, pine nuts and lamb sauce – if there was ever an offering to the gods of meat, this was surely it.

All was calm and well in the dining room. The doctor and his wife were enthralled by the bottle of wine Amy had recommended: a 2004 Pinot Noir from Alan and Nelly Cooper's low-impact vineyard, Cobar Ridge. Sitting at another table alongside the doctor and his wife, two friends were also immersed in their meal, enjoying the same wine. Amy, noticing that the doctor's wine glass requires topping up, takes three steps to the waiter's station, where both bottles are sitting. White linen in hand, Amy elegantly pours some of the fine Pinot into the doctor's glass, its dark ruby lapping the crystal. Within a microsecond, Amy realises she has poured from the wrong bottle. Her body pulses with the jolt of the mistake. Immediately she stops, offers an apology, and quickly moves to open a new bottle for each table, on the house. During a calamity, Amy knows it is essential to maintain focus, although hidden deep in her gut, Amy is feeling the physical manifestations of her split-second error, a dreadful feeling that we all know too well. But the doctor is now up half a bottle of wine – it is over, and it should end here.

However, the doctor becomes enraged, his anger escalating exponentially in the thirty seconds that it takes Amy to replace the bottle. As Amy returns to the table, he admonishes her; frothy at the mouth, he screams, 'You are completely fucking useless.' His wife sits silent, her eyes and hands on her lap. Before Amy has time to react, the doctor leaps up from his seat and, with a few broad strides, crosses the threshold of the dining room to the bar, where he picks up an open bottle of wine and throws it onto the concrete floor. Then he storms out of the restaurant. The restaurant manager rushes to the door and locks it behind him. In a second, the doctor is back at the door, hammering his fist into it. 'Let me in, you bastards,' he hisses. The restaurant manager tells him through the glass that he cannot come back in. He screams, 'Give me my car keys!' The manager refuses entry again. In the way a petrol-laced bonfire explodes, the doctor is engulfed by his rage and begins to kick the door in, smashing the bottom glass pane. But this door formerly served a bank, and eventually he gives up, yelling as a parting shot, 'Fuck you, I'm going to take the train.' At the table, the doctor's wife has been sitting silently through the entire episode, a picture of docility. Without a word, an apology, or even a whisper, she calmly takes out her credit card, settles the bill and departs in the car.

We call the police, and the officers who arrive are caring and sympathetic. They inform us that the doctor will be obliged to cover the cost of the damage, and they give Amy the choice of pressing charges or allowing him to apologise to her in writing. Being the exceptionally kind person she is, and genuinely not wanting to 'ruin' his life, she decides that the latter will suffice. Although I would really like her to press charges, I understand not to push – Amy does not want to relive any of this. The police go to the doctor's house to issue him a warning and the doctor writes Amy a letter. It arrives in the mail, and we read it together. I will never forget a line he wrote, on quality white paper with his medical practice's letterhead, in his pathetic attempt at an apology:

'Amy, it wasn't all your fault.'

Amy no longer works in hospitality.
Amy is many waiters.
Amy is almost always a woman.
The doctor is almost always a man.

You can tell everything you need to know about a person by the way they treat a waiter. I wish I could tell you that everyone treats waiters with the respect they deserve, but I would be lying. At times, waiters make an easy target for guests who have had a bad day, who are too entitled, or who think they have some form of ownership over the waiter due to the cost of a meal at the restaurant. Waiters belong to one of few occupations (including any based on the premise that the customer is always right) where it is considered socially acceptable, in some circles, to behave unreasonably towards them.

To me, and I don't say this lightly, the profession of the highly skilled waiter is one of the most graceful on the planet. Great waiters walk on rarefied air across their stage, the dining room, as they navigate humanity with the insight of a psychologist, the diplomacy of a Nobel Peace Prize winner, the intimacy of a best friend and the patience of a saint. All of this while carrying themselves with the humility of someone who has seen it all, and with impeccable personal grooming and dress sense. In unison, they can move with the elegance of the ballet corps, they can read a room like a socialite from a Jane Austen novel, and tell a story as if they were a direct descendant of Homer. On demand, and within a split second, they must be able to articulately share their knowledge about thousands of details, from food, to wine, to the art on the walls, and even the carpet on the floor (which, at Attica, in case you are wondering, was made in Geelong).

At their core is the most noble of causes: the strongest possible desire to make other people happy. This would be an achievement in itself if they were serving just one person, but skilled waiters must make this happen for ten or more people at once. Make no mistake, this is a deeply intellectual and emotionally draining undertaking, and one I am in awe of every single night, in part because I know I do not possess the skills required. (Many years ago, during a rocky period, I had to work in the dining room most nights for eight months, in a sort of hybrid waiter-chef role. I tried to compensate for my lack of authority as a waiter with my personality – but honestly, I sucked.) Waiters are responsible for some of the greatest times of my life. When experiencing a waiter's excellence dining out, I go out of my way to verbally acknowledge this excellence and always tip as much as I can – it's a matter of respect, of saying *I SEE YOU*.

Apathy from diners is especially tough on waiters because they are continuously asking themselves, are their guests happy? The newest form of apathy is customers glued to their phone the entire meal, ignoring the person trying to serve them. What can a waiter do with that? Nothing. It leaves them feeling unresolved because they are fuelled by the exchange of energy from the people they are serving. And it is utter madness from the diner's point of view, because a great waiter is your personal hedonistic agent for the evening. Who in their right mind would want to do anything to hinder another human being whose primary goal is your happiness? On a purely selfish level, it makes absolutely no sense!

Often, even chefs don't properly acknowledge waiters, and the view from my side of the pass is that chefs have historically per-petuated much more violence against waiters, than waiters have against chefs. Chefs need to understand that no matter how well they cook, it won't have the required gravity unless it's delivered with the dignity of a great waiter. Chefs can hide behind the kitchen wall;

waiters are at the coalface and must deal with the chef's mistakes. Who cops it from the customer if the food is slow to arrive, or isn't up to scratch? Not the chef. Chefs should acknowledge this kinship of interdependence and be more grateful for it.

How many average meals have you had that were redeemed by superb service? I've had plenty. But for me there have been no brilliant, ambitious restaurant meals, no matter how wonderful the cooking, where the service was bad. Dining outcomes are determined by service; the waiters are the human interface of a restaurant. It is dreadfully sad to think that in their professional capacity, and occasionally in social situations, they are made to feel bad about their vocation, as if it were a temporary option not befitting a serious career choice. As I've said, being a waiter is an incredibly difficult and stressful job. It's a vastly underrated skill and a valuable service to our society.

Chefs are celebrated the world over, but the chances are if you've had an amazing time in a restaurant, it was because of the waiters who served you. Waiters like Amy.

NEVER GIVE UP

Shadows hang over my 43rd birthday. In the distance, words are being spoken. The person speaking is Kylie, but it might as well be a stranger. I am lost in my own dark thoughts and grief. She's optimistic and persistent: 'We should give takeaway a go. Come on, baby, let's give it a go.' I respond with a touch of anger. I can't see how the small amount of income from takeaway could cover the wages of our forty employees. I remember saying something like, 'You must be kidding if you think that takeaway could save Attica. It will never happen.' Kylie continues, unperturbed. She's like that. 'We have to do something,' she says. 'Everything you've built, are you prepared to let it go?' In this moment, I believe I am – even though I've fought so hard to keep us afloat against the odds, I can't see a way of surviving with our dining room about to close.

Kylie isn't, though, and she's doing everything she can to lift me up, the way we always do for each other, even if she really doesn't believe it herself. She's following our unspoken rule: no matter how bad it gets, only one of us is allowed to be down. She's showing her real character, the character that saw her become the first-ever female blackbelt at her Muay Thai gym as a child. Her strength in this time will define her. It will spit out all the arseholes who denied her, who abused and underestimated her because she's a 'strong woman'. She will shed the self-doubt those powerful men inflicted on her and show her true self to all those around her – powerful and capable of making brilliant, split-second decisions. Her decisiveness will be like a comet, blazing through our community and acting as a template for adapting and managing a business in crisis. Even with all her intelligence, she will deflect the praise onto me and others, never seeking the tiniest bit for herself.

I go to sleep drained and exhausted. When I wake there's an email from my friend and business mentor, Bruce Dunlevie, an American gentleman in the truest sense of the word – he seems as if he comes from another, more decent time. Bruce co-founded Benchmark Capital, an investment firm in San Francisco whose string of start-up hits includes Twitter, Uber, eBay, Instagram and Dropbox. His email is brief, but it hits me hard, right between the eyes: 'Stay positive and radiate that to others.'

Seven words that change my life forever. Seven words that, for the next two years, I'll live by. The quality and brevity of his words, and Bruce's timing, is immensely significant. If Bruce hadn't sent that email, would Attica have survived? Would I be writing this book?

I don't know. Should I have just listened to Kylie earlier? Of course I should have. I acted like a man-child, turning my birthday into a pity party. But from the moment I received Bruce's message and started following Kylie's advice, everything began to change.

That Monday morning, I get out of my own way and finally agree with Kylie wholeheartedly: let's do this! Let's immediately turn Attica, a restaurant known for its exacting standards and singular vision of a multi-course tasting menu, into a takeaway and delivery business, serving lasagne with garlic bread and some of the most beloved dishes from across our fifteen-year history, with a bake shop hustle on the side. Not the first thing people would associate with Attica, but what do we have to lose? Absolutely nothing. By doing nothing we were going to lose the business anyway, so why not try something? Our mindset was, we might as well go down with a fight. How do we do it? No idea! But I recall Kylie's absolute excitement: to be planning to do something, anything, in the face of such gloom was energising, and that gave us something positive to work towards.

We are given five days before the restaurant has to shut down. They are five long and very hard days for our team. We have to cancel three months' worth of reservations and serve our current guests in a half-empty dining room, with a manic sense of impending doom in the air. I am like a man possessed, sawing up our tabletops to make a service counter for a bake shop, drawing up takeaway menu plans using the same standard of ingredients as in our restaurant menus, and utilising all of the skill and intelligence of the kitchen team, some of the finest young cooking minds in the world. I become a force of unrelenting positivity, running around motivating and consoling the team, who are experiencing the grief and fear of having to close down the restaurant. 'We'll be ok, you'll see. We've got to take care of each other, stay positive, focus on the present. It's the only thing we have any control over.' Even if I didn't know that was true, I'd say it, and the more I said it, the more true it felt. Stay positive, radiate calm.

The role of a leader in a crisis is to shelter those in your care from the storm. You should not be judged by how you lead in the good times, but how you handle the bad. No matter how bad things got, I didn't let them know; I protected them from the anxiety of my life and the company, because putting it all on them would be neither fair nor helpful. They had a job to do and their own sanity to keep, and over-sharing has been the failing of many a leader, myself included in the past.

Although I didn't admit it to anyone but Kylie, I set my first big goal: to keep every single member of our staff on full wages for the duration. I thought that if we could achieve that, then it would really be something to look back on. In that moment, when all around us businesses were being forced to close, it seemed like a ridiculous thing to attempt. This singular idea became everything to me, my whole reason for being. I had at times asked them to walk to hell and back with me before; would I bloody well stand up and do the same for them now, in their time of need?

It would have been much easier to fold up shop and blame it on the situation. But if Attica failed, half of our team, who were on visas, would be stuck in Australia with no help from the government and no family to turn to, with no employment to pay their rent with and ultimately no way of surviving. I took this responsibility personally. Let me carry this load. Judge me now. Radiate positivity. What sort of person am I? Will I be the leader that I said I am, the leader I promised I would be? Yes, I have to. I will do everything within my power to will this to happen. I shall be fucking defiant.

I spray paint 'Never Give Up' on the walls of the dining room and kitchen. Everything begins moving at the speed of light, and in a blink I am back to the early years here, to the memories of Jason and me in the kitchen by ourselves, scrubbing, scrubbing, scrubbing. I'm back in the countless harrowing stories of near-failure, the blood under the fingernails, the vomiting in the backyard, the hundred-hour weeks, the blur of everything. The restaurant that was never supposed to be, that shouldn't have survived, that wouldn't give people steak with their potatoes; the restaurant I was told was no good, where a guy once looked at the menu and said, 'Whoever wrote this must be on fucking speed.' We're still here, though. We succeeded against the odds. All that history was just preparation. This moment became the reason I went through all of that – it was the training for now.

Our action is swift. Thousands and thousands of biodegradable takeaway containers, in myriad shapes and sizes, are stacked up on warehousing racks – a sharp contrast to the beautiful walls of the dining room. All the restaurant's tables are pushed together in a snaking line that stretches from one end of the dining room to the other, the chairs stacked in our storage locker. The office is converted into an HQ for the new takeaway business, with Kylie at its nucleus – the conductor, manually working out the hundreds of delivery routes for the day, helping to build the online ordering infrastructure with our IT partners.

And oh, the stickers! Stickers to the high heavens, of all kinds and colours, with every conceivable allergy and menu component printed on them! Kitchen fridges are moved to the dining room to store prepared food. Our chefs are on their phones to friends all around town – 'Do you have any 100-litre stockpots we can borrow?' – then jumping in their cars to pick up whatever they have tracked down. There are endless questions for me, like, 'Chef, our wooden spoons are tiny in these big pots, can we please buy some big ones?' My son Kobe and I drive around for hours to collect a stupidly heavy 20-litre food mixer and a set of warming drawers borrowed from a friend's hotel.

The staff room turns into a dry store for all the extra food. Fine-dining cooking equipment like the Pacojet, pairs of tweezers and our magnificent handmade crockery is removed from the main kitchen and stored in the backyard, no longer relevant for this new business. I build a makeshift bakery next door to the restaurant, using stuff that was lying around and a track saw. There are a million trips to Bunnings to buy Perspex for screens. We park a second cool room on a trailer in our car park, which is only meant to stay for a month but ends up being there for two years. Everywhere you look, there's action – swarms of worker bees frantically preparing for a new way of life.

The exquisite madness of it all, the powerful belief in people coming together in the face of adversity, was at the heart of everything. Kylie and I knew that if we didn't put our people at the core of this, there would be no restaurant to return to. Attica was, is and always will be made by these exceptional people. I began to suspect that this was actually a once-in-a-lifetime opportunity, and I fully immersed myself in it. I will never forget the scenes of chaos and destruction at Attica. It was hard to comprehend in those moments, but after years of feeling frustrated with the system of external influences that affect a restaurant but aren't necessary, the damage marked a pendulum swing towards the honesty I craved.

In a quiet lull, Kylie and I wondered if all these efforts would turn out to be pointless. Under my ownership, Attica had always been community-minded, but you wouldn't have heard much about it; it's not written about on our website, nor posted on Instagram. It happened, quietly, privately, involving only our staff and a particular person or cause close to our hearts. I don't believe in making people who could use help 'sing for their supper', any more than I believe that if you do a good deed you should expect something in return, whether in the form of publicity or goodwill. Kindness is a privilege of those who are in the position to give it. Fundamentally, I believe that one function of a business is to be a force for good in your community – contributing, not just taking. In this brief moment of self-doubt, before we launched our takeaway, we sat in the office and Kylie said, 'Do you think anyone will care about us in our time of need, Ben?' She looked at me. 'I'm not sure,' I replied nervously.

Ostensibly, there were much bigger problems in the world than a restaurant under threat. I now feel like an idiot for doubting the love and goodwill of our community, because as Kylie pressed play on the ordering function of our new website and sent that first mailout, and as I posted our first menu on Instagram, the response was overwhelming. On the first day of the bake shop, the queue wrapped around the block. In a tender moment I shall keep with me always, a woman who had been waiting for hours for a slice of cake said to me, 'I have lost my job. I know what you stand for, you're a community guy, and I wanted to come here and support you with a little bit of money from my last pay.' She burst into tears, and we hugged and cried together, right there in our little makeshift bakery. I just couldn't believe that this person would choose to do that with the little money she had left. She could never know what that incredibly generous gesture meant to me.

In hindsight, it might seem obvious that takeaway was going to work, but to us it definitely wasn't. Maybe our fears helped us: a bit of controlled anxiety can be useful; it means you care. Conversely, if you automatically think you are going to crush something, then often that very arrogance means the opposite happens.

We launched Attica Bake Shop and Attica at Home on the same morning. I had been up for three days straight, baking cakes and rolling pasta through the night, powered by an endless stream of lattes and nervous hope. On the beginning of that first day, as four of us frantically served people in the bake shop, Kylie busied herself setting the first night's delivery runs – alongside a team of thirty-five, who were working like mad to prepare the night's delivery. Normally with a new business you have months to think about what you will do, and the ability to do trials and test runs. Yet here we were, with only a couple of days to set this whole thing up and fire it out into the world.

We lined up our highly skilled and trained front-of-house staff as co-pilot delivery drivers – dressed up to the nines for service, just as they would be in the restaurant, because I wanted to keep as much routine in people's lives as possible. If we were going to do this, then it had to be the absolute best meal-delivery service we could muster. If someone rocked up at your door in a suit, with a giant smile, a fine bottle of red and a lovingly prepared meal in hand, how would you feel?

Our other major point of difference was that we'd decided to cook food to order, then quickly pack it and head out on the road with a delivery run of several orders, to be delivered within fifteen-minute time slots, as chosen by the customer. Like everything else we have ever done in business, it was exceptionally ambitious and quite naïve. We had no real idea of how many orders we could deliver in one run while keeping the food warm and still staying on time. We had attempted to time the delivery runs using Google Maps, but there were so many hidden variables. Kylie did an astonishing job of planning the routes and sequencing of the deliveries – all done manually each morning and taking many hours of her time. Each driver would have a scheduled list of addresses to go to, and on arrival at the address the co-pilot would jump out of the vehicle, run around to the back and put together the customer's order from a packing list, taking into account what menu or menus they had ordered, grabbing food from hot boxes and cold boxes, factoring in their allergy requests, and adding any wine, beer or non-alcoholic drinks or baked cheesecake additions. Kylie would say it was a logistical minefield; I'd call it a complete mind-fuck.

On the very first night of Attica at Home, Kylie and I teamed up to do a delivery run of ten addresses in Southbank, an area close to Melbourne's city centre that is all modern high-rise apartment blocks. We hopped in the car, full of nervous excitement. This was to be the first night of our plan to save our business. Kylie drove to the first address on our schedule and I jumped out to pack the first order, sprint to the building and call the customer through a street-side intercom. 'Please come up,' they said. It took five minutes to get through the security door, into the elevator and up to their apartment. At the second delivery address, I couldn't get hold of the customer through their intercom, so I called their phone. They didn't pick up. I texted them. They didn't respond. Fuck! We'd lost ten minutes already. I couldn't wait any longer, so I ran back to the car, and we began to drive to the third address, when the person from the second address called me back, 'Sorry, I had my phone on silent,' they said. 'That's ok,' I said, but inside I was saying it most certainly wasn't fucking ok. We turned around, drove back to the second address and made the delivery. Now we were thirty minutes behind schedule, and dread was creeping in. Kylie was saying, 'Don't worry, we'll get back on track.' I dug my nails into the dashboard. We hustled through the next three deliveries and outside the sixth address I packed the order and ran up to drop it off. We were forty-five minutes late, but they were just grateful and happy to see us, which gave us a little lift. We headed to the next location. A call came through on my phone: the last address we delivered to was missing a bottle of wine from their order. *SHIT-FUCK-OH-NO.* We stopped and looked for the wine, but we didn't have it in the car. It hadn't been packed. *OH-NO, OH MY GOD.* We were on the cusp of a meltdown. I called Attica and our head chef, Matt Boyle, said, 'Yep, no worries, Ben, I'll jump in the car and deliver it.'

With each delivery we were getting further and further behind, and now calls were starting to come through to Attica. With no sign of their dinner being delivered, people were rightfully beginning to get upset – this was not what they, or we, expected from Attica. By the eighth delivery we were an hour and a half late. All was silent in the delivery car now, an abyss of smashed hopes and dreams. Would this relentless night never end? Mercifully, almost two hours behind schedule, we got to the finish, with cold food. Embarrassingly, I suggested to the final customer that they warm their dishes in the oven, as though it was meant to be like this all along, but I wasn't fooling anyone.

Our night from hell ended, and we pulled into the bumpy cobbled lane behind Attica. Kylie parked the car and turned off the engine. I was angry. 'We failed. We fucking failed. This is not our fucking standard!' I was venting, but there was no need for me to say anything: Kylie knew it as well as I did. The situation was so far below our expectations that it made me feel like vomiting. My self-loathing kicked in hard: *You are a fucking worthless piece of shit. What a fucking cunt you are.* We sat in silence for a minute that felt like an hour. Kylie began to cry first, just a glistening of her eyes caught in the backyard lumination, and then the shoulder-raising convulsions of full-fledged sobbing. My heart cracked, because she was so distraught. She was carrying so much of this. I dissolved into tears as well, and we grasped at each other, crying uncontrollably. Two despairing souls, completely and utterly lost.

WHAT WOULD
YO LA TENGO DO?

As we step from the darkness to the beach, the light blinds us. The stock tunnel – cut through the bluff so that livestock could be driven onto the beach and into boats – is wet and black, always. Without it, we would never be here. Nature has designed it so we shouldn't. There is danger everywhere: angry black sands, pitted volcanic reefs, the scent of kelp and sea water churning and spitting into the air. Dad points to where the English invaders would have loaded their livestock onto boats waiting to take the sheep and cattle to market, through the currents and unpredictable surf. As we tramp up the beach, bare feet sinking into iron sand, I hold my father's large hand. We walk past the rocks where two sets of fathers and sons were taken by the ocean. We dive into the drowning sea, flat-head screwdrivers in hand.

At first, the saltwater stings my eyes as I try to look around. Dad tells me to be patient: 'You'll see them, they are hiding.' I spot one pretending to be a rock, dappled in coral-like seaweed. As I kick down to reach it, depth exaggerates distance and I bump the pāua – clumsy pākehā! The mollusc tenses, locking its muscular foot onto the reef. It knows I'm here and I mean harm. I come up for air, then go back down, battling the strong current. This time I manage to prise the stubborn abalone off its rock. I come up to show Dad, who firmly says, 'It's too small, Ben. You have to put that back.' But the underwater hunt is a frequency illusion – once you've seen one pāua, they are everywhere. There are hundreds in our small area; we collect our limit of ten.

This is part of a family ritual. Driftwood is gathered and Dad builds a small fire. While waiting for the wood to turn to embers, he shucks the pāua with a pocket knife, removing the guts and tooth. Dad places the pāua in an old rugby sock and bashes it onto a smooth rock, over and over, until it is tender. As the coals turn ash-white, Dad grills the pāua on the old steel plate he carries around in the Kingswood, always at the ready for a beach feed.

Back at the car park is a lone station wagon, its tailgate open. I cast a look sideways and see that the back is loaded with pāua, hundreds of them. I feel sick to my stomach. Even a ten-year-old knows that this is wrong. I sense my father's rage and I worry about what he will do if he finds whoever took them. I've seen him dealing with illegal duck hunters on our farm. Dad thinks the culprits have fled: 'Must have heard us coming and hid amongst the flax.' There's nothing that can be done now anyway: those pāua are all dead, some two years old and undersize, some fifty and enormous. The sea is a way of life for many remote coastal people, the larder for those without access to shops. As Dad said, these selfish bastards risk ruining this precious resource for the whole community.

Twenty years later, I return to Whareorino with my five-year-old son Kobe, hoping to re-enact this tradition, but pāua no longer live here. I dive over and over, to near-exhaustion, desperate to find one, but this majestic, wild place has been 'stripped out', and in the place of abalone are kina. There are thousands of the spiky sea urchins, like underwater fields of globe artichokes. Kina has taken over, hoovering up all the soft algae that pāua depend on to survive. Kina's natural predator, koura (crayfish), is also overfished, and so with nothing to keep their numbers down, the kina spread. The greed of poachers has decimated this coastal ecosystem. It feels like no part of the world is safe from humans. It feels cruel attempting to explain this to Kobe, who cannot grasp why people would take every last one. It's unlikely that pāua will ever return to their home here, where they were once abundant, where they have lived for millions of years. On the way home, we drive past the Maniaroa marae (meeting grounds) and I think about how it must break the local iwi's heart. My family's ritual has ended here, but, much more tragically, sacred Māori culture and its ancestral and legal birthright to pāua and the sea had been broken.

Before dawn, I drive along the Great Ocean Road in Victoria, Australia, in the hope of sharing my father's pāua ritual with Kobe, who's six now. He is talking non-stop about the toilet paper we brought with us; he seems more excited about it than our adventure. Our small crew of four lugs film gear to a remote bay. We are making *Kobe and the Sea*, a short film I've written about the passing down of knowledge through generations of Shewrys, the destruction of the ocean, and the human disconnection with marine life. The ocean in front of us is untameable, violent and atmospheric – perfect for what we are about to make.

Today's project is a momentary escape from the desperation of my situation. Depression and looming bankruptcy are constant companions. Making short films is a creative outlet outside of the pressure and monotony of the kitchen. It's the way that I, as an introvert, find it easiest to gently communicate my dreams, experiences and feelings to the world.

The film is intended as a call to return to nature, for my family and for others. It briefly examines how the ethics of our food are hidden from us, like the abalone hiding beneath the surface of the sea. It's also a return to my childhood, with parents who taught their children to live with the land; before everything in my life felt out of control, there were quiet, vital memories of connection to and respect for the earth. The friction between the food we *need to eat*, and the food we *do eat* was always outlined by my father, with his rule that we were never to take more than we needed for a meal. I wanted to impart a little of that sense of custodianship to Kobe. In the film we make a meal from abalone, wild coastal plants, roasted bull kelp and handmade sea salt, cooked over fire on the beach.

Well before filming commenced, I had chosen a song for the soundtrack. I used it to visualise the script in my mind, over and over, for years. It is a song so completely and utterly perfect that I cannot imagine another song doing the film justice. It's called 'Green Arrow', by the iconic New Jersey indie rock band Yo La Tengo. An instrumental track, it remains, to this day, my favourite piece of music, and Yo La Tengo my all-time favourite band. Ira Kaplan's searching surf guitar glides across James McNew's gentle bass to the backdrop of crickets in the evening and a soft, gentle shaker. The song builds and when Georgia Hubley's atmospheric drumming kicks in towards the end, it reaches a calm but powerful climax. It's a reflective and deeply felt song that allows the listener to imagine they are watching a movie of their own life.

I make the film with my talented friends Johnny and Colin, who shoot, direct and edit, and we post it to YouTube. There is a tenderness and tension between the delicate filmmaking, the gentle song, the rugged beauty of the coastline, the imperfection of parenting, and the hopes and fears I have for Kobe's generation and the environment they are inheriting.

One of the distinct pleasures of running a creative restaurant is that it attracts many other creative people, from all walks of life, including, but not limited to, many musicians. By chance I met Jesper Eklow, guitarist for American psychedelic rock band Endless Boogie, who mentioned he was friends with Yo La Tengo. Sensing my opportunity for an introduction, I offered Jesper a meal at Attica if he would connect me with the band, which he kindly did over email. The words Jesper used to describe Yo La Tengo stayed with me. 'They are solid citizens,' he said.

Yo La Tengo didn't know it, but I'd been studying them for years. I'd witnessed the consistency of their output, and the genuine connection they have to their fans. There is nothing conceited or jaded about what they do. I see their way of being as a guide for a long and meaningful career, the kind I would like to have in the restaurant.

And so, in 2013, three years after making my film, I send Yo La Tengo a garrulous email to ask permission to use their song. Over-explaining is my usual style when 'cold calling' someone I really admire, especially over email. I've just re-read it and it's super-cringy, very earnest, way too long, going on endlessly about my restaurant, my life, my film. As if this wasn't enough, I follow up with a copy of my book and a card. I neglect to mention one small, crucial detail, however: I've already made my film using their song as a soundtrack.

Months pass and I don't hear back. I kind of forget that I wrote to them in the first place. I'm in Sydney for work, cooking at a corporate event, which is really just the bait on a hook for the client to lure more clients, many of whom don't give a damn about the food itself but enjoy the vibe, and would love a 'quick selfie' before moving on to their next event. I finish my shift and go back to my hotel. It has a glass wall looking out on the endless grey apartments of Bondi Junction. I hear the ding of an email on my phone. I get a sudden shock when I realise it's from Ira.

This is his email:

Hi Ben,

It's taken six months to write back, as you know if you have a calendar. Here's the reason. Looking around on the web, I saw that you had already posted your film, with our song, on youtube, before you asked for permission (let alone receiving it). Unfortunately, that's hardly uncommon, but it never makes us feel that good, and I didn't know how to respond, how to reconcile the feeling of violation that comes from our music being used without permission as opposed to the very thoughtful email you had sent (and of course the book that followed).

As you may know, we're coming to Melbourne next week, so I realized I'd better write.

best wishes, Ira

As I read his email, I reel with guilt and shame. I replay the words 'feeling of violation' over and over in my head. For several days I am frozen in embarrassment, distracted. All I can think about is Yo La Tengo and what I've done. The main scenario playing through my mind is a response to the effect of 'Dear Mr Kaplan, I'm so sorry for fucking you over. My sincere apologies, you will never hear from me again.'

But I don't have the guts even to send it. I don't know how to. I've insulted my heroes.

A few days later, back in Melbourne, I'm standing in Attica's kitchen garden, the sun shining on my face, picking aromatic herbs. In this blissful moment I've briefly forgotten about the mess I've created. The peace is interrupted by another email ding.

I check my phone and, to my disbelief, there's a second email from Ira.

> Hi Ben,
>
> I guess when it takes six months to write a reply to an email, it's hard to complain about not getting an answer within a week. But if you want to come to tomorrow's show at Hamer Hall, please let us know.
>
> best, Ira

This time my response is swift:

> Hi Ira,
>
> I'm sorry it's taken a few days to respond.
>
> Firstly, I owe you guys a massive apology for not being more straight up from the start. I should have told you that I had done the wrong thing when I originally made the film.
>
> When things progressed with my film-making, I realised that using your music without permission wasn't the right thing to do and I wanted to reach out to you guys to make things right.
>
> I feel your kind offer to come to your gig is more than I deserve, but would love to come.
>
> Can you make it in for a meal at Attica as my guests? What's your timeframe?
>
> We could do a late table this Sat if it suits? Attica is open Tuesday to Saturday for dinner.

Really appreciate your heart to reach out when you had every reason not to.

Hoping I can repay the favour.

Best,

Ben

At Hamer Hall the following night I pick up my ticket. Handwritten on the back it says, 'Meet us at the merch desk after the show.'

My seat is right in the middle, level with the stage. Yo La Tengo appear and open with 'Ohm', a song from the album they are touring, *Fade*. The first half is played in a beautifully quiet, acoustic style and the second half is rocking, electrified, loud. The show is incredible, one of the best I've been to, but I'm preoccupied with a deeply uneasy feeling, overcome with compunction at what I'd done. I keep thinking of a story I'd heard about Phil Collins, based on his song 'In the Air Tonight'. The story goes that the song is about a drowning that could have been avoided. Apparently, the man responsible for the drowning was invited to a Phil Collins show, where Phil asked the band to stop playing, and then in an act of revenge he pointed to the man in the crowd and said, 'That guy could have stopped another guy from drowning, but he didn't.'

This never actually happened, but knowing that doesn't help my nerves. In my mind I keep thinking the same thing is going to happen to me, that YLT will suddenly stop playing, a spotlight will shine directly on me, and in one chilling moment Ira will tell the audience: 'That guy right there, the guy with the Kiwi accent, he stole our music.'

After the show, after the standing ovation, it's a slow, guilty march up the stairs to the merch desk – I have a knot in my stomach as I join the queue. Each time someone else joins, I circle back and re-join, so I am always at the very end. It feels like the time I asked my mother for a boiled egg, even though I didn't like boiled eggs. I begged her to cook me one, promising I'd eat it. She cooked it and, of course, I refused to eat it. What came next was the slowest consumption of an egg in the history of humans consuming eggs, accompanied by my convulsing and dry retching. Mum was unmoved.

After forty-five minutes, the line has disappeared. I can no longer avoid the band. Finally, I'm standing in front of them. I'm not sure what I expected, but I receive a super-friendly, 'Hi Ben, it's so great to meet you.' We chat for twenty minutes. It's the loveliest conversation. They have a deep passion for food and restaurants. I pinch myself that I'm getting to talk to my heroes, but the whole time I'm thinking, *Why are they being so nice to me?* Before we depart, I can't help myself and I ask Ira the same question out loud. He responds simply, 'I could tell you weren't a bad guy.'

Over the next few years, Kylie and I become good friends with Ira and Georgia. When our travels align, we spend time together in many different places. The four of us hear Lou Reed's guitars feeding back at the Cathedral of St John the Divine in New York. We eat pizza at Bæst in Copenhagen while drunken chefs continuously interrupt us. At a dinner at Majordomo in Los Angeles, I lock our keys inside our rental car right before our booking time. There is a choice to be made between skipping dinner to extract the keys, or having dinner with the band, at the risk of missing our flight home to Australia. Of course, we decide to go to dinner.

My favourite time with the band involves a very late night in NYC, where after a meal at Atomix, Ira and Georgia suggest we go to a bar where their friend is DJing and, in Ira's words, 'has a huge collection of rare funk and soul 45s that you've never heard'. Over several cocktails and countless amazing songs, I get to go deep with Ira about his guitar playing and his approach to life. You are shaped by the people you spend time with, and here I am, at 2am, hearing all about the creative genius of someone I've looked up to all my entire adult life.

Before I met Yo La Tengo, I had never experienced this sort of kindness – the most sublime, redemptive form of kindness. To be treated like this felt like a form of love; their lack of anger at my transgression allowed me to step back from my internal ledge of shame. The gift of owning my misstep on my terms, meant I fully examined it and would never repeat it. Despite the fact that I had made a mistake and done the wrong thing, Ira politely let me know it wasn't cool, and in the process, he retained his dignity but did not seek pleasure by destroying mine. YLT found it within themselves to approach the situation with grace and class.

Initially I had been so bewildered by it that I had been suspicious, as if there might be an ulterior motive or a secondary move to bring down the gallows upon me, Phil Collins style. Until then, at every single interaction when I had done the wrong thing, I had received the full wrath of the person I'd wronged. Similarly, whenever someone had wronged me, I'd either yelled at them or cut them off completely, building a hard, cold wall of stone.

Their kindness made me question my own behaviour – my quickness to rise in anger when people made mistakes at Attica. The harsh way I sometimes handled relationships that had eroded. My inability to empathise with those around me who'd made a mistake, to imagine myself in their shoes. I began to consider how my anger was not only affecting the person I was angry with, but myself. I never felt good afterwards. Kindness is not only a gift to the person on the receiving end, but to the person who gives it.

I never forgot how Yo La Tengo made me feel. They made me feel that kindness is what matters most. The grace of that lesson would spread to every part of my life. When facing a tricky situation, or an ambiguous decision, something where the moral boundaries might be blurred, I now ask myself: *What would Yo La Tengo do?*

BATS AND HATS

'I thought of the clean linens at your table, the shining knives and
the flames of the candles, and I could not stomach it.'
Sharon Olds, refusing an invitation from the Bush Administration

'Critics are men who watch a battle from a high place
then come down and shoot the survivors.'
attributed to Ernest Hemingway

The phone rings in the Attica office. It's the assistant to a globally
famous chef. A King Chef, if you like. The King Chef is summon-
ing me to play table tennis with him tonight. It is a simple request
with simple instructions: 'Would you like to come? Okay, be at his
apartment at 10pm.'

As a young chef, but not yet a business owner, I'm excited about
this invitation, and assume it will just be the two of us hanging out.
After Attica's dinner service I go to the apartment, a penthouse in

a tall building in the city, surrounded by other tall buildings, with a private foyer lined with black marble.

I ring the bell and am buzzed in. Awkwardly, I enter the vast room. To the right are several large sofas and a huddle of D-grade actors doing drugs. In the middle is a massive bar, with two staff elegantly mixing cocktails. I immediately feel for these staff – all too often, those who work in hospitality are exposed to situations that are inappropriate, difficult, distressing and sometimes fucked up.

Further into the room is a table-tennis table, and towards the end is an annexed dining room with a buffet so grand it looks every bit the image of a feast from a nineteenth-century still-life painting, replete with whole glazed fish, piles of boiled lobsters on ice, wheels of aged Comté and a mountain of grapes. Among the rabid excess, in a tall white hat, a chef I know is carving a glistening ham. We lock eyes in recognition, but I quickly look down, embarrassed to be here.

A father and son approach me, struggling to string together a sentence. I enquire as to the King Chef's whereabouts and they point towards the bathroom, from which it appears they just came. I dare not enter. My physical discomfort is rising and I realise I have naïvely entered a zombie land. Although I have a strong urge to run out the door, I can't quite bring myself to do it. To avoid the awkwardness, I make my way to the vacant table-tennis table.

It's obvious that King Chef takes table tennis very seriously: the table's quality is apparent – and later I'm told it is Olympic standard, and that the King Chef has been receiving private lessons from members of the Olympic team. On the floor next to the table is a huge basket of table-tennis bats. There are at least fifty, as if the chef has been buying all the different bats that exist in the world to find the perfect one. I randomly grab a bat from the basket, and decide that the only safe thing to do in this situation is to play against the ball cannon mounted on the other side of the net.

I'm not much of a table-tennis player, and the machine is superior to me – it's firing out balls with a frenetic energy, half of which I miss, so they bounce across the room, which further fuels my discomfort. Mercifully, I see a friendly face, someone I know. We play a few games, and then the father and son stagger over again, slam an open bottle of champagne down on the table, and challenge us to a game of doubles. Having no choice, we play.

Soon, a line forms. The other creatures of the night emerge and want in on the action. We dispatch them all, winning game after game, until finally the King Chef and his sidekick emerge, and they want to play us. By this time, my competitive juices are flowing, fuelled by consistently trouncing the inebriated horde. We are on a fucking roll.

The King Chef grabs a bat and starts sizing up at the end of the table, gyrating his hips left and right. He's not happy, however, and goes back to the basket of bats. He tests another bat. No, wrong one. He rifles through, taking out every single bat and examining it with intensity. The King Chef is really fixating on the bats.

Finally, it seems as if he's given up. He can't find the bat he's searching for, the holy bat. As he rises, bats strewn about him like plastic soldiers on a child's bedroom floor, he looks over at me, eyes narrowing as his gaze lowers to my bat: 'You've got my lucky bat.'

I tell him that I just grabbed the first bat from the pile. He asks for it back. I'm not sure what comes over me, but I politely refuse. I tell him that I've been winning with this bat and he cannot have it back. He looks lost for words, dumbfounded by the little bastard at the other end of the table. He hasn't heard the word 'no' many times in his life, and he can't believe it's coming from a young, upstart chef.

His face has a crimson flush. His sidekick mutters, 'C'mon mate, don't be a cunt.'

I'm uncertain about what's going to unfold but I think, *Fuck it!* This night hasn't turned out the way I thought it was going to, so at the very least I should try and have some fun with these pricks. After giving me his best Terminator stare, the King Chef takes another bat.

The game begins. It's on, hell for leather. The intensity of it feels like restaurant service. Everything is on the cusp of chaos, but instead of dockets and orders and dishes flying back and forth, it's table-tennis balls, sweat and bravado. There's no doubt that the King Chef and his mate are superior players, but somehow I enter a flow state, helped by the fact that my friend and I are stone-cold sober. As the game tightens, the King Chef begins to unravel and starts to blame his bat. I smile through gritted teeth and the King Chef becomes more and more upset, veins pulsating in his forehead.

The horde of zombies have surrounded the table. My teammate can't believe what's happening. The scores are neck and neck. Match point. The King Chef serves to me, straight into the net. We win. He smashes his bat down on the table and screams, 'Fuck you!'

I decide it might be a good time to make a quick exit. My playing partner does the same. We take the lift in silence. Before we head out into the night, I ask, 'Was that a bit weird?' 'The weirdest fucking thing ever,' he replies.

My mother's hand hovers over a quince. Cloudy light glides through my father's stained-glass window, rippling across the quinces' yellow skins, which are placed in Mum's ripening spot on the sill. The fruit is from the tree above the porch, planted in the 1930s when our farmhouse was built. I am mystified by this tree and its mercurial produce. It smells how my grandmother's tinned guava tastes – heady with vanilla and orange, the scent of places far from here. The promise of the quince is so great, but the give seems so little: I have tried it raw many times, and the flesh is tannic and sour, granular and coarse. I think of it as an angry fruit. Why is it not like the others in our garden? Fruits of instant gratification, like Granny Smiths and Winter Nelis pears? Even the brutally acidic malus crabapples are palatable to my five-year-old tastes once I've cleaned out the orchard of sweeter things. I am a child who devours apple cores, whole feijoas, even the hairy skin of the kiwifruit. But this? No, this fruit is hostile.

The coal range stove warms the room as we sit at the wooden kitchen table and peel the quinces. Mum places them into her large wedding pot with sugar, water, cinnamon quills and a bay leaf. Oxidised, their flesh looks brown and ugly, like badly bruised spuds. For an eternity they simmer on the cast-iron stove. Despite my frequent requests of 'Are they ready yet?', Mum won't let me disturb them. Mercifully, just before bed, they are done. We remove the lid and I look up at Mum and gasp, 'Giant rubies!' The quinces have been transformed and shine a deep, dark red. To look into this pot is to see the soul of the fruit. I might be young, but this is all the evidence I need to confirm that cooking is truly magic. I am trans-fixed – the change in front of me is beyond anything imaginable. We spoon the quinces into bowls for my sisters, Tess and Tamie, ourselves and Dad, who needs two. Pouring cream runs through the crimson, pectin-rich syrup like a river meeting the sea. Silently we inhale the fruits of our labours.

Something shifts in me – the beginning of a great and captivating love. Cooking becomes an immense, heart-swelling feeling, teaching me that I can use everything inside me to make something special for other people. I see the glowing faces of my family and know that this is what I shall dedicate my life to, creating special joy from food.

Mum recently told me: 'From your earliest moment, you obsessed with pans and anything to do with the kitchen. I remember you boiling Dad's shoes in a pot with spuds on the kitchen floor. One of your first words was hot. You adored anything to do with cooking and food. At dinner, you would watch us eat intently from your highchair, following our every mouthful. Your cooking obsession as a little boy was almost like reincarnation, even though I don't believe in reincarnation. You recognised pots and pans like you had lived another life and you always wanted to cook, even when you were too tiny to be able to. It reminded me of children who can speak other languages early. It was so strange for us to have this little child who was so intense about it.'

Over time, as cooking becomes my muse, it is as natural as breathing. It draws me in and consumes me. I search for the feeling of those quinces continuously, within every new dish at Attica, for the ecstasy of creation that comes from being the first to imagine something, from making the seemingly impossible happen. This is the most brain-exploding feeling in the world for me; besides my family, it is the thing that brings me more joy than anything else in my life. The intoxicating, maddening perfume of the quince is always there, in each new challenge and new discovery.

When I first started at Attica, I remember the feeling of ambition I had as a chef. There was the ambition to be recognised for my hard work, the unrealised ambition to win awards. The night I won my first significant award, although I was terrified, I was beyond excited. It felt like a great privilege to receive recognition for my work and the work of our tiny team.

After the ceremony, I was invited for a drink with a group of famous older chefs, who said, 'Enjoy this moment, young man, it doesn't get any better than this.' There was an underlying sadness in their club. Sometimes it felt like the elation of winning awards was the only feeling they lived for. I felt so uncomfortable that I wanted to escape. It seemed to me that they were trapped by their success; while they knew that awards were fleeting, they were helplessly addicted to them, powerless to wrestle back their own narrative and find the original source of joy that brought them to this in the first place: food.

They had lost touch with their passion for cooking, gotten swept up in the hype that had begun to surround chefs of that time. Although they belonged to the second generation of well-known Australian chefs, they were perhaps the first to become celebrities, more famous than their famous restaurants.

At the centre of this is food media. It has played perhaps the biggest part in the building of chef legend. My approach with food reviewers is to be polite and respectful, but I never confuse these pleasantries with friendship – you cannot be friends with someone who is being paid to make judgements about your restaurant. I maintain a professional distance, out of deference for the job they feel they must do.

Of course, being a food reviewer could, and should, be an amazing job, spending one's life eating unique food, learning and writing about food culture and history, the major challenges facing the way we eat and the thoughtful storytelling of restaurants. The reality of how it is usually done, however, is very different. Many food reviewers justify their role as a service to the public, but few grasp the responsibility and privilege they have. Often, they work with little expertise. It takes a minimum of fifteen years of continuous focus to get good at all aspects of cooking; it can take a food critic one sideways promotion to find themselves in a position where they are judging the results of that cooking.

Over time, I have begun to call these people 'Jimmy'. One day Jimmy might be a reporter who gets promoted to 'chief food critic' because it's known in the office that they are an adoring 'foodie'. They wax lyrical about 'the croissant'. On Monday mornings, they bore everyone in the office with their weekend farmers market exploits. Their Christmas party BBQ skills are legendary. Once Jimmy has mastered sous vide at home, they decide that they would make a great food reviewer. The hospitality industry collectively sighs, the fate of our futures now in the hands of Jimmy. Jimmy is almost always white. Life has been good to Jimmy. Things just fall into place, and why wouldn't they, hey? Jimmy has been afforded every privilege. 'Jimmy' doesn't represent every food critic, of course, but does reflect my experience of some of the most powerful reviewers at major news sources and restaurant guides.

As the editor of a leading restaurant guide recently said to Kylie and me, 'You don't need a background in food writing to review and write about restaurants.' This person had taken the editor position after working as a direct-to-camera journalist for a television news station. That's an even bigger leap than me deciding that tomorrow I'll go from being chef to head sommelier – unthinkable, and seriously you don't want me selecting or serving your wine. The arrogance behind assuming such a position of authority so readily undervalues the mastery of restaurants, as if they are such a basic and easy-to-understand part of our culture that it takes no specialist knowledge to make informed critiques about them.

This is a story about Jimmy. It's about the sour impact food media has had on restaurants, the perils of hats, stars and best-of lists. It's also a call to our industry to step up and take control, to stop pandering to a system that no longer works, that was never truly independent, never properly informed, and never quite offered the expertise it claimed to.

Like Santa Claus, Jimmy is based on myth. As soon as you stop believing in him, he stops giving you presents. But the more we buy into this system, the more ownership it has over us. Have you been naughty, or nice, this year? It only works while we buy into it. What the fuck are we living for, my friends?

There's a phrase that enters my head when I think about hat ratings and accolades, and all that has been bestowed on me and Attica by these Jimmys: most climbers are killed on the descent.

I sit with my sister Tess and wait. Tess is often the nervous one, but today we both are. A beaten Dodge truck rattles into the car park of Sapp Coffee Shop in Hollywood's Thai Town. Behind the wheel is a hero of mine: Jonathan Gold, the belly of Los Angeles, food critic for *The Los Angeles Times*. I'm nervous because of how much I admire him – not only for his trailblazing cross-cultural writing, but for his life. He is much more than a food critic, despite being the world's greatest food critic. Gold is a devoted father and husband; a classically trained musician who played cello in punk bands; the first writer to pen a major article on hip-hop group N.W.A.; someone who could be found in the studio (or eating ramen) with Dr. Dre as he made his debut album *The Chronic*, earning him the nickname Nervous Cuz.

Jonathan sits down at our table without fanfare and suggests that we have the boat noodle soup, the one he'd described in an earlier review as 'a brilliant dish, a murky, organ-rich beef soup amplified with shrieking chile heat, the tartness of lime juice locked in muscular poise with the brawny muskiness of the broth'. I go for it. He senses Tess's discomfort, and suggests she try the gentler jade noodles with duck, which she does. After swapping a few stories about food, Jonathan is fascinated by Tess's career, working as an English literature professor at the University of California, Santa

Barbara. The dialogue turns to writing, punctuated by pieces of beef tendon and lung and observations on our blood-thickened soup.

Conversations with Jonathan were always like that, always curious, never self-interested, deeply thoughtful, trying to get to the heart of the matter. With a gentle awkwardness, he decoded what was being said, how it tasted, what was happening around us, where this or that had come from, and whether the unspoken contract between the creator and their audience squared up. Whether that creation was a meal, a musical performance, a work of art or a night at the theatre, he applied the same depth. In the food world, Jonathan was my favourite person to talk with, because nothing was wasted. The openness of his interest and the immediacy of his knowledge meant that in a world full of noise, his transmission was the clearest.

A few years before I got to know Jonathan, a publicist told me that Gold had been talking about Attica, saying it was going to be an important place, that at the time it was in his top five. When you feel misunderstood, to hear those words, especially from him, is to get the uplift you get when your favourite song comes on the radio as your car glides along the highway, the top down, the warmth of summer on your face and your partner there smiling back at you. That he was known as a champion of the little place, rather than the hallowed halls of fancy restaurants, made his words count that much more. He got it: he understood that deliciousness was not overrated, that going your own way was vital to the restaurant experience.

Jonathan wasn't only a gifted food critic: he was admired and respected by our gang for the humanity he brought to his profession. I think most chefs and restaurant owners sensed that they actually mattered to him; he knew that, in their distilled essence, restaurant reviews were stories about people, and those people have livelihoods. In the documentary of his life, *City of Gold*, he makes no secret of his love for those in the restaurant business: 'You want these guys to succeed.' Yet he is equally honest about his work: 'I've burned good friendships over bad reviews. You just have to be willing to do it.'

Jonathan wrote some extremely kind things about my work. The exacting focus he put on context is why it meant so much. In an interview, he once said, 'There are so many food writers that never vary their gaze six inches from what's on the plate. They'll describe one dish, then another dish and then another dish, and then they'll look around the room for a second and try to tell you what the people are wearing and then look at another dish. When you look at food without referencing who's cooking it and what the ingredients are and how they might've been produced, you might as well be describing a stamp collection.'

Succinctly, Jonathan is saying that a deep understanding of food systems and the people and culture behind the scenes is necessary to write about them with authority. To offer any less is an insult to readers, and to the intelligence of the cooks, waiters, farmers, makers, artists, designers and business owners whose efforts all combine to make restaurants what they can be at their best: life-changing.

Jonathan sought out diverse and often small restaurants, visiting them five or six times before reviewing them. While he researched meticulously, if he wasn't knowledgeable about the type of food they were serving, he didn't pretend to be, and would visit many more times, admitting his ignorance and showing respect for their culture. With deep love, he elevated his city's brilliant and exciting food culture, and brought attention to the meaningful work of restaurants and food trucks serving their local communities.

In Australia, we've never had a Jonathan Gold – but that's not surprising, as nowhere except Los Angeles has had a Jonathan Gold. LA was Jonathan Gold and Jonathan Gold was LA. I'd love to see a food critic here put a city ahead of themselves in that way. Too often critics are not truly interested in the culture of a place. More commonly, they are people who celebrate their own manufactured culture, or people who are self-interested, or people who have an agenda, rather than searchers with an open and curious mind, on a mission to discover the best of a city and link the food to its citizens.

The key to becoming a chef who can elevate dishes from good to great is a highly evolved palate, the ability to taste and differentiate flavours and to make the correct calls on the adjustment of season-ing. The key to becoming a great food critic is the same: it all comes down to palate. Many people incorrectly assume that being a good writer is essential. Certainly, it is helpful, but it is not what makes a critic great. There are many excellent writers who are poor food critics because they are let down by their palate and their lack of food knowledge. For chef and critic alike, palate is everything.

When Jonathan died from pancreatic cancer in 2018, the world lost a sage. More than anyone else I've ever read, the promise of his words made me want to jump up off my sofa, fly to LA and drive an hour across the city to El Monte and eat a slap-me-in-the-face-good burrito de *birria* at Burritos La Palma. This I did, and it was absofuckinglutely worth it.

There is a reason I am writing this chapter, even though it may land me in hot water. It is because the global restaurant industry has spent too long in the thrall of food media. It is a feckless system, built on hype. There are conflicts of interest everywhere. Experience and insight are almost non-existent. To those writing, it often seems like a game: who's up and who's down, who's worth a story because they have lost a hat; who has a pungent little line about how a dish was seasoned, or how the front-of-house were dressed; a joke that was too funny not to write, even if it wasn't quite true, even if it wasn't really funny – because to them, not being noticed is death.

Behind this desire for attention, though, are real consequences. It might sound like hyperbole, but this oppressive review system — the same one that has brought privilege and fame to a few chefs like me — has contributed greatly to bankruptcy, divorce, depression and suicide. Don't believe me? Google 'Michelin Guide suicide'. The stress and tension that restaurants often find themselves under are greatly intensified by the huge businesses that review us, businesses that want to sell more newspapers, magazines, or tyres — ratcheting and ratcheting and ratcheting up the pressure, which sadly has been too great for some.

Much the same sort of arbitrary scoring system exists in every food city. Hats replace stars, stars replace hats, 50 best whatever replaces a vapour of nothingness. Publications award restaurants scores out of 20 and chef's hats or stars from one to three. This system is hard to explain and it seems like no one, including the reviewers, knows how it works. You could be awarded a hat for making a sandwich or a hat for an ambitious restaurant cooking at the highest level. This just makes a hat seem arbitrary and meaningless. Why not just say these two very different businesses are great at what they do, and leave it at that?

Restaurants swallow the pill — we dare not speak out about it — and Jimmy understands their entitlement and position of power all too well. The merry-go-round of reviewers, guides, stars, hats, lists of top anything or world's best, all serve one thing and one thing only — themselves, their self-generated hype. They are constantly coming up with new ways to sell to you, and to use us. The churn and burn of superficial commentary is extraordinary: different reviewers, different organisations, but the same stale, decades-old system. Hospitality is the only industry I can think of where businesses get reviewed by major publications several times annually, year on year, for eternity.

It's 2am and I'm at the hospital with my young child, who has food poisoning. Why the fuck is this happening to me right now? I should be thinking only about my child's wellbeing, but instead I'm anxious that I'm also getting sick, while writing a menu and worrying about the food critic who will be reviewing Attica in seventeen hours' time.

Later the same day, as we hurtle through the preparations at Attica, I feel the first wave of nausea. In ordinary times, in an ordinary situation, at an ordinary occupation, I would go home. But I feel that I cannot leave: there is nothing ordinary about today; the restaurant is on the precipice of failure again, the critic is in the dining room and, with one bad review, it will all be over. I decide to stay because of the house I fear losing, the family life I'm trying to build, the job I love, and the jobs of our staff.

We are a tiny team of three chefs. No one in the kitchen questions my decision to stay. We all know I must. It's a Tuesday night, 'Chef's Table', our experimental menu, and I'm the only one who knows the dishes. As an overwhelming urge to vomit rises in me, we serve the reviewer their first course of hand-picked snow crab, sesame and grapefruit. Following this is 'The earth and ash: Cecil potato baked in earth, smoked cream and ash', the first iteration of 'A simple dish of potato cooked in the earth it was grown', the dish that put Attica on the map and a homage to my New Zealand childhood and Māori hāngī. We are so excited by these dishes, proud of the creativity that has gone into them, and what it means for the future of Attica – and yet, I also know that a single review could spell the end of it all.

I run out the back and, on hands and knees, vomit into the bin-washing drain, my face so close I can smell the rust of the steel grate. The night swirls around me as I lie on the cold damp concrete, trying to soothe myself through dry retching. I struggle back into the kitchen, despite being engulfed by a myopia-like fuzziness. From the kitchen I can see the reviewer eating his potato, but I can't make out the expression on his face – the place I always study for signs of approval.

The respite is brief and as the urge to vomit rises again, coming at me like the ground rushing towards the wheels of a plane at touch-down, the reviewer's main course of quail is called away. Making food while stricken with food poisoning is a cruel paradox: a personal pit of suffering, an unexamined fifth dimension as I attempt to prepare edible beauty, while suppressing my omnipresent gut of doom. I snap back to reality and, close to blacking out, I serve the critic their dessert of caramelised blood plums and figs, and a made-on-the-day honeyed fig-leaf cheese. On the edge of delirium, I return to the bin drain to vomit again, the reviewer thankfully none the wiser, and their forthcoming review positive.

When I took ownership of Attica in 2015, as part of my business plan, I wrote a list of the threats to our prosperity. Number one was a bad review, even after so many years of excellence and Attica winning almost all the awards possible.

Feeling under threat is hardly the sort of nurturing environment that encourages a person to push the envelope creatively. Awards can have the exact opposite effect, in fact – chefs and restaurateurs become paralysed, fearfully working to protect what they have, rather than taking risks to explore what is possible.

Recently a chef went on record to state that the restaurant they work for was undertaking a re-fit to the tune of three million dollars. His reason was very specific: it was not to provide a nicer environment for their customers, nor a better workplace for their staff, but instead to protect the award they hold.

After Attica won restaurant of the year for the first time, in 2008, I thanked the editor, who sniggered and said, 'Let's see if you can keep it.' He had given me something that wasn't mine; it was his. He was the king-maker, and he was letting me know it.

I'm not proud of the things I have done to comply with the system over the years. I can justify it any way I want to, that I do it to keep the lights on, that I do it begrudgingly, but among other things, this is a story of my complicity.

The crowd is rowdy. Football-fan-level rowdy. A food critic stands on a stage in front of the mob and tries in vain to speak over the noise. The mob is the restaurant industry, and it appears to have absolutely no appetite for what the food reviewers have to say. Individually, of course, we'd never dare to be so disrespectful, but collectively the crowd seems to be saying a noisy, two-hour *fuck you* to the reviewers. It's more like a scene from an anti-vax protest than a gathering of the finest chefs, waiters and restaurateurs in town. The reviewers don't understand what's happening and look a bit shaken. A decade earlier, this contempt would have been unthinkable, but in this time I understand perfectly: we've all been cooped up for two years and are about to be served another round of their reviewing hype-beast bullshit.

The food critic raises their voice through the microphone to try and gain control, but the mob isn't having it. For a moment I feel pity for the critic: they are getting angry, their discomfort is apparent. Through the din, I make out that they are trying to hand out this year's charity award. We all know what's up here: the organisation is trying to make itself look like it cares when it soundly and resolutely does not. We know this because the organisation never puts its hand in its own pocket to donate to the cause directly; instead, it uses our resources to hold fundraisers and events to do that. I'd hazard a guess that the hospitality industry, combined with the collective generosity of our suppliers, donates a higher proportion of our earnings than any other. Our skills and reputations are the reason why charity dinners can command vast sums of money and raise millions every year. Many of the charitable causes are run by society's elite, with a paid famous figurehead as host, but we are the mechanism and volunteer workforce that allows much of this kind of fundraising in the first place. A well-known restaurant or chef is the hook that sells out events that are otherwise a hard sell.

Additionally, the publishers of food guides and reviews regularly seek recipes from the chefs they review, and publish them without any form of payment. My recipes are my intellectual property, and they take huge amounts of time to produce. Yet it's expected that chefs will contribute recipes and photography for free, and the payoff is the supposed exposure that we receive in return. Not once have I ever been offered payment for my work. The fear for chefs is if we say to these organisations, 'No, I'd like you to pay me for my content and work,' then we will be punished when they next review us. Subconsciously or otherwise, it has been in our best interests to 'play the game'.

The awards are being called out, always with more suspense than is necessary, to make it as painful as possible for all involved. When it is announced that Attica is awarded two hats, down from three, a brief hush falls over the room. There's a part of me that always keeps my expectations in check, and I feel strangely freed by the demotion. Kylie, with her blackbelt in kickboxing, looks like she would like to kick someone's arse. There's been a changing of the guard at this particular guide, and she feared that the newbies might want to make their presence felt by making an example of us.

Both of our minds go straight to Anna, our general manager. Anna is deeply affected by the ebb and flow of the awards system, and her number one fear is to be the senior staff member 'responsible' for the loss of an award that Attica has held for over a decade.

Wrongly, she fears people would stop dining with us because of it, restaurants being as fragile as Fabergé eggs at the best of times.

As far as Anna is concerned, Attica is the most important restaurant in Australian history and stands for much of what is good in the world of hospitality. I do not write this to big-up ourselves but to show you the opposite: that, for some, it is a terrible burden.

Anna's belief in Attica is her bedrock, and she will do everything she can to protect the restaurant. As she came up through the ranks in hospitality, it was Attica that she admired, and at Attica that she had an influential dinner as a young hospitality professional. Anna went on to lead dining rooms around the world, until two years earlier – when, after being forced to move home during the pandemic, she took a senior management position with us. We were lucky to have her.

I know that Anna will be at home, anxiously watching every bit of news about the awards come through on social media. Concerned, I message her from the ceremony, 'None of this is your fault, and I'm ok with it. Hope you are ok.' There is no response. Kylie is worried, too. I call Anna; she doesn't pick up. I call Matt, and he's gutted but I know he'll be ok. 'Have you heard from Anna?' He hasn't. I message her again, 'Remember, I was at Attica the night of the final review, and I watched every detail, you have nothing to feel bad about.' Still no response. It's 11pm and I'm considering driving to Anna's house to check on her. Kylie says we need to give her some space. I'm terrified something will happen to her.

The next morning, as staff begin their staggered shifts, they are quiet, heads low. By the afternoon the atmosphere feels like a vacuum, as if all the oyygen has been sucked out of the room. Anna arrives and is distraught. She can't look at me. It's as if her greatest fear has been confirmed. She hasn't slept and looks like the wind has been knocked out of her. The whole team feels they have failed the restaurant, the place that each and every one of them care so deeply about.

I wish I could have done more to protect them. We all sit together and I tell them how I feel about all of this. I make a couple of points crystal clear: no one is responsible for losing a hat, and we are not disappointed or upset with the team. I tell them that what matters is how we react to this feeling – not to the loss of the award, but to the low feeling and to our understanding of the balance of expectation vs disappointment, and how in life this is something we all need to come to terms with. I speak of my journey here, and explain that, when you come from nothing, all this acclaim is surprising. I knew that all this could be taken from me at a moment's notice, so I had learnt early on that it wasn't the real reason to do any of it. What matters most, I say, is right in front of us: our connection, and the joy of the work that we do together daily, on behalf of our guests. I tell them to lift their heads, to feel no shame, to remember that we alone set the standard and the creative output. Lastly, I tell them I am so very grateful to each and every one of them.

That same night, with a frankness that makes me laugh out loud, a senior staff member says: 'Fuck the Good Food Guide. In fifteen years, Attica is still going to be around, and the Good Food Guide is not.'

Anna will resign within six months, before the next round of awards ensues. I tell her again and again that this is not her fault. Her eyes are cast downwards as she quietly nods in agreement, but I know she hasn't accepted it. She has tied so much of her personal value to this, and her sense of failure is like a black tide, as thick and hard to remove as an oil slick. I'm so sad about it, but I understand she is protecting herself and her mental sanctity by leaving.

The veneer is thin and worn, like on old Ikea shelves. If the fake, shiny things in the restaurant world had lost their shine before 2020, then the belt-sander force of nature that appeared in March of that year ripped off the remaining varnish and left only hard rubbish.

Dining rooms had been inverted, and what we thought we knew was so soundly shaken from its foundations that I was forced to question everything, but especially Attica's relationship with restaurant guides. As the restaurant industry was plunged into an abyss, the silence from these guides was deafening. The institutions that had built their businesses on writing about us – judging, selling, using and pigeonholing us – disappeared overnight. Collectively, we realised that we were alone. The feeling was fucking wild. My long-held suspicion that the guides were more dependent on us than we were on them was vindicated.

Globally, restaurants continued to serve their customers however they could, through takeaway and whatever side hustles they could manage – but the guides, whose professional identity relies on our work, they did nothing. Without restaurants functioning as restaurants, they had nothing to do, no one to write about. With the realisation that their business model really was as shallow as I felt it was, the power swung swiftly in our direction. We soon learnt that our restaurant could continue to innovate with new dishes and projects, as well as get by financially, in the absence of the major publications. For two years, restaurants in Australia received respite from being reviewed for guides. For the first time in my 27-year career, I was living without the pressure of an impending visit from a restaurant critic.

During this period Attica was judged by the only two sources that truly matter: our customers and ourselves. This feeling of freedom was widely shared among restaurant people. I came out of this time more resolute than ever not to give a fuck about the things that really don't matter, and to care more than ever about the things that really do: love, kindness and independence, and a vibrant and thriving restaurant — a creative enterprise that earns the right to do exactly what it wants, answering only to its staff, customers, community and environment, but never again beholden to or reliant on the global restaurant-reviewing machine.

One more story, though, while we're here. The night Attica loses its hat, I am bailed up in the bathrooms by a food reviewer, a 'Jimmy'. Jimmy is being overly friendly and apologising for not calling me; their friendliness is a bit suspicious but I'm cordial. A year earlier I'd been approached by this same Jimmy, who was also working in a different field and came to me with a commercial deal. We met, but I had my doubts, so I chose another direction, keeping this decision to myself.

Eleven months later (so just a month before the awards night), Jimmy DMs me on Instagram, asking, 'Did you end up doing a deal?' I didn't reply. Six days after this, Jimmy walks in the door of Attica with the editor of a restaurant guide. They are here to review us, and the service goes exceptionally well: the other tables are full of enthusiastic diners, the room has a buzz, our timing is on point. The nightly end-of-service report states that a dish of emu with caramelised bread and pickled rosella flowers was a favourite. We are on our game. The next day I say to Anna, 'If that's not three hats, I don't know what is.'

I'm concerned that Jimmy was dining with the guide's editor after approaching me with a business deal, but I try to think the best of them; they were probably just keeping the editor company, I reassure myself. But twelve days later my fears are confirmed, when Jimmy DMs me again, asking, 'Can you please tell me about your amazing petit fours?' and confirming that they are contributing to a round-up for the guide. I ask them to call the following day. They never call.

And here they are now, in the toilet, sheepishly apologising for not calling me, and continuing to act like a long-lost friend. Jimmy enters a cubicle and I get my chance to escape. An hour later, Attica is demoted.

Positive bias also exists within criticism, and it's a natural and easy-to-understand human attribute. I was once friendly with a journalist who asked for a table for themselves as a favour. I made the booking myself, under their name. When they arrived at the restaurant, I gave them a heartfelt hug, took them to their table, gave them drinks and extra courses, and spent time chatting and joking with them throughout the meal – all things I do when friends dine with us. Then they reviewed Attica.

To Kylie and me it felt totally wrong and, embarrassingly, the review was glowing to the point of gushing. Many food reviewers co-author, or ghostwrite, books for chefs whose restaurants they then potentially have to review. Recently an Australian food critic travelled to Europe with a restaurateur, on the restaurateur's dime, and wrote an article about their experiences. The publication declared this, but to us it felt like a new nadir for food journalism; perhaps no two occupations feed from the same trough as much as the food reviewer and the chef.

The public should be able to trust in experts and authority. Other professions that hold great responsibilities, with the power to change the course of people's lives – including teachers, lawyers, psychologists and doctors – have a transparent professional code of ethics to help govern their decision-making process. For example, a psychologist cannot treat somebody they have a personal relation-ship with, because that represents an obvious conflict of interest.

Food critics have the power to change the course of a business's life, and to define individuals' careers. Journalists have a code of ethics, too, but at times food critics don't appear to fall under that. Can food critics review their mate's restaurants? Sure! No problemo!

In my experience, Jimmy often struggles to understand the concept of subjectivity vs objectivity, layering their subjective views, thoughts and feelings onto restaurants, and expressing opinions often not based on truth or fact, and including many different biases, including the ones above. As the old adage that my father is fond of has it, 'Opinions are like arseholes, everyone has one.' Not everyone has the platform that reviewers have, however. A truly informative review should include more fact than feeling, and any feelings should be informed by fact. In short, more objectivity, more of the real facts and proven information about a restaurant. Objectivity requires a commitment of time, money and expertise in food journalism. I've lost count of the number of reviews we've had where, prior to publication, the writer hasn't asked us a single relevant question about Attica. Within their diminishing power, it seems they simply do not have the time, budget or interest. Unengaged editors lead to unengaged stories.

We never asked for Jimmy's observations and Jimmy hasn't published any criteria for restaurants to follow. Here is my declaration: restaurants should use any fucking means possible to combat Jimmy's potential castigation. Food reviewers are generally fawned over wherever they go because restaurants make a literal business out of knowing who they are. More often than not, we recognise them as soon as they sit down, yet the restaurant pretends it doesn't know that the reviewer is reviewing, and the reviewer pretends or hopes that the restaurant doesn't know who they are — what I call 'the dance of bullshit'. Visit the back office of any half-decent restaurant in the world and, on the wall, you'll find photos of reviewers, even those who go incognito. Restaurants are like spy agencies, covertly collecting and sharing intelligence with other restaurants to keep each other safe.

Two senior restaurant guide editors recently made a booking at Attica using the pseudonym Joanna Narlist. Get it? *Jo Narlist…* *Journalist.* As a friend pointed out, it's Bart Simpson calling Moe's Tavern. Aside from showing the lack of respect they have for us, it's even more disrespectful to the profession of journalism. If they can't take themselves seriously, then why should any of us believe a word they write?

Afterwards, Joke-anna emailed me a long list of the most painfully superficial questions for their review, among them this: 'Was Attica serving native ingredients pre-2005?' Fucking hell – check your own history! The publication you work for reviewed Attica in 2003, well before my tenure began, when, for the record, the reviewer wrote that the food had 'a nod to the Middle East and the Mediterranean'. Now, because I'm a helpful guy I attached a link to this original review in my sixteen-hundred-word response. Who's the Joanna Narlist now?

Here's the thing, dear reader, and I've known this for as long as I've been cooking: restaurant reviewers really aren't any better at judging restaurants than you are. The majority of food critics don't have a better palate than you, are no more an 'expert' than you are. How could they be? They don't actually make anything, can't hack it in other forms of journalism. Because they never have to pay for their meals themselves, they are even less connected to restaurants than you or I are. A vacuum cleaner review I recently read was more informative than any restaurant critique I've seen in the past year. Perhaps there was a time to care about what food critics said. That time was at least a decade ago.

Ever since I received my first award, my unease with the system has gradually grown, with every annual 'review season' and award adding to my private anxiety, like the apologue of the frog in hot water, where the temperature rises incrementally until the frog is boiled alive.

For a long time I've been pushing these thoughts away, reluctant to speak out because to write a 'takedown' of the system that I have benefitted from for more than a decade feels disingenuous. After all, it is partly because of this system that I am here, with this platform, to speak of these experiences.

Attica is one of the most-awarded restaurants in Australian history. A fair question is, 'But why, if you've always felt this way, did you not just turn down the awards, rather than accepting them?' My answer would be that this system existed well before I entered the industry, and initially I did not completely understand it. I thought it was all-powerful, and I did not have the same courage of my convictions that I have now. At first I didn't own Attica, and while I had autonomy over the creative aspects of the restaurant, making business decisions that would affect the outcome of it was not my call. In saying that, after I became the owner, I chose to stay inside the pot while the water continued to heat up.

I have also long been cognisant of the fact that the team I work with has taken more from the positive feeling of awards than I have. In those early years of my tenure neither Attica, nor I, would have survived without the merry-go-round of reviews, awards and hype. At that young age, when you are receiving benefits from something, it's hard to say you're not comfortable with it. This was also a time before the ability of restaurants to communicate through social media, podcasts and newsletters, which have been strong disruptors to the hegemony of guides and awards.

All of this, plus the hard truths we learnt during the pandemic, means we are no longer beholden to the opinions of a few, whose power, resources and relevance are now diminished to the point that if I were taking the helm at Attica in 2023, rather than 2005, I wouldn't need to rely on them to build our business. Thankfully, the landscape has changed. The era of the full-time paid food critic may well be over. Diners now have access to diverse alternative perspectives on restaurants, and it's a lot easier to be drawn to voices that resonate with your interests. Now, when making the all-important decision of where to eat, and who to spend your hard-earned money with, your choice may be informed by traditional media, but it no longer needs to be defined by it.

You might well ask why I would go after a system that continues to benefit me, especially as I run a business and I am conscious of how vindictive and punitive it can be? Well, beyond any personal fears, I strongly believe in personal responsibility, and my aim is to bring to light some of the unpleasant aspects of the world I've lived in. If I can help a single person avoid some of the pitfalls of this industry, then that alone will be worth any potential repercussions.

In addition, frankly, it turns my stomach to be complicit in what I consider to be a polluted moral ecosystem. Over the years I have helped perpetuate it, but it is part of my responsibility as someone with the creative freedoms that I've so painstakingly protected, to speak out about the things I believe in. We have not been honest; we have not spoken the truth. We have allowed our fears to control us, and by continuing to play Jimmy's game we have also become the farmers of this ecosystem. It is time to stop. We must plough into the soil these withered crops that we helped sow, or we cannot flourish.

Just before I handed in the manuscript for this book, a Jimmy returned. As usual, Kylie and I knew the moment they booked. The date for their dinner was Kylie's 40th birthday. We had planned a hiking trip to celebrate the milestone, but as soon as that booking came through, Kylie knew that I wouldn't be spending her birthday with her. I'd be spending it in the service of Jimmy.

This might sound to you like I've got my priorities mixed up, given my stance on the system, but really it shouldn't. I'd do anything to protect the people I love, and I reckon you'd do the same. Together, Kylie and I decided to delay the holiday so I could work that night to support and protect our team. I'd never want them to go through the pain of a bad review or a lost hat. And me? I fucking loved it. As Jimmy passed by the kitchen on their way to the bathroom, they cast a glance our way, caught my eye, and looked down. The game, friends, had changed.

Attica continues to push the boundaries of what is possible within food, service, art and culture. That's not to say that I think it's better or worse than any other restaurant, nor do I think that I'm too big to fail, or that I'm above criticism. Quite the opposite: our paying customers have the right to criticise our work via many means if they desire. This is not about fear of facing up to criticisms, as I'm demonstrably not scared to lead under fire, but instead I'm asking: who will hold the critics to account if judgements made about us are ill-informed or unjustified? Who are the experts in this industry? It's about questioning who holds the authority: the guides who think they uphold the standards, or restaurants themselves?

This is about a system, not any particular person. I have met many food reviewers who are genuine people, who care about what they do, and appear to also have doubts about the system they are part of, but that doesn't mean that restaurants have to take criticism lying down. We are entitled to a right of response.

As a business, Attica has a unique world view, and that view is in a constant state of evolution, not always in line with the tastes and expectations of food reviewers. This is something I'm comfortable with: it's our personal expression, something, as I've explained earlier in the book, that I protect closely. I've learnt to never assign any of my worth or value as an individual or as a company to external sources, because it will only lead to disappointment. Fundamentally, I've always wanted to invoke a strong emotion in a person who is experiencing our work: hopefully positive, but I'll also take negative, because to me that feels more alive than eliciting apathy. My values are to stay true to myself, not to forget where I've come from, and to only ever be the best version of myself that I can be, as not a single one of us can authentically be anyone else. These values, which also inform our restaurant, don't kowtow to reviewer scoring metrics, and I'm fine with that.

And I know this: through all of this madness, the quince will shelter me. As I am screamed at so loud that the spittle forms droplets on my face and rage rings in my ears, ducking and weaving between the excessiveness of success, past the spivs seeking to tear us down or overinflate us, the quince will protect me. All this noise that swirls around me, like a harsh wind battering a forest, has nothing to do with cooking, or restaurants, although it pretends to. I shelter my creativity from it, try to remember that fateful day and all the possibilities it opened up. It held me then, it holds me today, and will into the future. Where others lost their way, I invoke the foundation of everything I do: the quince, my surrender to the awe of cooking.

COLD BROWN TOAST

The Queen will arrive at any moment. We've been told to keep our hands at our sides. You do not touch the Queen. Standing erect, shoulders back, tin soldiers in a row, we are assembled like the *Downton Abbey* crew expecting the arrival of an eligible bachelor. After months of preparations, there she is walking towards us, the actual Queen. There we are, Māori and Pākehā, her appointed servants, graciously bowing back. For some of us, this is the pinnacle of a life dedicated to Her Majesty's service. For me, it's a cool story I can tell my grandmother Lois, who will absolutely use it to lord over our big-city cousins.

Several metres behind the Queen is Prince Philip. From memory, you could touch Prince Philip, no problem. He appears a jovial sort. He's smiling and shaking hands and we are smiling and shaking hands back. All's well, chaps. Prince Philip finishes his regal hand-shaking, and for a moment it seems he might walk on, but he stops suddenly, as if struck by a thought, and swings to face us. In his proper English accent, he demands, 'Where are all the savages?'

The Prince emits a chuckle. He seems quite pleased with his gaffe. We stand silent. Don't worry, servants, he seems to be saying; no need to respond, this one's on me.

Cold white and brown toast, three times a day, with every meal. Google tells me it was the Prince who craved the brown toast, while the Queen liked white. For six days in 2002, in my role as sous chef to the New Zealand Governor-General, as a 24-year-old, I followed the Queen and Prince Philip around New Zealand, making cold toast and dainty, perfect, crusts-cut-off club sandwiches. No meal tastes as bitter as the meal prepared for the racist. Ashamed is the chef who made those meals, who didn't have the courage to stand up for his Māori co-workers. It is my greatest regret.

Years later, as I shared a sandwich with my friend and Yorta Yorta man Adam Briggs, I thought of Prince Philip and this story. Adam told me that he finds it easier to deal with the 'out and out racists' than with the subtle ones: 'I know exactly where I stand with those types. It's the racist comment, unexpectedly out of the blue, from someone you trust that really hurts.'

As with a lot of families at the time, when I was growing up I witnessed racism in some of the older members of my extended family. My memory is that anyone who looked different to them, especially Māori, could be in their firing line. The intention of this racism was the same as any: to make one human feel badly about themselves and another feel superior, to push down one community and pin them there with a boot, to reinforce fears and prejudices. It is the same as Prince Philip's racist quip, so natural that it was unconscious. It sharply tells its intended victims to stay there – at arm's length, right where you are.

In restaurants, we are fully prepared to eat the eggs of fish, the blood of pigs, the unethically fattened livers of geese and ducks. But we are particularly resistant to kangaroo, saltwater crocodile, Australian ants of any kind and many native fruits that are just 'way too sour'. Most Australians know far more about Italian foods than they do about the foods of the country they live in.

When we began cooking with saltwater crocodile at Attica, we began to work with its most difficult cut: the ribs. The farm told us they couldn't give them away. Until we approached them, they had been forced to throw the ribs out. This seemed like a senseless waste of food, so we began to experiment with this ingredient. Every food that is new to us, we are beginners at preparing it. Our first try is always a simple, well-worn path – in this case, liberal salt and pepper, a kiss of oil and a long, slow smoke in an offset smoker. Although this idea proved terrible – the rib was dry and tough – the benefit of the first failure is arriving at ground zero. It was obvious from the start that the ribs lacked the fattiness that pork ribs have, but there was something there. As bad as our first test was, once we got past the car-tyre texture, there was a hint of savoury richness. We took that hint and worked and worked and worked at it across eight months, fully committed to learning how to cook crocodile ribs.

Our team landed on a method using a plastic vacuum bag that rendered the rib moist, tender and true to its flavour. Then, when I banned single-use plastics at Attica, we had to begin all over again. Today, the rib is slowly cooked for hours, before being grilled aggressively over fire, then glazed with soured honey, Dorrigo pepper and Geraldton wax leaves. Of the twelve courses on our menu, it is the overwhelming favourite, the charred, moist, flaky meat giving way to the salty-sweet-sour wrestle of the glaze; our guests pick the meat from the bone and wrap it in small discs of handmade white bread, like a reimagined tea-party version of BBQ. Beautifully cooked food is an expression of care and knowledge. Poorly cooked food is always culinary illiteracy. Whatever the outcome, it's never the food's fault.

I am always prepared to be humbled by native foods. They have been around far longer than I have. It is me that needs to learn about them, they don't need to learn about me. I always strive to seek the permission of the culture that they come from. I learnt in my earliest years that the truest cooking I could do was the cooking of the place where I stood. With Māori friends and family, I laid my first hāngī earth oven when I was a small child, and my life changed forever. The country itself was cooking.

When I arrived in Australia, my parents having shared with me some knowledge of historical wrongs, I moved like a snail for fear of being another whitefella who does further harm. Eventually I found my way to the food of this place, as I began experimenting with seaweeds and coastal native plants. I met Elders who showed me how to prepare their food. I met people on Country who began supplying the restaurant. This education helped inform me as I developed my own cooking with these ingredients. Every time I work with native food, I listen. And by serving it, I am also asking Australia to listen, to pay attention to the culture that is here and the rich and complex food that has sustained it.

This approach is not always popular. At the restaurant it is not uncommon to be asked, 'Why would you bother using these foods?' – to which the answer is that these are the country's oldest, most important foods and provide a deep connection to culture, land, and climate in this part of the world. Another line is, 'These foods are only for the tourists, mate' – to which I can only express incredulity and sadness at the special racism reserved for Indigenous people, and by extension their food.

A critic once described a dish of ngerdi (Gurr-goni for native Australian green ants) served inside a caviar tin as 'perhaps a little mean'. I was incensed. The critic made clear that when she saw a caviar tin, she expected caviar: anything else would be a letdown to 'soaring expectations'. The tin in question was painted beautifully in Kamilaroi iconography by Reko Rennie, my friend, in memory of a picnic we once shared. Ngerdi, aside from being incredibly tasty, and as zesty as the spittle of a lime against a grater, is also highly valuable – culturally and financially – and has been eaten and used as a medicinal food by people in Arnhem Land for millennia. It had cost Attica $700 per kilo, the proceeds of which had gone straight back to the person harvesting and the Maningrida community. The tin also contained the incredibly rare sugarbag honey, from the native Australian stingless bee, which, in my opinion, is the single most celestial ingredient on Earth. The critic said nothing about the quality of the dish, just that it was tasty and an interesting experiment, but they wanted caviar, an imported food, not ngerdi, an important cultural food to northern Australia. Much of this information was relayed to the reviewer when they dined, the rest was there for the asking. We were making a very explicit and delicious point, which they seem to have missed.

There will be some who say, 'Oh, Ben, you are being too sensitive; you can't blame everything on racism.' To that I would say, respectfully, that foods and peoples are seldom able to be separated, and that mainstream Australia has picked and chosen the culture that it wants from Aboriginal and Torres Strait Islander peoples when it suits them, on their terms, and profited from it greatly – through dance, sport, music, art and some would say, more recently, food. But not really food, actually. These foods are still not commonplace in the broader culture in any significant or real way, and the people who spend their livelihoods caretaking these ingredients aren't supported by mainstream industries. We only eat the tiniest amount of what is out there – the more than 8000 edible native Australian foods. Most Australians only eat between fifty and a hundred different ingredients annually, almost none of them native.

Multiculturalism is a rightfully celebrated part of modern life in Australia and contributes to making this country one of the greatest places to live on the planet. We were early adopters of many other foods from different cultures: Italian, Greek, Chinese, Vietnamese, Thai, American, even the occasional Kiwi dish (pavlova, avo toast, flat whites), are ubiquitous in cities and small towns across Australia now. Many minority groups have initially had racism projected onto their foods, only to overcome this later as their cuisine made its way into the broader Australian culture, often after white chefs and white-owned restaurants more easily benefitted from their food culture, at a higher price and at a more celebrated level. I've always believed that one of Australia's truly great strengths as a culinary nation is the diversity of its food, and the integrity of the representation of this diversity, outside of the countries of its origin. So why not the true food of this place?

Perhaps I shouldn't be surprised. I've seen it with my own eyes. You can lead the Commonwealth, your head can be on our money, you can have nearly infinite privileges and resources, but if you don't take an interest in what's around you, then you'll spend your whole miserable life eating cold toast.

THE BOTTOM
OF THE APPLE

Harold McGee is sweating. I've put him under the pump. 'How are those onions coming along, Harold?' I ask in my half-question, half-command style. 'You need to cook them until they are sweet, a little caramelisation, golden brown but not too dark. We don't want them to be bitter. Put your nose right in there – it's the fragrance we are looking for as much as the flavour.' Harold, the consummate gentleman, nods gently, listening to every word. It's at this moment that I catch myself. Here's the guy who literally wrote the book on what happens scientifically when you caramelise an onion – and I'm telling him to watch the colouring and smell. I stop what I'm doing and say with equal parts horror and shame, 'Oh, but you already know that, don't you?' Harold smiles modestly and says, 'But Ben, I enjoyed hearing it from you.' That, right there, is the thing about truly knowledgeable people – they never need to tell you how knowledgeable they are.

Harold and I cook side by side, late into the night. Like a pair of deep-sea divers on the hunt for treasure, we sift through a foreign kitchen to make a meal to go with our one luxury – a bottle of cold champagne. I have a QUESTION™ for Harold, but after my onion performance I decide it will have to wait until tomorrow.

The warmth of summer is beating down on the strange dark berries in front of us. Harold and my friend Daniel are amused that I don't know what they are. For context: I'm a self-described 'fruit obsessive' who on discovering fresh lychees for the first time, purchased five kilos of them, went back to my hotel room to scoff them in one sitting and promptly broke out in a rash. I can barely contain my excitement for this latest fruit discovery. I shimmy up the gnarled tree trunk to reach the intriguing fruit. It has blushes of different shades of red and I pop a pale one into my mouth. The shock of its intense sourness nearly causes me to fall out of the tree. My companions laugh and tell me to go for a dark one. I grab at one just slightly out of my reach and it spits its black juice all over my hands. I get a taste and it's marvellous. 'Your first mulberry, Ben?' Harold chuckles.

In 1984, which feels like a lifetime before we were obsessed with food, Harold wrote a seminal book, *On Food and Cooking: The Science and Lore of the Kitchen*. Those who haven't had the privilege of meeting him would rightly admire him for this book, and I'm here to tell you that he is as advertised. What I really admire him for, however, is who he is as a person, and for the way he treats everyone he meets with kindness. (And although I would never admit it to his face, and I know it is an absolute bible to chefs and cooks everywhere, I have never read his book.)

We continue to wander through the park, blissfully relaxed. I think about THE QUESTION™. This question is like the itch you can't scratch, the itch that you also can't find anyone to help you scratch. So it stays with you, always there, since childhood, unconfirmed. For 25 years I've been carrying THE QUESTION™. I've never shared it because I have never met the right person to share it with. I wouldn't just waste THE QUESTION™ on anybody. This question needs just the right somebody. And now, finally, that right somebody is walking right in front of me with Daniel. As Daniel runs to kick a ball back to a child, I have Harold to myself.

'Harold,' I say. 'I have this question. It's one of the great questions of my life. I guess I've held an observation since childhood and I'm trying to confirm why something is the way it is. Would you mind trying to help me answer it?' Now of course, Harold was never going to say no; he's far too lovely. He says, looking through his glasses, his eyes friendly with curiosity, 'Well, Ben, I'll do my best.'

'So, Harold, here's the thing,' I say. 'When I eat an apple – in fact, almost every apple I've ever eaten in my life – I notice that the bottom always tastes better than the top. Why do you think that is?'

Harold pauses for a moment, weighing what I have said, and replies, politely, 'Well, I've never had that question before, Ben. Let me think on it for a minute.' We walk for a moment, enjoying the warmth of the sun, and then Harold answers. 'I'd need to confirm this, Ben, but my take is that the cells at the bottom part of the apple contain more juice than the cells at the top of the apple,' he says. 'And when you bite into those different parts, what you are experiencing is actually the delivery of more juice in the bottom and slightly more air in the cells on the top of that apple, and thus less juice. Also, the bottom of the apple was the first part to grow and therefore it is more mature and may have higher sugar levels.'

I beam, unable to hide my adoration. Harold has solved one of humanity's great unanswered questions.

Another time, in Philadelphia, Harold, Kylie and I walked from our hotel to a restaurant that we'd been told about, braving the freezing cold on the chance we might get a table. Outside, Harold and Kylie decided I would have the best chance of getting us a seat, so in I went. One of the perks or pitfalls, depending on which way you look at it, of being a successful chef is that you sometimes get recognised when you go into a restaurant. I stood waiting for a moment before the restaurant manager looked at me blankly and politely explained there were no tables. By this time, Harold and Kylie had followed me in to escape the cold. The restaurant manager looked up, saw Harold and took on that particular expression that front-of-house staff often get when they recognise someone famous but want to play it cool. They quickly re-checked their reservations again and all of a sudden there was a table available. Harold was so kind to the staff, and they were so excited and happy to have him in for dinner. Such is the gentle power of Harold McGee.

CHIPGATE

The cultural significance of hot chips is impossible to overstate. Don't tell lasagne, but hot chips are my favourite food. Big-noting fish comes first in fish and chips, but it's always been about the latter for me.

As with many New Zealand families, fish and chips was a big treat in my youth, but for me this combo was solely a mechanism to get intimate with chips. Our spot was called Seaview Motor Camp. Beachside, next to a river mouth, black sands stretching beyond a child's vision, the camp office doubled as a fish and chip shop. For reasons that escape me now, we'd grab our order, ignore the view, and drive home in our Holden Kingswood. I'd nurse the newspaper-wrapped parcel – couldn't risk it burning my younger sisters, Tess and Tamie – and tear a hole to allow the steam to escape. This would save the family from soggy chips and would allow me to extract a chip or two and place them on the inside of the roof rail. I've known folks who get excited about air-cooled Porsches, but the chip equivalent is even more breathtaking.

I realise that you, of course, do not need any convincing that a hot chip is really the ultimate food. Few accompaniments maintain as much positivity, in the face of such historical disrespect from steak, burger and pie. Despite their often-thankless support role, chips have a quiet confidence. A crispy on the outside, fluffy on the inside, salty and savoury, 'look at how much oil we can use' rich-country marvel. Every time I dive-bomb one of those golden motherfuckers into tomato sauce, the Robin to its Batman, new neural pathways are created in my brain. (For the record, my mum is comfortable with the offensive language. She raised a better son, but this is how I ended up.)

Like untrustworthy lumpy bolognese-makers (I'll deal with them later), I don't have any faith in people who decline tomato sauce with their chips, especially those who do so for health reasons. You do realise you are eating potato impregnated with fat, right? Declining tomato sauce is like hiking all day to a beautiful waterfall, then not enjoying the view. Just like lasagne (much more on that to come as well, trust me), chips are good hot or cold. But before they can be eaten cold, chips must first be served piping hot, straight out of the fryer. I like to exercise my locus of chip control and eat them through a rainbow of temperatures for the full experience.

I could come up with a gazillion technical reasons to rationalise my chip habit, but the single most important factor in global chip addiction is much simpler than the science of millions of microscopic potato cells exploding in hot oil. According to social psychologists, the proximity effect is central in the formation of many human loving relationships, but I'd argue that the same applies to relationships between humans and their shoestrings, crinkle-cuts, steak fries, wedges and all the other chip cuts in between. It's a convenient and beautiful love. Our addiction can be fed, anywhere, at any time. Hot chips are all around us, not only because of the global ubiquity of a giant chain of restaurants hosted by a creepy clown, but also because of air fryers, food delivery services, the supermarket frozen aisle, pubs and family-owned takeaway shops, and us, *El Restaurantes!* (Winks at you in an inappropriate way.)

It's time, though, that I drew your attention to the darker, uglier, less well known side of everyone's favourite salt, starch and oil delivery system. For I have conducted a years-long investigative exposé of hot chips in restaurants: I call it Chipgate. So. Have you ever noticed that restaurant French fries often seem remarkably similar to the ones down the road at the gigantic fast-food chain? That's because, most likely, they are the fucking same! In Australia, hardly any restaurants make their own chips. I'm not talking about fast-food joints, but actual reservation-only fancy restaurants. Most restaurant chips are manufactured by one of the three enormous North American companies that dominate commercial chip production globally. These frozen frankenfries are dumped into fryers from the same industrially manufactured, five-kilo white plastic bag. It's both hilarious and sad that the bowl of fries served to us on linen-clothed tables is made in the same factory as the ones we get at the drive-thru collection window. Now, if one is intentionally dining at a multi-national fast-food restaurant chain, then one accepts the fact that one's chips will comprise all the additives and processes that industrial food manufacturing can throw at us. It's part of the deal. But your side of fries at a nice restaurant?

You might assume that such restaurants would make their own chips, right? Surely they would buy their potatoes from the same small local farmers they promote on the rest of their menu? Chips are difficult and messy to make at home, but at a restaurant, a place whose whole purpose is to do all of the hard work for you, surely they would make good on that promise and cut and fry their own potatoes? Wrong on both counts. In short, they have gotten really lazy and snuck one by us here. This is as much of a scammy card-trick as bottled water landing on the table (and bill) without being ordered – and it turns out that bottled water and frankenfries are on a restaurant's menu for the same reason: pure, simple, lazy profit. French fries are an irresistible add-on, and we are paying four times the price for the exact same product as we'd get at a fast-food joint. There's an important distinction, however, which makes it even worse. Massive fast-food chains have more advanced, expensive deep-fryers and chip-cooking systems than serious restaurants, which means their execution of the same frozen chips is undeniably better. I'm looking you straight in the eye: it is a fucking con!

This wouldn't be such an issue if some of these restaurants weren't wheeling out the old 'farm to table' ethos – which, broadly, is a load of shit anyway, because all food, at some point in time, came from a 'farm'. On menus where 'everything is sustainably sourced' it confounds me that so often this isn't applied to chips. It would be refreshing to read on a menu, 'We use a combination of small local farmers and gigantic industrial food factories.' On their way to becoming chips, those potatoes have jumped through the hoops of a chip factory's Pulsemaster, which, according to the manufacturer, achieves 'the disintegration of biological tissue', and 'is a key function in food processing to enhance winning of valuable intracellular compounds from cells'. We sure are a long way from a potato, a chopping board and a knife. Is it too much to want something potato-esque, not a chip made by a machine with a name that sounds like it belongs in a sex shop? The food element of this commercial chip equation becomes as difficult to see as the bottom of a dirty deep-fryer.

I grew up harvesting Rua potatoes from the raised beds in my grandmother Lois's garden. We'd scrub off the moist dirt and peel them in her hand-cranked 'rumbler' before cutting and frying them. Lois had inexhaustible patience with me, as I would make chips in her kitchen nearly every time I visited. In the early 90s, when I was a teenager, I worked as a bicycle mechanic at a bike shop next to a takeaway shop. The owners cut their own chips at a bench in the car park and twice-fried them long and hard in tallow until they were thick, stumpy, potato-flavoured barnacles, as crusty as treasures found in the briny deep. Every lunchtime I'd scamper next door for a brown paper bag of these gems, the fissures in their deep golden-brown surface the perfect place for the flecks of salt to nestle. Those, friends, where truly the times. And they're also the reasons why Attica has always made hand-cut chips from seasonal varieties of potatoes sourced from 'Spud Sisters' Kerri and Catherine, third-generation potato farmers in Millbrook, Victoria. I'm sure you wouldn't expect any less of us.

And look, I'm the first to admit that I'm a complete sucker for a bowl of French fries at a restaurant. My argument for writing this is a selfish one. I want to be able to order something superior! If five dudes from Virginia can hand-cut fries from fresh potatoes in every one of their 1700+ fast-food joints worldwide, then why can't restaurants? But until the day that restaurants place equal value on all the foods they serve, you'll find me, the eternal optimist, ordering hot chips at every new bistro I visit, praying that what will come makes me think of potato, rather than Skeletor: a crispy shell of nothing, with key notes of salt and grease.

A GUIDE TO GETTING OUT OF TRICKY SITUATIONS

Loose noose

At the back of Awakino Primary School, the older boys held me high up on the tree-hut platform. This was a different era for school-yard play. Once, they had put me inside a barrel and rolled it down the steep incline from the school to the rugby field. Another time, during bullrush, the entire school's favourite game, a girl had tripped over in front of me. She accused me of ankle-tapping her. I protested my innocence, but to no avail. The principal caned me. I would not be long for this school.

On the platform, one of the boys tied a rope to a branch. Another formed a noose and put that around my neck while the third boy held me. They were just about to hang me when my mother, Kaye, who was relief teaching that day, flew around the corner of the building. I have never forgotten the look on her face: pure rage and complete focus. Like a big cat defending its young, she let out a reckoning shriek, so deep, guttural and wounded that it reverberates with me still.

As she sprinted at us, the fires of Armageddon at her feet, the older boys froze in fear. 'YOU LITTLE FUCKERS!' she screamed, exaggerating each syllable as she verbally ripped them to shreds.

I have thought many times about this day, but I've only recently begun to talk about it. That's because I didn't recognise it for what it was until I had a conversation with friends, years later. It was a seriously extreme form of bullying. Although I wasn't friends with the older boys, I think I had framed it in my memory as just friends playing, because I didn't know how else to process it. I have contemplated what would have happened if my mum hadn't been at school that day. I don't think it ends well for me.

Every moment in life is interconnected to another, and each extra day you get to take a breath is a good one. My mother is a bad-ass and the absolute backbone of our family. A whip-smart, anti-racist, straight-shooting, powerful woman, and also a deeply kind person, so long as you don't fuck with her kids! That was the day I first learnt about the value of getting out of tricky situations, and I hoped that I wouldn't always need my mum to help me.

Hit, run, replenish

George Street, Sydney. It's 5pm and it's rush hour on the footpath. I'm ducking and weaving around pedestrians like I'm playing a game of Frogger, 'the game with the most ways to die'. I'm zipping along the edge of the kerb and ahead of me is a pole. To dodge it, I take a quick step right onto the road, and suddenly I'm flying. Not a cool, dreamy state of flying, but more in the vein of a-bus-just-hit-me flying. This is because a bus just hit me.

Now I'm lying on the road ahead of it. The bus, which had stopped temporarily, now drives away. People keep flowing on the footpath.

Two men jump in to help me. They barely speak a word of English, but the universal sign of need called 'lying on the ground helplessly' transcends all languages. One of the kind men stays with me while the other runs after the bus, swearing and yelling. I'm winded, in shock and unsure if I'm ok. The men want to call an ambulance, but I temporarily put on a brave face as they help me off the road, telling them I'm alright. I sit in the doorway of a closed shop and try to pull myself together. I have a 6pm booking at Marque restaurant, so I struggle up to Surry Hills on foot.

Limping up to the slick black bunker-like dining room soon after 5.30pm, I realise the restaurant isn't even open yet, but I knock on the door and a waiter asks if they can help me. Still out of it, I tell them, 'I've been hit by a bus.' Immediately they help me to the bar, prop me up and make me a stiff drink. This is my first year at Attica, and they don't know me, but they take great care of me. As I drink the liquor, I try to evaluate myself. My clothes are torn, I am bleeding from several places and I'm in shock, but miraculously, I don't think anything is broken. The bus hit me squarely from behind and must have braked suddenly before impact.

Most of the serious pain is coming from my calf muscles where the bumper hit, and my shoulder blades and the back of my head. The grazing is superficial. I raced downhill mountain bikes in my teens, and if there's one thing that sport teaches you, it's to take stock of your body after a crash. The bus impact reminds me of the time I hit a tree head-on at speed during a race, jumped straight back on my bike concussed, rounded the next corner and fell again, breaking my collarbone. A cameraman ran over while I lay on the ground and said, 'Dude, that crash was so gnarly, wanna see the video?!' That day ended with a helicopter flight to hospital.

The restaurant was keen to call an ambulance, but I didn't want to miss dinner. Eating in great restaurants is one of the most important forms of education for young hospitality workers and, at the time, Marque was one of the most acclaimed in Australia. The meal that followed was a revelation and totally saved the rough start to the evening. In my state, I was not an ideal customer, but as the Marque team worked their magic, delivering invigorating and startling snacks, and uplifting things to drink, I began to forget the pain and my worry about whether I was internally bleeding to death. Instead, I became transfixed by their care and craft. They helped me out of a tricky situation and gave me a memory much greater than the feeling of being hit by a bus. That is one of the incredible roles a great restaurant can play – to create a deep emotional reaction. At our best we have the power to turn around a bad day.

Strong handshake

I once worked for a chef who told me repeatedly: 'Look after your hands. For a chef, hands are the most important tool you will ever own. Always protect them.'

A lifetime later, dusk is coming quickly and with one hand I am wrestling with a solid wooden door. With the other hand I'm watching a YouTube tutorial on how to install a door. Heavy it be. Stressful it be. I'm knackered from an eighty-hour work week. And, having driven home to the Bellarine Peninsula, I'm rushing to get this door installed so I can lock the house. Finally, I've mounted it on its hinges. I grab the corded drill my father gave me.

If drills were cars, this one would be an HSV Holden Commodore: beefed up, overpowered, high torque, muscular and awkward to use. I take a 54-millimetre hole saw, tighten it in the chuck on this V8 drill and begin to cut the hole for the lock. By now it's dark and as I'm halfway through cutting the hole I hear a sound behind me. Concerned it's a small child, I turn my head slightly. My shoulders follow and I lift my left drill-bracing hand. In a split second the hole saw grips the hardwood and the drill violently whips around, slamming into the back of my right hand. The action is so sudden and violent that I immediately slump on the floor and scream for help, clutching at my hand. As I am going into shock, I curse my stupidity.

Later that night at Geelong hospital, they seem to think it's only a very bad sprain, but because of the intense swelling they are unsure. I return to work the following day. As my right hand is my knife hand, it's a long week of painful chopping. On Friday the kitchen receives an unexpected visitor. It's Ray, who used to work with us. Ray is really excited to be back, and I have my back turned as he enters my area of the kitchen and rushes up behind me like a bull at a gate.

As I turn to say hello, he grabs my right hand and gives it the hardest handshake I've ever received. Instead of a handshake, though, Ray kind of folds my hand in half, lengthways. I feel the bone break. Although the blood drains from my face and nausea rolls over me, I don't want him to know he broke my hand, because he'd be mortified. I grimace and say, 'It's good to see you, Ray. Thank you for coming.'

Sitting in the office, I feel my hand throb with the rhythm of my heart, making it difficult to dial the number of a regular diner at Attica who also happens to be one of Melbourne's leading hand surgeons. He diagnoses my injury as a spiral fracture of my fourth metacarpal. My hand is broken in three places. I have two options: 1. Let it heal naturally, or 2. Have surgery. Although he attempts to tell me I need two weeks off post-surgery, I opt for this as it presents the quickest return to work. He thinks I'm a maniac but understands the pressure I'm under.

During the operation he puts a titanium plate and five pins in my hand, so it will be 'immediately stronger than it was before'. As the effects of the general anaesthetic wear off, I lie on the sofa at home, listening to the muffled sound of birds tweeting and the rolling surf in the distance. It is the most peaceful I've felt in a long time.

The following day I return to work, arm in sling, my post-surgery hand burning with the intensity of our charcoal grill. Working with my left hand all week is slow and awkward, but at least I'm able to contribute during dinner service by calling the pass. Like all the forms of pain I've endured, both mental and physical, the mind softens the experience over time. Nowadays, if I injured myself I would be able to take time off, but to get through this lean time I resolved to stay away from powerful drills and men with strong handshakes.

Too much to bear

To finish my dish, what I really need is 800 baby wasabi leaves. Not 200, nor 400 – only 800 will suffice. I am quite certain that Earth will spin right off its axis if I cannot fulfil my quixotic desire for 800 tiny, majestic wasabi leaves, not a bug-hole in a single one of them. Ten leaves will complement each of the eighty serves of my crystalline broth of shiitake mushrooms, with its small and seductively plump sweet shrimp. The shrimp are so fresh they are translucent and will poach ever so lightly when I pour the hot broth over them tableside. Combined with this are the first freshly dug peanuts of the season, from which I have painstakingly removed the papery red skin so they now shimmer in the swirly ivory-glazed handmade bowl like pearls. All of it will be in vain, however, without wasabi leaves!

Thanks to my most accommodating hosts, it just so happens that I find myself transported to a forest in Ishikawa Prefecture, Japan.

This forest has a wasabi carpet. Everywhere, as far as the eye can see, there is the foliage of wasabi plants growing wild under the canopy of venerable old trees. I'm dumbfounded. I had never considered the notion of wasabi as a wild plant. This is foolish of me, as almost all of the cultivated foods we consume can be traced back to their wild origins. As I taste the leaves, stems and roots in the forest, their potent spiciness reminds me that the plant is screaming at me. The next time you eat wasabi, consider for a moment what exactly the plant is trying to tell you – it's saying, 'Fuck right off and leave me alone. I will fuck you right up.'

Every person who has eaten just a little bit too much wasabi in one hit subconsciously knows this already. But scientifically it is a fact, too. The volatile, stick-up-the-nose, neck twistin', eye waterin' pungency of wasabi is caused by allyl isothiocyanate, a chemical that by design is wasabi's defence mechanism. Technically speaking, allyl isothiocyanate translated into wasabi language means 'fuck you'.

I've enlisted Swedish chef Magnus Nilsson, my compadre and roommate on this chef-junket trip, as my chief picker. Magnus is diligent. He clearly knows his way around a forest and together, with a couple of journalists in tow, we harvest the required 800 leaves in no time.

Stepping out of the canopy into low misty light and onto a steep road, we are approached by two Japanese hunters. No one in our wasabi gathering party can speak Japanese, and the hunters do not speak English. They wave us over towards a modest hillside building, beautifully clad in shou sugi ban charred cedar, which blends harmoniously with the landscape, appearing as if it grew alongside the forest. The hunters offer us a plate of food. As we approach, they hold it out in front of them excitedly, gesturing for us to help ourselves. It is a plate of raw meat, carefully cut into thin slices like carpaccio. It is naked; no salt, no oil. In colour it is a dark, deep burgundy, tinged with violet. The coarse grain of the cross-cut muscle shimmers like oil on a wet road. I don't want to be crass, but it looks a bit fucking scary.

From a distance, Magnus takes a glance at it and subtly hangs back. Although I have no idea what meat this is (I presume it is wild venison) I don't want to cause offence, so I take a piece and pop it in my mouth. It's bland, slightly frozen, and a little bit chewy, with a fibrous texture, but generally it is unremarkable. The two journalists follow suit and take a piece, too. Magnus does not. He's waiting for meat verification. Soon confirmation arrives in the form of our hosts, who earnestly tell us that it is the leg meat of a bear. *Ooft*, I think, not something I'd eat by choice.

Magnus tells the group, in his matter-of-fact Swedish tone, that in Sweden bears carry trichinosis and if a person eats it raw, then a near-certain and painful death follows. A panic comes over us. The journalists google trichinosis and discover that it's a disease carried by certain wild animals, including bears. Parasitic larvae can squirrel from the ingested meat into a human's intestine, growing and multi-plying and entering the bloodstream before eventually making their way to the skeletal muscle, where they make a cosy home deep in one's bones. After that, one becomes death.

For the poor journalists, it is just too much to bear (sorry). The two of them run across the road and, fingers down throat, force themselves to vomit up the bear into the ditch. I'm less flummoxed. Eating is a tricky business, but I will not stoop to the indignity of forced vomiting. I take comfort in the knowledge that I have never had a bad meal in Japan, and trust that these hunters are no fools. If this is to be my last day, then fuck it. Lay me down to rest in a wasabi forest.

The mule

The top of the unpainted, difficult wall was fifteen metres from the ground. The painters said they couldn't reach it without specialist scaffolding. I told them to leave it to me. Kylie said, 'Don't you dare go up there to paint that, Ben.' Kylie went home, having reinforced her orders, and I was all alone at the site of our new venture in the Yarra Valley. The wall still wasn't painted, and every time I walked past it seemed to say, 'Please paint me.'

On my first attempt, I climbed to the fourth-last rung of a five-metre extension ladder, armed with a paint roller on a long pole, but even with my body fully outstretched I was still a full metre short. As I gingerly climbed down, I saw the painters' scissor-lift sitting all alone in the corner of the building. This scissor-lift was a big, heavy sucker and could happily hold three people at once. I flicked the key on and gave it a test drive on the flat concrete driveway. Seemed pretty straightforward to operate.

The problem was that the ground level of the wall that required painting was on an incline. Scissor-lifts don't like inclines. I knew this because of the big warning sticker by the controls picturing a scissor-lift on an incline with a big red 'X' through it. Just a guide really, I thought to myself. The other problem was there was lawn between the base of the wall and where I was on the driveway. Turns out, due to their immense weight, scissor-lifts don't like lawns very much either. This part I didn't know yet.

I slowly tested the scissor-lift by inching its front wheels out onto the lawn. They immediately sank into the grass and soil. I reversed it back and decided that if I was going to get it onto the concrete pad in front of me I would need a run up. I got a long run up, came in hot off the driveway, and managed to skid it across the lawn onto the base of the wall, which was just slightly larger than the scissor-lift.

Paint pole in hand, up I went. Now, despite not knowing much about inclines, it was impossible to ignore the fact that the higher I went, the more extreme the lean on the scissor-lift became. The Leaning Tower of Pisa has a 5.5-degree lean perpendicular to the ground, and I'd estimate that my scissor-lift was at least the same, based on the scientific observation of my tools rolling away from me on the platform.

Adding to the drama was the scissor-lift itself, which was letting off a series of alarms. I got to the top of the lift's range and it was wobbly as all hell. Petrified, I wasted valuable seconds planning a spot to jump to if the lift toppled over, but given how high I was off the ground, that would have been totally futile. I quickly smashed out the painting job and lowered the lift as fast as I could, heart pounding, the whole time thinking about how I really dodged one there, but ultimately feeling very pleased that the wall was now painted.

Now I only had to return the lift across the lawn and back to its parking spot. I attempted to make a fifteen-point turn on the small pad but immediately got the back wheels beached on the lawn. Fuck. Further manoeuvres only served to get the lift more stuck. After thirty minutes, the scissor-lift was on the lawn on its belly, its four wheels fully sunken into the soft ground. Swearing and sweating, I stood back, scratched my head and wondered what to do.

First, I placed sheets of plywood onto the lawn and attempted to drive it up onto these, but the wheels just spun in the dirt. I got my car jack out, but that just sank into the dirt. Lamely I tied a ratchet to a pole and attempted to pull it out with that, but it wouldn't budge. All useless moves from a desperate man. Wiping my brow after two hours of failed attempts, I searched for a way out of this.

I was well and truly wrecked by this point and imagined how I was going to explain to the painters, who were an already cranky bunch, that I had got their expensive piece of hire gear stuck on the lawn. That was going to be an embarrassing conversation. As the light faded, I heard a tractor in the paddock nearby. I jumped the fence and ran over to the farmer to explain the tight spot I was in. He said, 'Yeah, no worries, mate, I'll come over when I've finished feeding the horses.'

When he arrived and saw the situation, he didn't say much but gave me a look that said, *Mate, you are an absolute dickhead.* We fixed a chain to the lift, then painfully inched the lift back onto the driveway, using wood to chock the small wheels. An hour later and job done. I said a grateful thank you. The bottom of the lift and wheels were caked in dirt. I set to work and made sure it looked cleaner than before I borrowed it, then parked it back in its spot, the painters none the wiser. That only left Kylie to deal with. I didn't say a word, but as soon as she arrived the next day she noticed the painted wall, shook her head and said, 'You total arsehole.' Smiling sheepishly, I said, 'Would you like a hug, baby?' 'Fuck off,' she said.

THE PIG

The light is low across the dining room in North Atlantic House, Christianshavn. This is a new restaurant, but the stone walls anchor this place to the past. Two hundred years earlier, leather and oak were shipped from this sixteenth-century warehouse in Denmark to the North Atlantic colonies. Now these materials adorn the tables, chairs and menus of Restaurant Barr. Materials that are the natural palette of the Scandinavian design aesthetic provide an effortless duality between the old and the new, a look so ersatz elsewhere that it's a cliché – but in Copenhagen it is home, it is calm. The space is cavernous, warm and friendly. Food tourists on the inside, and beyond the glass, tourist-tourists wander the docks in the late summer sun.

On the eve of an important speech I am to make at the MAD Symposium (an international gathering to discuss and shape the future of food), Kylie and I both feel drained. She focuses her attention on a saison ale. I bury myself in the menu: brown crab with southern Jutland waffles, Swedish meatballs, proper Wiener schnitzel with brown butter and anchovy and, for dessert, acidic

Danish strawberries, calyx elegantly attached, nature's handle. All interpretations of 'Northern Sea Cuisine' by chef Thorsten Schmidt.

Kylie is unusually quiet. Normally she maintains a child-like wonder for eating out that balances my occasional cynicism of fine restaurants. Across the table, I reach for her hand and ask, 'Are you ok?' She brushes off my question, but her moist eyes say something else. Softly, but with an edge, she says, 'You know, Ben, a woman should be telling the stories you are going to tell. Men always get the platform and it's frustrating.' Looking down, I tear at my waffle and drag it through the crab, letting her words sink in. This is during the height of the re-emergence of #MeToo in 2018, and also the early stages of our relationship, where we are feeling one another out and challenging each other's perceptions, and I recognise her words as the truth. Although she wouldn't want to make the speech herself, many of my views are informed by her experiences, those of my mother and of my women colleagues. I knew it was a fact the first time they had asked me to give this talk, and I had initially said no. It wasn't my place. But they came back to me and asked again, saying, 'We need a male chef with the moral authority.' I'm not sure if I am that man, but because it was a woman doing the asking, and because I had the support of Kylie and the encouragement of Lisa Abend, my friend and an acclaimed journalist who would be interviewing me on stage the following day, I reluctantly agreed.

As Kylie divides the meatballs between our plates, I ask, 'Has any of that stuff ever happened to you?' 'Of course it has, Ben. It has happened to all of us.' Kylie bites her lower lip and smiles uneasily; I move my chair closer to comfort her. She grips my hand tightly and, like the first rains of a storm approaching in the distance, Kylie begins to tell me a story.

'I worked at a place for two years that was owned by an acclaimed chef – let's call him "Cerdo". I was so excited about getting a job at his restaurant. The public adored him for what he had accomplished. Slowly I worked my way up to a supervisor position and became a big part of the business. I was locking up the restaurant at nights and I was opening up for the lunch shift during the day. I had a lot of responsibility. Cerdo seemed kind of awkward around women; he would always remember all of the guys' names but not the women's names. He'd arrive at the restaurant and say "hi" to all of the male chefs or the male restaurant manager, but never to us. If I or another woman would greet him, he'd say, "aww aww, yeh yeh" and walk away. He didn't engage with the women employees very much. It was quite odd, he just seemed weird.

'Despite him, I made some really good friends there, but eventually I left and started working at another restaurant where I took care of the reservations and worked nights on the door, hosting. I'd usually come in from the office at five o'clock when all of the other front-of-house staff would break for dinner briefing. There would be hardly anyone in the place and I'd look after the restaurant by myself while the team discussed the reservations, and food and drink specials for the night's service.'

Kylie's courage builds and, although I can see she's struggling, she takes a deep breath and a gulp of water and continues. 'One night I started my shift and I saw that Cerdo was dining with three mates. They'd been there since lunchtime and had moved from the dining room to the bar. You could tell they were quite intoxicated, and I was like ugh, I REALLY don't want to serve them. Not because it was him, but because it was a group of guys who were drunk and that is never a pleasant experience. All the other staff went into briefing, and his table had empty glasses, so I went over to clear them and to see if they needed anything else, and Cerdo was like, "Hey, Kylie!" I was so excited and pleased that he remembered my name. I felt really good, because he seemed so happy to see me and he'd never said my name before. And then he started telling his friends that I used to work for him and that I was really good at my job. I was feeling even better about myself, and I thought that it was a nice thing for him to say.'

Kylie begins to choke up and raises her hand to her face. My throat tightens. The feeling is like walking on the crest of a dark country road, dressed in black, and hearing the sound of a car hurtling your way, but unable to see its lights. She regains just enough control to continue and says, 'With a smirk, one of his friends said, "She was good at her job, was she?" Cerdo replied, "Well, if you'd like to know just how good she is at her job, you can take her into the toilets and find out."

'The table erupted into laughter, and I was just standing there, in front of them, holding empty beer glasses. I felt so humiliated and ashamed. Just a moment before, I'd felt so good about myself. I felt stupid for feeling good about him remembering my name which made his words even more painful. They were all looking me up and down and laughing loudly and without saying anything, I just kind of walked off and didn't go back to their table. All I'd wanted was to do my job, you know? I felt dead inside. I wished I was invisible, like this wasn't really happening. I've never told anyone this except you.

'Straight out of high school I'd been groped and insulted by male customers and, as a woman working in hospitality, there's a part of me that kind of pre-loads the expectation of highly sexualised insults. But it is still, no matter how many times it happens, shocking to me. I can't blunt the trauma. You put in all this work, and I tried so hard at his restaurant. I had looked up to him, and it knocked my confidence for years to come and made it hard for me to trust mentors. I felt bad for his wife and children, because they used to come into the restaurant all the time and were really nice. Years later when I saw that vase they sent you, congratulating you on everything you had accomplished, I wondered why he would have such high regard for you, someone he doesn't even know, and such a low level of respect for me.'

We're sitting in the middle of the full restaurant, waiters whirling, the walls spinning around us. We hold each other, the grain of the wooden tables reflecting the lines on our faces. There's been few times that I have felt more angry than in that moment. But deep down even my rage feels like an entitlement of my gender. By birth I've never had to endure any of this, and outraged men are accepted in society, but outraged women talking truth to power are generally portrayed as scary, angry and bitter. I want to do something about it, but Kylie begs me not to say a word to anyone. It's too painful and it has taken everything she has just to voice her story. She feels deeply embarrassed, ashamed and powerless, as though somehow she was the one who had failed. 'Really, what can I do, Ben? It's not like we can prosecute him. I don't have a voice, and right now I don't want to talk about it, nor do I want anyone else knowing he did this to me,' she says. We are quiet for some time and then she tells me that, in a small act of defiance, Cerdo 'tried to get a table at Attica a few years ago, but I let him know that none were available'. Through drawn faces, we manage a sad chuckle, but in different ways neither of us will ever be the same again.

The following day at the symposium, I continue to digest stories, this time told by two heroic women, Trish Nelson and Lisa Donovan, fellow restaurant peers who share their harrowing tales of sexual assault and harassment in the hospitality industry. There's not a dry eye in the house, and their stories are poignant reminders of the power of hearing someone's experience first-hand. These stories originate from the USA, and some of them had been uncovered through investigative journalism by *New York Times* writers Kim Severson and Julia Moskin, who won a Pulitzer Prize for their reporting. In the audience and backstage, men are visibly grappling with what they are hearing. They seem not to know what to think or how to act. After my speech, a guy asks me, 'What should I do about my urges? Am I not supposed to be sexually attracted to the women I work with?' 'Dude, get professional help, that's not cool,' I tell him. Another pillar of the restaurant community says, 'But you've always thought differently, Ben,' as if I held the proprietary rights for attempting to make the changes necessary not to be a dick (my speech was titled 'No More Cock Rock') and was somehow preventing him from addressing the culture in his own restaurant.

It's a strange, troubling afternoon and, even though it's not helpful, I feel somewhat resentful towards the men who are looking to me for guidance. Momentarily, the dial has shifted, and suddenly it's a good thing to be sensitive and vulnerable as a man (nothing new for women, just sayin'), and this is the first time I've felt this. I'm used to being mocked for my sensitivity. Over the years, I've been called 'weak', 'soft' or a 'pussy', and told on multiple occasions that I'd never lead a kitchen because I wasn't 'alpha enough' and that 'no one will ever know you are the head chef'. It's a bizarre twist of fate when the outsider becomes the insider, yet it shouldn't be remarkable to behave and lead with basic decency. Some of these men remind me of herding dogs who've bitten a sheep and know they are about to feel the wrath of the farmer. I don't know how to feel or act, so I just smile and internalise it all. Clearly, sexual harassment and assault is a men's issue, but cruelly, women become the victims, survivors and educators. But we are not here for the sympathy of men. More positively, the symposium provides a glimmer of hope that just maybe someone will be brave enough, and well supported enough, to research and publish these sorts of stories back home.

Now, more than five years on, without a single article of any significance published, and with the sad saga of Brittany Higgins currently making headlines, I've concluded that in Australia it is almost impossible for men to be held accountable for serious misdeeds, let alone for the victims of sexual assault or harassment to achieve justice. Watching this unfold, it will be a miracle if any woman comes forward publicly with stories of impropriety by powerful men. In our culture, women have nothing to gain and everything to lose. In the years since Kylie told me her story, I've heard other women speak unprompted about their experiences with Cerdo, about how he tilled a kitchen fertile with misogyny and instilled crippling self-doubt in the women chefs he employed.

What lies in the heart of men like Cerdo is a deep hatred of women and, simultaneously, fear. Sexist men are fearful. It's a fear of losing something – POWER, and it's a fear of not getting what they want – CONTROL. In kitchens, along with most parts of society, it's a well-known fact that men have always held most of the power. But in 2018 we began to see that women weren't going to put up with this bullshit anymore, and it felt like a real moment of change, a moment that many hoped would last, but instead it now feels more like a pause. Although we saw a few powerful men ousted, we have not yet seen the sort of societal transformation that would develop fully realised, safe and equal opportunities for women in workplaces. We've taken our foot off the gas on this issue, which has given rise to a second, more emboldened wave of misogyny. Society has given men the right to act a certain way for so long, and now in the worst-case examples we see a few awful men doubling down on it, as though their fear drives them to hate even harder. As men, our sexism is something we need to be conscious of daily, I think. And until gender equality is achieved, it needs to be something that society discusses continuously. This is a critical issue, and one faced by other marginalised sectors of the industry who are also discriminated against, or not given the same opportunities or treated with the respect they deserve because of race, sexuality or disability.

In restaurants, many of the worst stories that came out of #MeToo had two main things in common: problematic men, and drug and alcohol abuse. Not for one second is the latter an excuse for indefensible behaviour. But it is a hard, cold fact that any workplace culture of regular partying, excessive consumption of alcohol and drug-taking will lead to problematic and likely unsafe environments for their staff. A business owner, restaurateur, head chef or head waiter who oversees this type of culture is putting the people they employ at risk of serious harm, and holds us all down by damaging the reputation of our profession. Which leads me to 'The Book', a spectre that hangs over every chef who writes a memoir.

The first time I read the 'The Book', aka the late Anthony Bourdain's memoir *Kitchen Confidential*, it made me uncomfortable. Not for its lack of truth, but rather because of its unabashed telling of the truth, and the perpetual celebration of that truth, which continues to this day. The truth of bro culture, overt sexualisation of women, glamourisation of excessive drinking and drug abuse, and general poor behaviour in restaurants. You may say, 'But Ben, that was a different time.' To that I would say, 'But *WHEN* will it be a *DIFFERENT* time?' This behaviour continues in the hospitality industry while the book and its author are still held up as heroic by millions, to what effect? I recall, not long after his tragic death, being called out by male chefs on social media for not honouring him with an epitaph (which, of course, would have been disingenuous of me) and one message stuck with me: 'Why couldn't you even give old Anthony a shout out when he died?' Such is the total devotion of some of his male chef fans, that they would heckle another chef about not paying him his dues, as if all chefs are bound to feel the same reverence for him. To many chefs, his book is sacrosanct, above any rational questioning. I'm certain they will be sending hellfire my way for this, but this is not a shot at him. Rather, it's a shot at blind devotion by toxic meatheads.

For the record, I did not know Mr Bourdain. I met him once in Japan as he filmed us, an all-male group of chefs, for his show 'No Reservations'. He seemed shy and nervous around us. I know he lived to have significant regrets about the sexist, male-dominated world he portrayed in *Kitchen Confidential*, with lines of biting cruelty like, 'Women who can survive and prosper in such a high-testosterone universe are all too rare.' *Kitchen Confidential* does not exactly promote a hopeful picture of equality. Of course, the behaviour he documents did not begin or end with his book, and it is not a crime to reveal the truth of it, but in restaurants it lives on – and with well over one million copies sold, and hardly a decent bookshop on the planet that doesn't have a copy for sale in its food section all these years later, it still has the potential to cause further damage.

In his own words: 'I would go to signings a few years after *Kitchen Confidential* came out, and people would come up to me, mostly guys, they'd high-five me over the table with one hand and slide me a packet of cocaine with the other. And it was like dude, have you not read the book? What the fuck is wrong with you?' I think that's the problem, though, they *had* read the book. Of course, people don't become serial killers just because they play violent video games, nor am I saying that no one should read it. But language shapes thought, especially for young, impressionable would-be chefs looking for heroes, and with sexism being a root cause of gender inequality globally, I doubt it is helping.

Hospitality is built less on a questioning of principles and more on the dedicated replication and authoritarian rule of senior figures. Generations of male chefs, young and old, WORSHIP *Kitchen Confidential*, so the question is, how much of an effect has this had on women in restaurants? It's unquestionable that we learn from people we admire, both the good and the bad. Was there a copy on the bookshelf in Cerdo's office? Did he laugh when he read it? Mr Bourdain and Cerdo are from a similar era, raised in kitchens which were, at the very least, unfriendly places to women. They grew up part of the same cultural movement and are products of that time, albeit one was Don Draper charming, the other, well, a swine.

From male attitudes towards women, to the drug and alcohol abuse I've witnessed in restaurants over the years, I'd say that *Kitchen Confidential* offers validation, however misguided, of poor behaviour for men who are looking for it. If you listen to parts of the audio book now, or read the printed edition, it's hard to argue otherwise. If, as male chefs, *Kitchen Confidential* is our most sacred tome, then what does that say about us? To me, it says that an industry that celebrates the flawed will remain flawed.

What Mr Bourdain's devotees may not fully appreciate is that his early attitude towards women slowly grew from him thinking of them as sexual objects, that he gleefully described a career-defining moment as being shagged by the head chef out the back by the rubbish bins, while the kitchen crew looked on, after which he said: 'And I knew then, dear reader, for the first time: I wanted to be a chef.'

Just a bit of a joke between the boys, right? Fuck off. Tell that to a woman, any woman you know, who will definitely have been on the receiving end of male 'jokes'. Shame on you, Mr Bourdain.

Later in his life, after listening to women involved in the #MeToo movement and seeing his powerful male chef, restaurateur and musician friends get taken down as a result of their own horrendous conduct, he wrote, 'To the extent which my work in *Kitchen Confidential* celebrated or prolonged a culture that allowed the kind of grotesque behaviours we're hearing about all too frequently is something I think about daily, with real remorse.'

Anthony Bourdain was 43 years old when *Kitchen Confidential* was published. He never added a preface expressing his changing views to later editions of his book. Was the joke on us, Anthony? Perhaps it was, but the book was not the man, only a snapshot of the man, at a different point of his life. No more than this book is me; for it to be 'me', it would never be finished, I would be writing it forever. The same goes for the vast majority of us; our story is not finished yet. We have the potential to be better. Will we realise that potential?

'The Book' wasn't Bourdain's only legacy, or the only thing he should be defined by. But it's time to dump the sexist outlaw shit and egomania at the door and leave the emulation of that book to its reverence for stocks and sauces. If 'old Anthony' can wake the fuck up, then men, so can we all.

A LETTER TO ELLA

Darling, there's been times during my career where I've felt like if I had a kid that there's no way that I'd let them enter the hospitality industry.

I first stepped inside a professional kitchen when I was a child. It was a rough and tumble world. Some sank like stones. Others swam. In kitchens you learnt to survive fast. I was punished for not being a smoker. I was punished for not being much of a drinker. I was punished for my curiosity. I was yelled at for not yelling. I was abused mentally and physically. Many times, I felt like an outsider in what was most definitely an outsider's world. Bruised but not broken.

Earlier this year, at thirteen years old, you came to me and said, 'Dad, I want to become a pastry chef.' My reaction was one of both immense pride and horror. The horror was the history. My history, the hospitality industry's history. The pride was that you have grown up at Attica, spent time in the kitchen from the day you could walk. Countless weekends and holidays here. Played bunnies in the dining room. Played waiter with the staff. Called the pass with Attica head chef Matt. Picked and portioned thousands and thousands of flowers and herbs. Even lived here temporarily. Was I blind to it? I honestly didn't see it coming, although for years you worked here every Friday night by your own demand. I never noticed how much you loved it, how you, like me, had fallen in love with hospitality. Whenever you spoke of Attica, you spoke of the people. 'So interesting and so kind, Dad.' Always nagging me to take you to the restaurant if the staff were there.

Slowly, the plates shift beneath us. There's hope and it will be applied to your generation. While the times have changed in hospitality, they have not changed nearly enough. We speak of sustainability often but seldom do we ever apply it to our humans. The next generation, with the support of my generation, can be the first to make our industry into a true profession, a calling. Something that is attractive for young people to join. A place where women have the same opportunities that men are afforded. Where diversity is not tolerated but instead celebrated. The rotten actors will be weeded out and composted. Your generation will know not to put up with what I did, nor carry it forward. Your generation should expect more.

I'm hopeful that you will find the same joys that I find. The most amazing friendships, the camaraderie. The family spirit that exists in caring restaurants. I've been around almost every kind of business in my life, and none of them have the spirit that exists in restaurants. Non-hospitality people are fascinated and horrified by the tell-all books and television that glorify the dark side of working in kitchens – and that still exists, but within the good side there's also a depth, a richness that to me has been far greater than money. It's worth fighting for. Soon it will be your fight. Lead with your heart, trust your gut, learn that a sustainable restaurant is a profitable one – but profits can never come before staff or community. Dive in, eyes open. Run your own race – never compare yourself to others. Work your arse off – that never goes out of fashion. Hold on, find the good people – stick with them – through some

of the greatest times of your life. All the tears and all the laughter together.
They will be there for you, as they are for me.

Good things have happened, better things will come.

All my love, sweet girl,

Dad

EAT THE PROBLEM

A key rattles in the lock as a weary Kylie arrives home from her shift, slipping in as I prepare to slip out. The kids are wrapped up tight asleep, oblivious. Despite our exhaustion, we kiss in the hallway. Her shoulders rise slightly as she pulls me close, then rests her head on my shoulder and takes a deep breath, as if she is exhaling her stress onto me. And, with an 'I love you,' I'm off into the night, driving through the ghostly streets to still and dark Attica.

The click-boom-spit of the lighter igniting the just-washed gas hob, the familiar whir of the extraction hood, suddenly drowned out by the sound of Television's 'Little Johnny Jewel' on the kitchen stereo. Three 60-litre pots lined up in a row, 100 kilos of beef mince on the bench. The kitchen is coming to life at the time it traditionally gets to rest. I'm on a solitary lockdown bolognese shift. The kitchen has been struggling to make enough bolognese and bechamel so I'm working from 11pm to 9am, for fourteen days straight, to help ease the burden. The bulk cookery skills I learnt in catering kitchens in my teens, which I once found embarrassing and discarded in favour of ambitious cooking, have become furiously valuable in this time.

Within the loneliness, my mind occasionally drifts to dark places – will the roof cave in? Do I have my clothes on? Tom Verlaine's virtuosic guitar helps bat them away, keeping me sane. By the end of my shift, my clothing will be soaked with sweat. This is the cross-fit of cooking – I'm simultaneously managing 200 kilos of bolognese and 100 litres of bechamel in a flat-out race to the finish line, which is 9am, when I return home for another handover with Kylie, who will already have gotten the kids up, in the shower, made them breakfast and baked her signature zucchini slice for our home-school lunch. She'll hug me like she's trying to collapse a balloon, then she'll be off to organise the new day's delivery run of over a hundred lasagnes.

Bolognese and lasagne first made their appearance in my life in the late 1970s, when I was two years old. They quickly became staples in our family and represented the closest thing we had to family dishes, without having many ties to our own cultural identity. Lasagne was also the pasta dish that my father, Rob, thought was 'real food' – unlike all those other weak and pathetic pastas that can't provide any sustenance to a rugged man putting in a hard day scrub-cutting on the farm. And so, in our family, we regularly made bolognese and lasagne, but not a single other 'Italian' dish, although over-cooked boiled spaghetti with grated cheddar cheese on top was often served as a birthday breakfast treat to us kids. What's that sound? Oh, I hear it, it's Italians the world over screaming in agony.

Bolognese and lasagne became the way we celebrated every special occasion – birthdays, neighbourhood pot-luck dinners and, most importantly, Christmas Day. These dishes became so intertwined with our lives that they now form part of our culture and identity as a family. How did this happen to a family living in the middle of nowhere in New Zealand, with zero knowledge or passion for Italian food, and 18,000 kilometres away from Italy, a country we had never visited?

One reason: the supermarket. More precisely, from a recipe on the back of a bag of dried lasagne pasta that my mother picked up from a supermarket in 1978. Mum thought she'd give it a whirl, why not? Always the consummate problem solver, she needed a creative and delicious way to use the near-endless supply of beef mince that dominated two 500-litre chest freezers in my parents' garage. It's hard to imagine lasagne as a punk move now, but it was totally trailblazing, and turned out to be life-changing for our family. Keep in mind that at that time in New Zealand there was almost NO point of reference for this exotic dish, with its fancy, hard-to-pronounce name.

But how did that packet of lasagne pasta end up in our supermarket in the first place? Turns out that at the start of World War II, to get the country through this difficult period, the New Zealand government decided they needed to start manufacturing international foods locally, and they licensed the Timaru Milling Company to make pasta. In 1941 small-scale production began, although pasta wouldn't catch fire in the hearts of Kiwis until the 1970s.

For the uninitiated, New Zealand lasagne pasta, in its 'traditional' form, comes in a plastic packet as domino-sized frilly rectangles that require significant pre-cooking in salted water (translation: boil the shit of them – overcooking is impossible) before they are painstakingly laid out across bolognese and bechamel.

As a child, teenager and young adult, my obsession for this baked pasta dish only grew. Before I was ten, I had mastered both bolognese and bechamel and laid (what we call lasagne building in the big leagues) many lasagnes. My style was to stay true to the foundations of my mother's recipe, but slowly add flourishes and begin experimenting. I committed very deeply to perfecting bechamel, as we always had butter in the fridge and milk in the freezer (backcountry living dictated that we'd freeze our milk, as there was no delivery and 'the shops' were hours away). I loved to eat it on toast with peas. Early on, I discovered that I can make bechamel velvety smooth with only a wooden spoon, a trick I later adored teaching the professional chefs in my team. From that moment on, I would look down on those using whisks for their bechamel.

Listening to the Violent Femmes when making bechamel stresses me out. Don't try it. Or do. At Inglewood High School, in home economics, all the other kids made toasted sandwiches and milkshakes. I took the opportunity to perfect a microwave lasagne where, scarily, everything including the mince goes into the microwave raw. Later, living in Canada for a winter, I supplement my board in a house of fifteen snowboarders by whipping up batches of lasagne for breakfast, lunch and dinner. By the end of the season, desperately broke but too proud to ask for help, I frequented the Salvation Army, who kindly fed me with their bolognese. As a young man, I often poured my heart (and too much red wine) into lasagne as a special meal for lovers (with mixed results) and friends (who, kindly, always told me it was great). And sure enough, my children fell madly in love with lasagne too, and so our family tradition continues alive and well into the third generation.

The ten commandments of bolognese and lasagne

1. There's no such thing as a bad lasagne. In culinary wastelands such as shopping malls, hospitals, ski resorts and airplanes,

it can sometimes be hard to identify lasagne as lasagne. Under normal conditions, it would be the stuff of nightmares. But during the second leg of a twelve-hour, long-haul flight, when lasagne's heady fragrance comes wafting down the aisle, it's been known to make this grown man's heart swell with anticipation. Even when it's bad, it's good. Even the poorest, most mechanised attempts have a redeeming characteristic. Plus, who am I to judge? I've committed some heinous crimes against lasagne.

In New Zealand, we are responsible for a dish (loose term) called lasagne topper: a crumbed, deep-fried slab of lasagne found nationwide in dairies (convenience stores) and, joyously, in the bain-marie of my chef-school canteen on Fridays. Even this low-brow bastard cousin of lasagne is good, as far as I'm concerned, although now I only eat it discreetly in private (along with the occasional secret listen to its perfect accompaniment, Coldplay). The dish may be a source of great shame to the nation, but its fatty, cheesy, crispy pie-warmer pleasures are known and loved by tradies and schoolchildren throughout Aotearoa's twin islands.

2. In the history of the world, there's been only one exception to the rule above. A young apprentice chef, who shall remain nameless (Matt Boyle), once cooked the worst lasagne I've ever eaten for an Attica staff meal. He was nineteen years old and full of misguided confidence about his lasagne-making abilities. Having never made the dish before, and despite my repeated questioning of his experience and conveying of my family's affection for it, he said, 'Come on, maaate, how hard can it be?' and charged ahead. Poor Matt did not correctly calculate two fundamentals of lasagne – flavour and moisture. It was completely devoid of both. It was one of the saddest staff meals ever

served. The post-meal atmosphere was morose; it felt like a member of the family had died. A huge amount of time, money, effort and attention to detail are put into our staff meals – they are served daily at 4pm and are the soul of the team, the fuel that powers them through high-performance nightly services. When someone gets it wrong, it's an abysmal occasion that can negatively affect the whole business. Counter-intuitively, many restaurants serve their staff much lower quality meals than their guests, but not Attica. But the importance of our staff meals had been lost on Matt, and we all suffered hungrily through that night.

Instead of getting angry, I expressed a deep disappointment, then told Matt we would be having lasagne for staff dinner the following night, and to meet me in the kitchen at 7am. Together we painstakingly made lasagne from scratch. I taught Matt every single detail, from a slow-cooked, deeply flavoured beef ragu, to handmade egg-pasta sheets blanched in boiling salted water then refreshed in iced water, to a perfect rich, velvety bechamel. We made two huge trays of lasagne, and it took the two of us absolutely hustling from 7am until 4pm to complete the task. The team adored the meal, and Matt was shocked at the effort it took to make this simple dish at a high level. Eleven years later, Matt Boyle is the head chef of Attica, makes a seriously mean lasagne, and I couldn't be prouder of him.

3. Lasagne hides brutality. My father was known as 'the butcher of Awakino'. I just made that up, but really my dear dad should have been called that because his butchering skills on our family farm were rudimentary, to put it kindly. I recall a steak that he once served me that had a huge piece of artery jutting out of the middle of it. I sat at the table staring at it, half expecting

the steak to burst back into life, spraying blood throughout the kitchen. I was eight. I didn't touch another steak until I qualified as a chef at eighteen. Which brings me to the dark side of lasagne: it can hide anything, even arteries. Trust me, I know. My childhood lasagnes were filled with them. Feeling squeamish? Don't be: bolognese is a result of that most magical of human activities, cooking. We take raw ingredients and through the use of fire, mind and hands, a transformation takes place that turns these modest ingredients into a dish far greater and more delicious than the sum of its parts. Lasagne is a celebration of the best and worst of humanity!

4. Garlic doesn't belong in bolognese. Reread that line. Don't feel bad, I only recently learnt this myself on a trip to Bologna, the spiritual and actual home of bolognese, and it shook me to my core. (Somebody tell the rest of the world.) As the aftershocks reverberated, I calculated that I must have spent over $12,000 on garlic for bolognese in the last two years alone. I was further flabbergasted when, at 45 years old, I made my first bolognese without garlic and didn't miss it. Strap yourself in: some of you might be even more surprised to learn that not only does bolognese not have garlic in it, but it's not called bolognese either. Are you questioning your very existence? In Bologna, on restaurant menus, it is listed as tagliatelle al ragu. One could correctly assume that in Bologna there would be no need to remind ourselves of where we are by calling ragu (stew) 'bolognese'. By now, you may also have guessed that there is no spaghetti bolognese in Bologna. As if these facts weren't perplexing enough for those of us who live outside of Italy, the pasta used for lasagne in Bologna is Teenage Mutant Ninja Turtle green from the addition of spinach: la pasta verde. In one swift daytrip,

everything I thought I knew about bolognese and lasagne had completely burst, like the tears of northern Italians every time they eat 'Italian food' outside of Italy. On behalf of Shewrys worldwide, I would like to formally apologise to your ancestors.

5. Screw tradition. Again, with apologies to northern Italy. Fuck rules: this is, after all, a book that's in part about breaking them. Make your damned lasagne however you like to eat it. Just as it is for the rest of us in the family, my mother's is still my favourite. Even if I once told Kylie that hers was the best I've ever tasted. Even if Kylie and I once told a very stern cook inside a food court (DeGusto Coop, Mercato di Mezzo, Bologna) that theirs was the best we've ever tasted. Every time I eat lasagne, I honestly believe it's going to be the best I've ever had. I'm irrepressible when it comes to lasagne. Of course, I'm human, so am often disappointed, but fortunately I benefit from a super-short-term memory and just keep picking myself back up to head for the next plate. The quest continues.

6. Hot lasagne is a dish best shared. All my favourite early memories of lasagne are from the potluck dinners my folks used to hold with other families from our district. Scrapping over the crispy-edge bits is a favourite Shewry pastime. If I'm feeling generous, I'll serve my dinner guests all the crispy edges first and serve myself the sloppy middle last, but only if they arrive with special bottles of red wine. Self-sacrifice at its finest. Fights over left-over cold lasagne the next morning should be a blood sport, with families rumbling over it straight outta the fridge. As a child, I'd always be the first out of bed to devour whatever was left. Call me a heretic, but lasagne is one of those rare dishes that I'd argue is as good cold as it is hot. Cold lasagne should

always be eaten straight out of the dish – standing, spoon in hand, alone, with eyes on the door and a quick exit in mind.

7. Lasagne is the world's greatest natural high. Making lasagne was the highlight of my early career. At the now-closed Time Out Café in New Plymouth, New Zealand, when I was fourteen years old, I progressed from dishwasher to lasagne maker, the greatest honour of my fledgling career. I watched for the first time as a serve of my lasagne floated across the dining room to a guest whose huge smile of approval as fork was brought to mouth was like a shot of lightning to the heart – if a shot of lightning to the heart, rather than being fatal, was the best thing that had ever happened to you. I let out a glorious internal shriek, my hair stood on end and, in that single euphoric moment, lasagne and I were bonded forever.

8. Lumpy bolognese is a sin. Lean in close, this is serious. It has been brought to my attention that some people don't even know that lumpy bolognese is a problem at all, which sends a chilling shiver down my spine. I shall indulge them with an explanation. Lumps* will form when the mince is not stirred properly (duh!) during the browning process at the beginning of the recipe (don't even get me started on people who skip this step), because if you don't stir properly to break up the mince, then the protein in all the thousands of tiny pieces of meat that make up mince will coagulate, re-join and create lumps. We are not making meatballs, people! You can tell everything about a person's

---

* In the interests of clarification, lumps are not to be confused with a coarse bolognese. In a coarse bolognese the maker has deliberately chosen to mince their meat using a larger-holed mincer plate, resulting in a chunkier style. Of this I approve.

character by the quality of their lasagne's bolognese. The most mean-spirited people I have ever met have one thing in common: lumpy bolognese. Studies have conclusively shown that lumpy bolognese is a sure indication of a fatal character flaw, right up there with the creepy people who cook their bolognese for less than an hour. Do you make lumpy bolognese? Yes? Eeeek! Scary!! But, I BEG OF YOU, please do not put this book down. At the very least, finish this chapter – I'm certain I can help you knead out this 'imperfection'.

9. A caveat to commandment 5: lasagne and bolognese are never vegetarian. Never ever. The beauty of writing this in book form is that you have no mechanism to counter the above statement. I am incredibly fond of vegetables and eat a mainly vegetable diet, but aside from a small amount of soffritto (onion, carrot and celery), olive oil (the blood of olives) and a modest amount of tomato, vegetables have no place in bolognese. The first bologneses didn't even have tomato in them, because tomato is not an Italian plant (it's an Aztec fruit brought to Europe by the Spanish), as I recently took zero pleasure in pointing out to a young Sicilian-Australian cook in my employ who I am very fond of, but who was ignorant of this fact. I'm lying. Correcting him was the best feeling I had that week, maybe even that year…

Again. There is no place for vegetables in lasagne or bolognese. To suggest otherwise is blasphemy. I know what you are thinking, 'Aren't mushrooms a bit meaty?' or 'I love a good pumpkin lasagne.' Rubbish! Both are desecrations! I have been forced to eat mushroom and truffle lasagne in many a fine-dining restaurant and, every time, as the wine wore off, I was left seething with hatred both for them and myself, the realisation dawning upon me that I had wasted a meal of my life on such an appalling dish, and I would never, so long as I lived, be able to get that meal back. The power of vegetables' flavour is completely weak in the face of a fine salty pancetta, the iron of grass-fed beef chuck, the funk and complexity of chicken liver, or the soft richness of pork neck. The gently simmered combination of these ground meats is an absolute tour de force that the plant kingdom, its natural beauty notwithstanding, shrinks in the face of. It isn't pretty, but the fact is: we must kill to make bolognese.

10. Lasagne is best at home. It is often disappointing when made by chefs. WTF, chefs! Why you do lasagne like that? What has lasagne ever done to you, except make you money? Lasagne must be seriously pissed off about all the bad shit chefs do to it. I once heard about a very famous seafood chef who shall remain nameless (Rick Stein) who made a fish lasagne. Fuck me, Rick, I love you, but seriously, putting fish in a lasagne is worse than putting vegetables in lasagne. Fish, of course, is innocent in this conversation, its lean, delicate flesh defenceless against the long and constant barrage of heat, cheese and heavy caramelisation of lasagne. Throughout the cooking process, fish is screaming, 'How did I get here?' Poor fish. I apologise to you on behalf of Rick and his country of England (the country also responsible for the abominable fish-and-chips lasagne – England, keep fish in your fish pie). Lasagne itself is without guilt here too, Rick. Lasagne never even asked for fish! It was quietly minding its own business, hanging with hard-hoofed animals, and along you come, all free-wheeling and reckless with unsuspecting aquatic creatures of all kinds.

The hard truth is, leave lasagne at home. I run a restaurant, so I'm really shooting myself in the foot here, but good lasagne-making is the ultimate handmade love language for a fellow human. How do I know? My twelve-year-old daughter Ruby made her first lasagne for me last night, on Father's Day. She was so pumped about it, she physically couldn't keep her excitement contained. With a sort of shaky, squealy energy, akin to performance art, Ruby delivered it to the table with her small hands. It was the most memorable lasagne of my life. Rick, take note, Ruby used beef. BURN! (As Ruby would say.)

There's absolute beauty in bolognese. Its depth of flavour, history and culture. As I write these lines, I have a pot of it gently simmering on the stove. It's a version I've never tried before, but it's familiar territory; bolognese has become a sort of meditation to me these past months. I've been making it a few times a week. Each time a different recipe or a tweak to the recipe I'm working on. I'm constantly amazed by how the same group of ingredients brought together in slightly different ways can taste so different, and yet retain similarities, like members of the same family.

As deep as I'm going into new bolognese horizons, I'm always trying to bring it back to something that feels right to me, that feels respectful. I guess you could say that, even though I'm a grown man, with each attempt, I'm also reflecting on my younger self. I think bolognese can reflect someone's personality. And like a personality, one's bolognese recipe should become more well-rounded as one ages. Like a person, it should become deeper, more inclusive and more thoughtful. I think back to the first bologneses I was making for flatmates in my late teens: very one-dimensional and basic. Those bologneses, like their maker, viewed the world through blacks and whites, and absolutes. There was only one way to make them; they tasted meaner, less inclusive, more insecure, and less capable or willing to reach out to people and meet them in the middle. There was no richness to them. I regret those bologneses now, as they were missed opportunities to spread kindness, and although they are a part of my journey, I could have done better with them.

These new bologneses have been the stuff of wonderment. Such was the joy that there have been a few times when, for a fleeting second, they were the only dish in the world, the only dish I felt like making for the rest of my days. In looking to learn something new, I've returned to something very old, and it has rewarded and enriched my life.

Uses for obsession include buying a mincer to mince one's own meat for their bolognese. But not just any mincer, oh no, only a mincer made in Bologna would do. And not only a mincer from Bologna, but also a copper saucepan made by the same family in Bologna since the 1950s, because only that pan would be adequate to make their fine bechamel in. What sort of pot would this kind of person cook their bolognese in? A huge, hand-thrown terracotta pot, with a rich red glaze, of course. Where would the person find such a pot, you might ask? Bologna. If you question the obsessive person on the point of their fastidious equipment selection, they might say that you're missing what's important here, that the magic lies in the unexplainable. This person (*moi*) intends to let the universe withhold some things on bolognese.

Is my obsession with bolognese just an outlet for considering my own flaws and failings and addictive personality? Or is it 'just' a recipe? Most of my life, I've had enough self-awareness to know when my personal pursuit of excellence was in danger of hurting those around me. With this bolognese pursuit, it's only myself in danger, so it's mostly healthy – except for the girth of my family who, like surfers pinned down by a set of giant waves, are repeatedly subjected to bolognese for dinner over and over again. So much so, that this morning Kylie audibly sighed when I cheerfully told her that I'd been to visit our butcher and friend, Gary McBean, to discuss my latest Google translations of Italian cuts of meat and what they meant. 'Babe! Gary reckons the end of the pork loin, yeah! The end down by the rib cage! He thinks *that* might have the perfect blend of lean meat, fat, and collagen!' Sure, this obsession has all the hallmarks of a problem habit, but I prefer the word fascination over addiction.

When I recently returned from a northern Italian holiday, I questioned one of my firm rules at Attica: NO PASTA ALLOWED ON THE MENU. I had made this rule (and many others like it) in 2006, in a quest to develop my own cuisine. I had imposed these creative limitations on myself so that the cooking would feel like it could only come from one place (Australia), and therefore I attempted to remove almost every other international influence, in the way that only a naïve 28-year-old can.

This was not out of disrespect: I adore food from everywhere, along with the stories it tells of migration and culture. It was out of practicality, as I wasn't very skilful at cooking the classics due to my modest early career, and I had an overpowering desire to create a personal identity through my cooking. Across the Australian restaurant landscape were references everywhere to cuisines from other places, but nothing that truly felt like here. In addition, 'the classics' hadn't worked on the menu at Attica prior to my arrival, so my plan was to be bold to survive.

Some seventeen years later, I found myself questioning my rigid approach with thoughts like, 'But Ben, you love lasagne more than any other food.' With an expansive attitude towards Australian cuisine, based largely on foods endemic to Australia, I had forgotten to be generous to myself and my own personal history and culture, to recognise the one dish that felt more like something I had ownership and knowledge of than almost any other.

If you were thinking of questioning my authority on this topic, my credentials are provided below and come straight from the bastion of truth that is The Attica Bureau of Lasagne Statistics, an institution I founded in 2021.

What is the Attica Lasagne Census?

Every five years, the Attica Bureau of Lasagne Statistics counts every lasagne released from the Attica kitchen. We call this the Census of Lasagne.

The Attica Lasagne Census is the most comprehensive snapshot of lasagne in Australia and tells the story of how we are changing our lasagne-eating habits as a nation. It includes around 10 million households and over 25 million people.*

The Census of Lasagne data helps us make important decisions about transport, schools, doctors, the number of babies born, and how much wheat, beef, milk and tomatoes will be needed in the future. The information you have provided to us is essential for maintaining a constant supply of lasagne, not only in the present but also for future generations.

Attica Lasagne Census Data 2020–2021
8661 lasagnes made
17,322 customers served
43,305 layers of pasta blanched and hand cut
1732 kilos of pasta used
2087 kilos of bechamel made
2771 kilos of bolognese made
1820 litres of milk used
7361 kilos of lasagne made
1732 hours of labour used

After these statistics were collated in the Attica Lasagne Census master computer, we then calculated this hard data:

- Over the 262 days that Melbourne was in lockdown, an average of 66 people per day ate Attica lasagne.
- Of the 262 days that Melbourne was in lockdown, Attica made lasagne on 210 of them.
- Following extensive objective research conducted by the Attica Lasagne Census, lasagne's true origins have been confirmed as being Taranaki, New Zealand.*
- In the region of Taranaki where Lasagne Zero originates from, lasagne is referred to as 'Lasagne al Farm-o'.*
- By the end of 2021, the total weight of Attica's output of lasagne was almost double that of the Guinness World Record holder for the world's largest lasagne, which was made by Magillo Restaurant in Poland in 2012 and weighed in at 4865 kilos.
- Annual growth of lasagne-eating in Australia during 2020 was 1,000,000 per cent.*

Our team lovingly made more than 8661 takeaway lasagnes for two in the previous two years. We applied the same exacting attention to detail to our takeaway lasagne that we did to our twelve-course tasting menu, building each lasagne on a set of scales, weighing each layer. We kept ourselves sharp through this time, providing a set of rigorous standards that could be relied upon by our customers. The dish that I had such a deep love and affinity for, my greatest culinary friend, had saved us. It had put a smile on the faces of thousands of Melburnians, who endured the world's longest lockdown. Lasagne, the quintessential hard-times food, back in its rightful place.

---

* This statement may not be factual.   –

But while I was happy to sell thousands of lasagnes on our takeaway menus, how did I treat lasagne when my restaurant's tasting menu came back? Like trash, like something that I was embarrassed about. Lasagne's ungrateful son, I took everything from it and then kicked it to the kerb, thinking it wasn't worthy of the dine-in Attica menu. A person who has dedicated my creative life to looking from the outside in, celebrating the familiar in previously unobserved ways. But when it came to my family food?

As I examine this, how painful is my own cultural snobbery and prejudice? I'm crying now, crying over lasagne. Tears rolling down my face. An absolute snob, who didn't deserve this dish in his life. A dish that had been a part of every celebration, success and near-death experience in my life. What a fucker I am. Rick, I owe you an apology. I'm sorry, I take back everything I said – I'm the real lasagne-abuser here.

Fortunately, no relationship is ever truly irredeemable. And while I have some work to do to make amends with lasagne (and Rick), much of the conflict in life exists because we are unprepared to cross the bridge to say sorry. I've found judicious use of that single word most powerful. When you've fucked up, an early sorry takes the wind out of the conflict. A heartfelt sorry when I've over-reacted restores relationships. But make that sorry count. I was once a chronic over-user, instinctively apologising for everything out of fear, and diminishing sorry's effect. Appropriate, timely and proper use of sorry has been one of the most powerful learnt skills of my life. Real acknowledgement of my mistakes has brought me closer to others, and increased my happiness and mental health.

So, lasagne, it's time I issued you a heartfelt public apology. I'm truly sorry, no excuses. I'm going to put you on my menu. I hope you'll be happy there. I wish for you to shine.

I'm well-known for pushing boundaries with cooking. Sometimes it has been said I push too far. What is less known about my practice is a core philosophy and principle behind every recipe and piece of food that I serve. Before you can change something, you must understand it. Only then can you subvert it.

Many of the world's problems (and poorly conceived dishes) can be ascribed to people who rush in with arrogance, never taking the time to study the history, culture, context and people who came before them before they attempt to change something, often with horrendous results. This can be applied to virtually anything: art, politics, business, education and even love.

To avoid this problem as much as I can, before I subvert something, I will submit to completely learning it. I'm prepared to go deep. I will sacrifice. I will test and test and test, over and over again. Days blend into weeks, months and even years if that's what it takes. I will not stop until the work is done. I'm relentless and I can be insufferable. You may think that this is a privilege of my position. You are wrong. I have always been this way. Bechamel, Christmas cake, hāngī or some obscure (but important!) detail, it doesn't matter. I probably don't have to spell it out by now, but I know obsession well.

But I digress: back to lasagne, Attica lasagne. With the renewed focus and energy that only a first-ever proper holiday (one that wasn't a work trip with a couple of days tacked on the end) can bring, I return to the restaurant kitchen to work on the very first pasta dish for the Attica menu.

My idea for a new lasagne is based loosely on the visual memory of my mother's pinwheel scones. This lasagne will be literally flipped – with the layers of spiralling pasta pointing towards heaven vertically, rather than the traditional horizontal layering.

After months spent working on it at home, I have the bolognese recipe in my back pocket. By now it's taken an 'eat the problem' direction: rather than my standard practice of using only animals native to Australia, I've utilised introduced wild pest species like deer, buffalo, and wild boar – animals that are destroying biodiversity and putting pressure on native Australian animals and plants.

Together, with intensity, my team and I commence work on a green pasta dough. Fortuitously this begins to come together quicker than expected – and after testing daily, within a mere month, we have a recipe for green pasta made from Australian wheat, native warrigal greens and ngerdi (green ants). After the pasta is rolled out and blanched, I use a scalpel and steel ruler to cut a piece 88 centimetres long and 3.5 centimetres wide. Rolling out an unwieldy strip of moist fresh pasta, and then cooking it while keeping it whole is putting us all through the wringer, and we've been close to tears.

I carefully spread bechamel (made from Jersey cow milk, that my father fondly calls 'bovine wine') along the entire length of this pasta strip, making sure not to get any on the edges. I follow this with coarsely ground, locally made two-year-old parmesan and then the cold bolognese, into which I've whipped Jersey butter ('bovine gold'), and this is spread along the length of the pasta.

This entire undertaking is then painstakingly rolled into 'pinwheels' (I've since learnt that Italians have something similar called rotolo, can't reinvent the wheel...sorry, couldn't help myself) and placed into a metal ring before being baked in an exceptionally hot oven for 3 minutes and 20 seconds. After resting for 2 minutes, the fragile lasagne is then carefully placed, using every ounce of skill I possess, onto a handmade red terracotta plate. Commissioned from local artist and former Attica chef Claire Ellis especially for this dish, it is made from Australian terracotta clay and has images of Australian grains carved into the rim.

The plate matters, its relationship to the food – how it looks, how it feels, how the dish eats when served on it. Every detail, no matter how small, is connected and helps to complete a circle of thoughtfulness.

We stand and taste it. My lips are the first to break into a smile. The euphoric hit shakes me, as my mind flashes back through a wormhole of previous lives, dreams, connections, and the culmination of an adventure. This is the moment we live for at Attica. Brian Eno's incredible song 'The Big Ship' captures this sensation: go listen to it! This feeling is completely addictive. It only happens once every few months, but it is my motivation to continue to do the difficult, obsessive work. The promise of feeling this feeling again is always just around the corner, but almost always out of reach: a mythological carrot. This is what drives and motivates me. If I couldn't feel this way anymore, I've often said that I would stop, close the restaurant, and move onto something else, rather than let my career and business die a slow, sad death.

Authentic lasagne? Authentic to me.

Jonathan Gold once said that 'cuisine has never been static, and the idea of authenticity is a constantly moving target'. Culture changes, cuisines change and evolve and swallow new ingredients. Could one imagine Italian cooking without tomatoes, or Thai food without chillies? Both were introduced relatively recently, and are both part of 'authentic cuisine'. In 2019, during a visit to my friend Auntie Leila Nimbadja's traditional lands of Djinkarr, near Maningrida, in Arnhem Land, I incorrectly assumed – assumption being the mother of all screw-ups, as my mother regularly reminded me throughout childhood – that local people would see the feral buffalo population, introduced to Australia between 1824 and 1886 for meat, as separate to the native plants and animals of the area, and was surprised to learn that buffalo were considered to be as 'native' as any of the other plants or animals living there. Perhaps I shouldn't have been surprised, as people in that area had traded food with the Makassar people in Sulawesi, Indonesia, prior to the European invasion of Australia. Makassar words had entered the local vernacular and are still used today, and Makassar influence on the local cuisine is evident.

The point being that culture evolves, it adapts; new things are added or taken away, for better or worse, but it never stands still. Humans have a habit of viewing culture in a romantic sense – the way we pine for another time, when culture was somehow better. But few of us are old enough to have really experienced what we fantasise about, and most of what we remember is romanticised. It's a modern concoction of something that never really existed in the way we think it did – more a manufactured view, embellished by story, manipulated by marketing, and borne out of our desire to connect. The restaurant is a perfect example of the romanticisation of culture.

All cuisine was once new. And with it the food we eat, including my family's lasagne. Do you love lasagne? Then do what every good ragu, pasta and bechamel obsessive would do: grab your wooden spoon and join my bolognese cult.

Now, I want you to listen very carefully. Hey! Pay attention!

Sit on the floor with your legs crossed, hands at your sides. Close your eyes. Relax and listen to my voice calmly whisper in your ear: *bolognese, booloooogneeese, boooolooooogneeeeeseee*. You will fall into a dream state, where all your bolognese dreams come true, and the world's problems fade away. If you don't know what your bolognese dreams are, then just think of the most delicious thing you ever tasted, multiply it by ten, and then imagine it was bolognese. Visions of rivers of bolognese are flowing steadily downstream, its heady aromatic steam like the hypnotic notes of the Pied Piper's flute. This is the Stairway to Bolognese Heaven. Would you like to reach it?

Yes? Let's continue.

AWAKE! to the snap of my fingers, alert and prepared to do the following without hesitation:

1. Shewry family bolognese
2. 'Authentic' ragu bolognese
3. Obsession-level bolognese (don't try and skip 1 and 2 before attempting this).

Bolognese wisdom, tricks and tips

When using store-bought mince, a whisk is a great way to break up lumps (because the meat is not freshly minced, it will be harder to break up). Use it like a potato masher, cheerfully smashing the blades of the whisk down upon those dreadful balls of protein – the more savagely the better, Norman Bates style. Lumps, as we now know, are the enemy.

Invest in a large heavy-based stockpot or saucepan. I own a 10-litre one, which is perfect for larger home quantities. You'll only need to buy it once in your life, and your bolognese will thank you. Although they are a sturdy investment, I adore All-Clad Copper Core pans (not a sponsor).

Never use pre-ground black pepper. It is too fine, and it has the flavour and musk of pepper that's been ground too early and 'aged' for years on the concrete floor of a spice warehouse. Buy the best whole black peppercorns you can find, a good-quality pepper mill, and grind at will. The French make the most robust grinder mechanisms, and that's what we use at Attica.

Always season bolognese with salt from the beginning. I like to add a little salt to the mince as I fry it, right at the start. Then I add small amounts of salt throughout the cooking, slowly building up the salt level. I'm always mindful that bolognese reduces its water content by 30–50 per cent as it cooks, and therefore I keep in mind that it will become saltier as this happens. But always be bold with the salt; under-seasoned bolognese is almost as bad as lumpy bolognese. Adding salt from the start, and throughout the cooking process, makes for a 'less salty', more flavoursome and well-rounded bolognese. If you add all your salt at the end, your bolognese will always taste salty and harsh. I add pepper in the last 30 minutes of cooking – I find it tastes tired and worn out if I add it at the start. Sugar should be judiciously added at the very end, if at all, and never so much that you can taste it – just a touch to balance out the potential roughness and acidity of the tomatoes (the quality and flavour of tinned tomatoes is incredibly variable between brands).

Taste, taste, taste, taste and taste again – drink glasses of water in between to keep your palate fresh and to avoid fatigue. One of the biggest differences between professional chefs and home cooks is the large amount of time chefs spend focused on seasoning and tasting. Commit to spending time to train your palate on seasoning, and your cooking (and therefore your life!) will take a huge leap forward.

When you taste your bolognese, do not use a teaspoon. You need a full dessertspoon to really understand what's going on; a teaspoon-sized amount is like dipping a toe in a swimming pool rather than going for a swim. Just dive on in. And never taste it piping hot. Blow on it a little bit, or even better, set the spoonful to the side to cool, because bolognese cannot show its best self when it's like lava. Swish the bolognese all around your mouth, allowing it to coat the palate, and meditate on the flavour. Analyse the tenets of bolognese – salt, savouriness, richness, acidity, sweetness, meatiness and texture. This is a learnt skill, and with time, dedication and practice, you will know how to adjust your sauce to suit your own palate.

A flat-edged wooden spoon is an essential bolognese tool. It has been said that ancient Egyptians first designed the ridiculous round-edged wooden spoon. Gnarly dudes! If only they'd squared the bottom off their spoons, they could have spent so much more time taking milk baths, which sounds much more pleasurable than standing around all day stirring. A round-edged wooden spoon has approximately one-twentieth the surface-contact area of a flat-edged wooden spoon. Bolognese needs regular stirring, so efficiency across a 5–6 hour cook is important, as is minimising the risk of burning your sauce. A flat-edged wooden spoon is, therefore, the kitchen implement of the enlightened.

All the recipes below make more than you need for one meal. Bolognese freezes very well and keeps in the fridge for several days when stored correctly in airtight containers. Always allow your bolognese to cool completely before freezing or refrigerating. Great bolognese is a commitment of time, money and effort, so you may as well enjoy the fruits of your labour for a few weeks (if it lasts that long). Bolognese also cooks much better in larger batches, and these recipes are for a volume that will give you greater control of the slow and proper reduction of the liquids, rendering of fats and tenderisation of meats. A smaller-scale recipe would simply be unkind.

If you cannot discuss the meat, you cannot trust the meat. My rule is to never buy meat from a store where I cannot have a conversation with the butcher. Real butchers have nothing to hide. And it's easier to pin someone down on the murky depths of animal husbandry when you're looking them in the eyes. I think the least we can all do is get to know the meat we eat a little better. A side-benefit of getting to know your meat through your butcher is that if you ask kindly, they will gladly mince your meat with a number 8 mincer plate for the Obsession-level bolognese. But cool your jets! First, let's begin at the beginning.

Shewry family bolognese

This is training-wheels bolognese, modest and simple. The place where it all started for me, and the best place for you to begin your ascension to bolognese heaven.

Serves 6–8

3 tablespoons olive oil

1.6 kg (3 lb 8 oz) beef mince (ground beef)

2 brown onions, finely diced

⅓ cup garlic cloves, peeled and finely chopped

2 carrots, peeled and finely diced

350 ml (12 fl oz) red wine

1.2 kg (2 lb 10 oz) tinned tomatoes, pureed in a blender
    or food processor

2 bay leaves

½ bunch of thyme sprigs, left whole (don't pick the leaves)

salt and freshly ground black pepper, to taste

pinch of white sugar, if needed

1. Heat your largest frying pan and your largest stockpot or saucepan over a high heat. Add a few drops of oil to both pan and pot, and then a tennis-ball sized amount of mince to each, along with a good pinch of salt. Fry until browned, working quickly to break up lumps. Add the browned mince in the frying pan to the pot and turn off the heat under your pot. Keep frying batches of mince in the frying pan until all the mince has been browned, adding it to the pot as it's done.

2. Add the onion, garlic and carrot to the browned mince in the pot and cook over a medium heat for 5 minutes, stirring regularly.

Add the red wine and simmer until reduced by half – this will take roughly 5 minutes. Add the tomatoes, bay leaves, thyme sprigs and 500 ml (2 cups) of water and bring to a gentle simmer. Cook for 30 minutes, then check the seasoning. Continue to simmer gently for another 2–3 hours, stirring frequently and working on your seasoning. Towards the end, add pepper to taste and a pinch of sugar (if needed). Finally, adjust the salt, then remove and discard the bay leaves and thyme sprigs.

3. If you're not eating your bolognese straightaway with freshly cooked pasta (page 162), allow it to cool to room temperature before storing in airtight containers – it will keep in the fridge for up to 5 days or in the freezer for 2 months.

'Authentic' ragu bolognese

This bolognese is perfect for tagliatelle al ragu (page 162) or, as we call it around these parts, spaghetti bolognese. Shewry family and Obsession-level bolognese recipes (pages 158 and 165) are better suited for lasagne, though they can of course be eaten with other pasta too.

Serves 10–12

250 g (9 oz) butter

200 ml (7 fl oz) extra virgin olive oil

160 g (5¾ oz) brown onion, finely diced

160 g (5¾ oz) carrot, peeled and finely diced

160 g (5¾ oz) celery, finely diced

500 g (1 lb 2 oz) fatty pancetta, coarsely minced (ground)

1.2 kg (2 lb 10 oz) beef chuck, coarsely minced (ground)

850 g (1 lb 14 oz) pork neck, coarsely minced (ground)

1.5 litres (6 cups) Nebbiolo wine

1.6 kg (3 lb 8 oz) tinned Italian tomatoes, pureed in a blender
     or food processor

130 g (½ cup) tomato paste

250 ml (1 cup) beef stock

500 ml (2 cups) cream

salt and freshly ground black pepper, to taste

good pinch of white sugar, if needed

1. In a large saucepan, melt the butter over a medium heat with half of the olive oil. Add the onion and a pinch of salt and gently cook, without browning, for 5 minutes. Add the carrot and celery and continue to cook over a low to medium heat

for 20 minutes. Add the pancetta and fry until golden brown. Remove from the heat.

2. Heat two large frying pans over a high heat and add a little of the remaining olive oil to each pan, followed by a tennis-ball-sized handful of beef and a sprinkling of salt. Brown the meat, breaking up the lumps, then repeat until all the beef is browned, adding it to the saucepan as it's done. Clean the frying pans and repeat the process to brown the pork neck.

3. Add the browned pork to the saucepan and pour in the wine. Simmer over a medium heat to reduce the wine by half. Add the tomatoes, tomato paste and beef stock and bring to a simmer. Cook gently for 2 hours, stirring frequently.

4. Add the cream, then check the seasoning and cook for a further 1–2 hours, adding the pepper in the last 30 minutes. When the meat is tender and the sauce has a good consistency, not too thick and not too thin, check the seasoning. If it tastes acidic or a little rough, add the pinch of sugar.

5. If you're not eating your bolognese straightaway with freshly cooked pasta, allow it to cool to room temperature before storing in airtight containers – it will keep in the fridge for up to 3 days or the freezer for 2 months.

Pasta for tagliatelle al ragu, otherwise known as 'spaghetti bolognese'

Resolutely, this 'look at how many egg yolks I can use' pasta is right up there with chips in the category of 'rich-country marvels' (page 105). Guilt-trips aside, these gilded ribbons from heaven are totally worth the indulgence. The dough is best made on the day to avoid oxidation, but you'll need to allow for several hours of resting time. Don't waste this pasta on lasagne, as its fine texture is not robust enough for baked dishes; turn to page 175 for my recipe for lasagne pasta.

Regardless, don't use a stand mixer for kneading this dough (or the one for lasagne), and definitely don't ask my mother what happened to her mixer when I used it to make pasta dough. All I will say is that I recently purchased her a new one.

Makes enough pasta to serve about 8

350 g (12 oz) '00' pasta flour, plus extra for dusting
290 g (10¼ oz) egg yolks – from approximately 17 × 60 g (2¼ oz) eggs

To serve
large knob of salted butter – let's say 100 g (3½ oz)
splash of olive oil – let's say 2 tablespoons
freshly ground black pepper, to taste
a hefty amount of freshly grated Parmigiano Reggiano
    and/or Pecorino Romano

1. Place the flour in a large bowl, make a well in the middle and add the egg yolks. (I like to use a bowl at the beginning because I can't stand a messy kitchen, but if you prefer chaos, then knock yourself out and start this directly on the bench, you reckless

animal.) Use a fork to combine, then use your hands to knead until you have a rough dough.

2. Tip the dough out onto the bench and keep kneading. After a couple of minutes of kneading, rub the dough around the bowl to collect any remaining flour, then continue kneading on the bench. You're aiming for a total kneading time of about 10 minutes, or until the dough begins to relax and can be formed into a smoothish round ball.

3. Tightly wrap the dough in baking paper and refrigerate for at least 3 hours – but use it on the same day. (Don't be tempted to roll and cut this pasta too far ahead of serving it. Many a stressful dinner party was had by buffoons who rolled their fresh pasta too far in advance and it stuck together like a tube of superglue spilt on a precious vintage table. On both counts I'm speaking from experience here!)

4. Remove the dough from the fridge and cut it into four quarters, then roll each piece through the thickest setting on your pasta machine, passing it through several times and reducing the thickness each time until you reach the number 6 or 7 setting. Lay the pasta sheets on a lightly floured benchtop and use a 'bench' knife to cut each one in half, then cut each half into 4 cm (1½ in) wide strips, lengthways. (A bench knife is chef-speak for a knife that has been intentionally allowed to become blunt, so that it can be used to cut things like pastry or pasta dough right on the bench – but if you don't want to sacrifice that special Japanese blade you got for your birthday, feel free to cut your pasta on a chopping board.) LIGHTLY dust the tagliatelle with flour – too much flour diminishes the delicate nature of this pasta.

5. When the time comes to cook the pasta, bring a large pot of salted water to the boil. At the ready, sitting next to my pasta

pot, I like to have a huge warmed bowl containing the half-melted butter, olive oil and a grind or two of black pepper. My bolognese will be gently heating in a saucepan and I'll give it a last-minute seasoning check, then a splash more cream perhaps.

6. I blanch my tagliatelle for 1 minute max (always taste a piece to check doneness) and then drain it, reserving some of the cooking water. Next I throw (we are working VERY quickly now) the pasta into the butter bowl, add a good pinch of salt, and a small ladle of pasta water. I then toss and gently stir the pasta in the bowl until the butter and water emulsify and coat the pasta with a glossy sheen – the liquid should be a little bit saucy, but thin.

7. I serve the pasta in warm bowls, ladling some bolognese into the middle of each serving. I add a generous amount of freshly grated parmesan and/or pecorino and demand my guests stop talking and eat the damned pasta. Traditionalists will question why I don't toss the bolognese through the pasta. Well, traditionalists, that's because I am a non-homogenous man, who likes to taste the pleasures of buttery pasta and bolognese separately, and then together. (Cut to a choir singing the Hallelujah Chorus.)

Obsession-level bolognese

*Before you rush out to source these ingredients, this is my advice to you –
and it doesn't just relate to bolognese making, but to all of cooking. The
better the ingredients are, the better your cooking will be. It sounds like a
cliché, but it isn't – it's a hard-and-fast rule to live by – but one that even
many professional chefs overlook, to their own detriment, as the cooking
follows the ingredients, not the other way around.*

*Why start at the base of the mountain with inferior ingredients,
when you can begin at the summit and elevate from there? Eighty-five
per cent of the success of my cooking at Attica has been built on this
simple philosophy. The careful and proper sourcing of the best food to
work with is like a cheat code, catapulting a cook miles ahead of their
competition – whether that competition is a family member you want to
outdo, a highfalutin friend, or a frenemy from work. The easiest way
to give them a cooking beatdown is by buying better food than they do –
you must outsmart them on sourcing – execution is only ten per cent at
this level. So, take your time, because we are not fucking around here.
Thoughtfully research, talk about, obsess, feel and taste each one of the
ingredients below. None is more important than another, and the tiny
increases in quality will compound across this recipe, slowly turning into
something extraordinary.*

*When I started developing this recipe, I was using a fine wine that
Attica head sommelier Dom Robinson had made with our good friend
and winemaker Mac Forbes. Dom was quite offended when he saw me
pouring bottle upon bottle of his hard work into bolognese, but to me using
his wine was the highest compliment! I recommend you buy very good
quality wine, as I've designed this recipe to allow for a perfect left-over
glass of each variety for the bolognese-maker, to aid in the creation of a
successful sauce.*

Always make this a day before you need it; it's a huge job and you will feel stressed as you make it. For that I make no apology, I may even take pleasure from it. Because of your intense proximity to it during 6–8 hours of preparation and cooking, psychologically, it's going to taste better to you the following day. After tasting and smelling your bolognese dozens of times, your palate will be overwhelmed by the end; your mouth will feel as if it has been forced to perform Tom Waits' gravelly song 'The Piano Has Been Drinking' in a smoky bar over the fracas of a room full of noisy drunks. In short, you will be unable to make informed decisions about the seasoning. The following day your bolognese will almost certainly taste better to you.

Note: If you are making the wild boar bacon, it needs to be started at least 8 days before you begin this recipe.

Serves 8–10

120 g (4¼ oz) brown onion (or yellow in North America)

120 g (4¼ oz) carrot

120 g (4¼ oz) celery

100 g (3½ oz) cultured butter

120 ml (scant ½ cup) extra virgin olive oil (I prefer a milder style)

1 kg (2 lb 4 oz) wild buffalo (can be swapped for well-marbled
    beef chuck)

500 g (1 lb 2 oz) wild venison (can be swapped for beef sirloin
    or pork neck)

85 g (3 oz) chicken livers, soaked in milk overnight (in the fridge)

500 g (1 lb 2 oz) wild boar bacon (recipe below, can be substituted
    with pancetta)

600 ml (21 fl oz) Pinot Noir (or Pinot Nero, as it's known in Italy)

600 ml (21 fl oz) Chardonnay (I know it's not Italian, but it's
　　my favourite)

1.5 litres (6 cups) full-cream Jersey milk

1.5 litres (6 cups) buffalo stock (recipe below, can be substituted
　　with beef stock)

1.6 kg (3 lb 8 oz) tinned San Marzano tomatoes (can be substituted
　　with your own fresh home-grown tomatoes), pureed in a blender
　　or food processor

⅓ whole nutmeg, finely grated

freshly ground black pepper, to taste

1 tablespoon freshly ground pepperberries (can be substituted
　　with more freshly ground black pepper)

sea salt flakes, to taste

2 teaspoons white sugar, to taste, if needed

Equipment

A benchtop mincer, with a number 8 mincer plate
　　(ideally from Bologna)

A heavy-based 10-litre (10½-quart) stockpot and/or a 10- to 15-litre
　　(10½- to 16-quart) terracotta earthenware cooking pot. I'm
　　obsessive, so I think a terracotta pot is totally necessary, but a
　　good result can be achieved without one; it's worth noting that
　　terracotta will only work on a gas cooktop or over a fire, and you'll
　　need a diffuser, otherwise you run the risk of cracking your pot.

3 × 2-litre (70 fl oz) or larger saucepans

2 large frying pans

A fine Microplane or grater

A very sharp cook's knife

A very sharp boning knife

A flat-edged wooden spoon

1. I suggest you listen to Wilco's album *A Ghost is Born*; whole albums only for bolognese making.

2. I also suggest you pour yourself a glass of wine.

3. Read my instructions from start to finish, then repeat.

4. Peel the onion, wash and peel the carrot and wash the celery. Cut all the veg into 4 mm (⅛ in) dice.

5. Melt the butter over a medium heat in your stockpot. Add half of the olive oil.

6. Add the onion and a pinch of salt and cook gently for 15–20 minutes, stirring often. Don't let the onion brown.

7. When the onion smells sweet and delicious, add the carrot and cook for a further 5 minutes.

8. When the carrot is beginning to show its best side and smells delicious, add the celery. Continue to cook the soffritto until it is harmonious. The total cooking time from onion to end will be around 40 minutes.

9. While the soffritto is cooking, there is time to prepare the meats. Go through each cut and remove any big pieces of sinew, using a boning knife. Then dice your meats into 4 cm (1½ in) pieces so that the mincer can take them easily, but don't mince them yet. Keep each meat separate.

10. Place the diced meats into the freezer for 15 minutes. You do not want to freeze them, just make them exceptionally cold. The colder and firmer the meat is, the better the cut you will get from your mincer. If your meat is at room temperature when it goes through the mincer, then the mincer and friction will mash it, which would be unfortunate. You need a nice sharp and clean cut. Pop your mincer parts in the freezer too.

11. Drain the chicken livers, discarding the milk, and pat dry with paper towel. Remove any connective tissue from the livers with a boning knife. Use a cook's knife to chop the livers very finely.

Once they are finely chopped, turn the blade of the knife on its side and carefully use it to further puree the livers by pressing them against the chopping board, millstone style.

12. This is where the rubber hits the road, so put your glass of wine down and crank up the stereo, as shit is about to get real.

13. Mince the wild boar bacon, using a number 8 mincer plate – don't force the meat through the mincer or add too much at once, otherwise you won't achieve a nice clean cut. Let the mincer do the work.

14. When your soffritto is ready, add the chicken liver, spreading it across the bottom of the pan. Add a small amount of salt and allow the liver to cook over a medium heat for a minute without stirring – it should begin to set like an omelette. Increase the heat slightly and stir quickly to 'scramble' and brown the liver, breaking it up until it has completely combined with the soffritto. Turn down the heat and cook gently for 4–5 minutes, or until any whiff of urine has dissipated.

15. Increase the heat and add the minced boar bacon, frying it until it is brown. Turn off the heat under the stockpot and set to the side.

16. Place your two large frying pans over a medium heat.

17. Mince the wild buffalo, again using the number 8 mincer plate.

18. Add a small amount of olive oil to each pan and increase the heat to high. Add a tennis-ball-sized handful of minced buffalo to each pan and quickly spread it out to cover the bases of the pans. Add a little salt and fry until brown, then turn and brown the other side. When the meat is browned, break up the lumps, then add the browned buffalo mince to the stockpot. Repeat until all the buffalo meat is browned. Be careful not to add too much at once, or the mince will 'stew' instead of browning, and don't let your frying pans burn – after two rounds, deglaze each pan with a tablespoon of water, scraping with your wooden

spoon to release any stuck-on food particles, and add this to the stockpot – these food particles have a lot of flavour, so you don't want to waste them.

19. In a saucepan, combine the two wines and bring to a simmer. In a separate saucepan, gently heat the milk, stirring frequently. In a third saucepan, combine the stock and the pureed tomatoes and gently heat.

20. Repeat the mincing and browning processes with the wild venison and the boar neck. After this, all your meats should be browned and in the stockpot.

21. When the wine is simmering, add a quarter of it to the stockpot and cook over a medium to high heat to evaporate the wine by three quarters. Repeat four times until all the wine is used.

22. Add half of the hot milk and simmer over a medium heat until reduced by two thirds, then do the same with the other half of the milk.

23. If you are using a terracotta pot, it's time to transfer the contents of the stockpot into it. If not, just stick with your stockpot. Add the hot stock and tomato and bring to a simmer, then reduce the heat to low.

24. At this point I like to check the seasoning. You don't want it to taste too salty, as the bolognese will reduce by at least 30 per cent and up to 50 per cent as it cooks. You can keep an eye on how much it's reducing by watching the sauce-ring on the inside of your pot. Before each taste, cleanse your palate with a mouthful of water – a clean and clear palate helps immeasurably with seasoning.

25. Your bolognese should be gently simmering now. Cover it with a lid, leaving a 20 per cent gap to allow for partial evaporation.

26. Set a timer for 15 minutes, then stir. Reset the timer and repeat the stirring every 15 minutes for approximately 4–5 hours, or

until all the meat is tender and the bolognese is thick; if, after 3 hours, it doesn't seem to be thickening, remove the lid. Continue to taste throughout this time, taking note of the changes.

27. About 30 minutes from the end of the cooking time, check the seasoning and add the nutmeg and both peppers, plus the sugar if needed.

28. Do not be tempted to skim off the fat that has risen to the top – it's an essential part of the bolognese and needs to be emulsified into the sauce – so give it a real good stir. If it refuses to combine, give the bolognese a quick whisk once it has finished cooking and is off the stove.

29. Allow to cool completely to room temperature before storing in airtight containers – it will keep in the fridge for up to 3 days, or in the freezer for 2 months.

30. If using this bolognese for pasta other than lasagne, I like to finish it with a knob of butter and a dash of cream when I add the pasta to the sauce, along with a ladle of pasta cooking water – not so much that it seems creamy, just a touch. In addition to Parmigiano Reggiano, I like to use aged Pecorino Romano, the hard sheep's milk cheese, which gives the dish a slightly more complex character.

Wild boar bacon

2 kg (4 lb 8 oz) wild boar neck (can be substituted with pork belly),
   boneless and skinless
55 g (2 oz) salt
1 g (0.035 oz) freshly ground black pepper
5 g (⅛ oz) celery juice, from freshly juiced celery

1. Butterfly the wild boar neck by placing it on a chopping board and, with one hand on top of it to secure it in place, firmly hold your knife horizontal to the board and slice into the meat lengthways without cutting all the way through – leave about 3 cm (1¼ in) to act as a 'hinge' so the meat opens out like a butterfly. Ideally, you'll make one clean cut, using a smooth action; don't saw at the meat. Pat the meat dry with paper towel.
2. Mix the salt and pepper together, then scatter evenly over the meat. Sprinkle the celery juice evenly across the meat and rub it in all over.
3. Place the meat in a non-reactive shallow dish and cover with a tight-fitting lid. Refrigerate for 7 days, turning the meat every 24 hours.
4. After 7 days, remove the meat from the dish and, using the blade of a knife, scrape off any visible salt and pepper. Pat dry with paper towel.
5. Place the meat on a wire rack so that air can flow all around it, then refrigerate it for 24 hours so the meat dries out a little.
6. Your wild boar bacon is now ready. It will keep for up to 4 days in the fridge, or for 2 months in the freezer.

Buffalo stock

5 kg (11 lb) buffalo bones (can be substituted with beef bones –
   ask your butcher for meaty ones)
2 tablespoons olive oil
2 large brown onions, approximately 180–200 g (6–6½ oz) each
2 large carrots, approximately 150 g (5½ oz) each
1 bunch of celery, leaves removed

1. Preheat your oven to 180°C (350°F).
2. Divide the bones evenly between two large roasting trays, spreading them out and lightly coating them in the olive oil. Roast the bones for around 30–35 minutes, or until they are golden brown, turning them occasionally to ensure an even colour.
3. While the bones are in the oven, you can prepare the vegetables. Peel the onions and cut them in half, then place in a 10-litre (10½-quart) stockpot. Peel and wash the carrots, then chop into 5 cm (2 in) pieces. Wash the celery, then cut into 5 cm (2 in) pieces. Add the carrot and celery to the stockpot.
4. Once the bones are roasted, add them to the stockpot. Drain the roasting trays of any fat and discard it. Add ½ cup (125 ml) of water to each roasting tray and scrape with a wooden spoon to deglaze, then add the deglazing liquid to the stockpot.
5. Add 7 litres (7½ quarts) of water to the stockpot and bring to a gentle boil, then turn down to a low simmer. Using a ladle, skim off any scum, impurities and fat from the surface of the stock. Simmer for 8 hours, skimming frequently throughout the cooking process.
6. Strain the stock through a fine sieve, discarding the bones and vegetables. Strain the stock a second time through a muslin-lined sieve, then allow to cool to room temperature before storing – it will keep for 6 days in the fridge, or 3 months in the freezer.

A lasagne manifesto

You, me and lasagne, bonding together like starch gelatinisation and protein coagulation in the boiling pot of this crazy old world. Here is where I answer the urgent and pressing lasagne questions of today: To make your own pasta sheets or buy them? To roll pasta by hand or by machine? To blanch pasta or not to blanch pasta? To start layering with bechamel or bolognese? How many layers of pasta? Vegetables or no vegetables? *C'mon, I was testing you with this one.* What kind of cheese? *No ricotta, the fodder of cheeses.* Herbs? *Gotcha! Herbs are a subset of vegetables. No herbs!*

Let me be clear: when it boils down to it, lasagne is five things only: bolognese, pasta, bechamel, cheese – and, most importantly, you. Once you have all five assembled, you're ready to start building your lasagne (page 180).

Pasta for lasagne

I recommend you make your own lasagne pasta – it is miles better – and pre-cook the sheets before layering. Otherwise, you'll have little control over how moist or dry the lasagne will turn out (I'm winking at you, young Matt Boyle).

Some puritans might insist that this pasta should be rolled by hand, using a spianatoia *(pasta board) and a* mattarello *(rolling pin). I'd suggest they live perfect lives that are frankly impossible to replicate. A hand-cranked benchtop pasta machine gets a great result – and for lasagne pasta, no one, puritans included, can tell the difference.*

Makes enough pasta for a lasagne to serve about 10

350 g (12 oz) '00' pasta flour, plus extra for dusting
150 g (5½ oz) whole egg – approximately 3 × 60 g (2¼ oz) eggs
55 g (2 oz) egg yolks – from approximately 3 × 60 g (2¼ oz) eggs

1. Place the flour in a large bowl and make a well in the middle, then add the whole egg and yolks. (Feel free to do this directly on the bench, if you don't mind mess!) Use a fork to combine the egg, yolks and flour, then use your hands to knead until you have a rough dough.
2. Tip the dough out onto the bench and keep kneading. After a couple of minutes of kneading, rub the dough around the bowl to collect any remaining flour, then continue kneading on the bench. You're aiming for a total kneading time of about 10 minutes, or until the dough has relaxed and feels smooth and silky; note that this is a softer dough than the one for tagliatelle on page 162.

3. Roll the dough into a ball and flatten it with your fist, then wrap tightly in baking paper and refrigerate for at least 3 hours – but use it on the same day.

4. Once your bolognese and bechamel are ready, remove the pasta dough from the fridge and cut it into four quarters, then roll each piece through the thickest setting on your pasta machine, passing it through several times and reducing the thickness each time until you reach the number 6 setting. On a lightly floured benchtop, use a table knife to cut each sheet in half.

5. To pre-cook the pasta, bring a large saucepan of salted water to the boil. Have ready a large bowl of iced water, a tea-towel-lined tray and a pile of clean tea towels. Add the pasta to the boiling water in batches of 4 or 5 sheets at a time and cook for 30 seconds, stirring gently so they don't stick together.

6. Remove the pasta sheets from the pan and drain for a few seconds before plunging them into the iced water to refresh. After 2 minutes, remove the sheets from the iced water and drain again. Lay the drained pasta on the tea-towel-lined tray, placing a clean tea towel between the sheets to stop them from sticking together.

7. Repeat until all the pasta is pre-cooked, refreshed and drained. If your ice melts, add more to the bowl for the remaining batches of pasta. Cover the pasta sheets with another tea towel and set aside at room temperature until needed – aim to use them within 2 hours.

Bechamel, or as it's colloquially known where I grew up, white sauce, or just sauce

This recipe is especially designed for those of us who look down on whisks – but if going it alone with a wooden spoon, then prepare to sweat. A roux is a combination of fat and flour that is cooked together and used to thicken a sauce. There are three types of roux, white, blond and brown; bechamel uses a white roux, so it is very important not to caramelise the butter and flour as you cook it. Bechamel is best made fresh on the day.

Makes approximately 1.5 litres (6 cups) bechamel, enough for a lasagne to serve about 10

125 g (4½ oz) salted butter

140 g (5 oz) plain flour

1.5 litres (6 cups) full-cream Jersey milk

small pinch of freshly ground nutmeg

pinch of freshly ground white pepper

salt, to taste

70 g (2½ oz) good-quality parmesan and 50 g (1¾ oz) cheddar,
     both grated – if using the sauce for lasagne building

Equipment for a smooth bechamel

A red suit – always dress for success when making bechamel

A wooden spoon

2 × heavy-based medium saucepans – one for making the bechamel,
     the other for heating the milk

A 120 ml (4 fl oz) ladle

A rubber spatula – the heat-resistant ones with the red handles
     are best

Additional lasagne-building equipment

Baking paper, to make a cartouche (see step 2 below)

A whisk (for cheese only)

1. Put on your red suit.
2. If your bechamel is for lasagne building, you'll need to make a cartouche – otherwise known as a round piece of baking paper – before you start. To do this, take a square of baking paper and fold it in half to form a triangle, creasing the fold firmly, then fold that triangle in half to make a triangle that's half the size of the first. Repeat this three more times, each time making a narrower and narrower triangle – it will look a little like a paper plane. To cut your cartouche, place your triangle of folded baking paper over your chosen bechamel saucepan, with its pointy end at the centre, then measure the distance to the edge of the pan and cut your cartouche so it's 5 mm (¼ in) larger than this. Unfold the cartouche into a circle and scrunch it into a ball, as if you were going to throw it away – the scrunch helps the paper fit to the contours of the pan and the sauce – then unfold again and flatten it out on the bench. Rub a little butter on one side of the cartouche to make it non-stick, then set it aside.
3. Add the butter to the bechamel saucepan and melt it over a low heat.
4. In the other saucepan, warm the milk over a low to medium heat.
5. Add the flour to the melted butter, stirring constantly, and cook over a low to medium heat for 3 minutes. It's important that the butter and flour simmer, but that no caramelisation occurs – this part is called 'cooking out' the roux, and it is one of the foundations of a smooth sauce.

6. Remove the bechamel pan from the heat and add one ladle of hot milk, stirring vigorously with the wooden spoon, then return to a medium heat and cook for 30 seconds, stirring constantly.

7. Repeat step 6, making sure to cook the milk and roux mixture well after each addition of milk. This is key. If the mixture is not cooked each time, then the bechamel will turn out lumpy, especially as the roux loosens and begins to form a sauce. Scrape down the sides of the pan with the spatula after every second addition – if you leave lumps of roux on the sides of the pan, they might fall into your sauce later.

8. Keep repeating step 6 until all the milk has been added, then simmer gently, stirring constantly, for 4 minutes, or until you can no longer taste raw flour in the sauce. Season with nutmeg, white pepper and salt to taste. Your bechamel is now complete.

9. For the purposes of lasagne building, add both cheeses to the bechamel and whisk over a low heat until smooth (a wooden spoon cannot break down cheese protein, so I allow the use of the 'devil' utensil here).

10. Remove from the heat and scrape down the sides of the pan, then place your cartouche, buttered side down, directly onto the sauce, covering its surface completely and taking care not to trap any air pockets underneath. This stops a skin forming.

11. Set aside at room temperature until needed. Refrigerate if not using on the day – this sauce is best when freshly made, but will keep in the fridge for up to 2 days.

Lasagne building: a step-by-step guide

First up, you'll need a baking dish for your lasagne. These quantities have been designed around my enamelled cast-iron roasting dish, which measures approximately 32 cm long, 25 cm wide and 7 cm deep (about 12¾ in wide, 10 in wide and 2¾ in deep). It doesn't really matter what material your lasagne dish is made from, so long as it is ovenproof, but a similar-sized dish (or two half-sized dishes) is necessary.

An offset palette knife is not essential, but if you make lasagne often (or decorate cakes), it is a very useful tool for spreading bechamel and bolognese (or icing). I use one with a blade that is approximately 15 cm (6 in) long, and find it the perfect size.

Serves about 10

2.25 kg (5 lb) bolognese, either Shewry family (page 158) or Obsession-
  level (page 165); both recipes make more than this,
  but the rest can be happily stashed in the freezer
1 full recipe of Pasta for lasagne (page 175)
1 full recipe of Bechamel (page 177), with cheese added,
  divided into thirds
60 g (2¼ oz) freshly grated parmesan
60 g (2¼ oz) freshly grated cheddar
60 g (2¼ oz) freshly grated mozzarella

1. Preheat your oven to 220°C (425°F) – use the fan-forced or convection setting, if your oven has this feature.
2. This lasagne has five layers of pasta, and three layers each of bolognese and bechamel, plus a layer of cheese on top: twelve layers is perfect for this size of dish.

3. Evenly spread a 1 cm (½ in) layer of bolognese over the bottom of your dish. Cover with an even layer of pasta, measuring and cutting your pasta sheets to fit. No gaps!

4. Evenly spread one third of the bechamel over the pasta, then cover with another layer of pasta.

5. Divide your remaining bolognese in half and spread one half of it over the pasta. Cover with another layer of pasta.

6. Spread the second third of the bechamel over the pasta, then cover with another layer of pasta.

7. Spread the remaining bolognese over the pasta, then cover with another layer of pasta – this is the final layer of pasta.

8. Spread the remaining third of the bechamel over the pasta, then evenly sprinkle the three cheeses on top of the bechamel.

9. Bake for 30–40 minutes, depending on how fierce your oven is, or until deep golden brown and hot in the centre (insert a metal skewer or table knife into the centre of the lasagne, then remove and check the temperature by carefully touching it to the back of your hand – it should feel very hot).

10. Remove from the oven and leave the lasagne in a warm place to rest for 20–30 minutes. This allows the lasagne to cool and firm up slightly as the temperature becomes evenly distributed throughout the layers. Serve.

FALSE PROPHETS

Let's start with a home truth: restaurants rip off other people's dishes all the time. Now, before we go on, there's an important difference between copying and paying homage. Restaurant lover and hip-hop impresario Adam Briggs once said to me, on the difference between sampling and plagiarism: 'In sampling we are doing history, it's part of our musical journey, some of these producers are on a genius level of understanding jazz, funk, soul, all these things that are the cornerstones of hip-hop and electronic music. Homage means that you are open. If I tasted something at your restaurant, and I was like, *Holy shit, I gotta put this on my menu at my pizza joint*, I'd ask you. It's about respect. This is what artists strive for too. You have to approach it with humbleness, otherwise you'll be humbled. Only a person who doesn't know themselves would try to hide their influences. That's just facts.'

Some of the most established restaurants have 'borrowed' ideas and not attributed them. There was a time in recent history when a dish of 'Lobster on a rock' was served, unattributed, in nearly every large city around the world, and that idea only came from one place: Copenhagen.

It's happened to me too. I recall a meal at a high-profile restaurant overseas (not in Copenhagen) where, prior to my visit, the chef had eaten at Attica and, flatteringly, been very excited by his meal. During my meal at his restaurant, he took me out of the dining room to another part of the building for a different experience, resplendent with art and food – a signature Attica move – and, embarrassingly, whispered in my ear that this was directly inspired by our work. He only said this because it was so obviously a rip-off. Unfortunately, he failed to mention this to any of his other guests.

That's short-term shitty behaviour, but even before this, several other chefs from his own country had complained to me about him 'borrowing' their ideas. Many of those chefs were not in the same position of power as this chef was, and that's when it really hurts and has impact. Plagiarism is an emotional and economical gut punch when you are starting out. But who gave the power to this chef in the first place? Of course, it was a 'Jimmy', one of the faceless critics who wanted to be first to celebrate this fake dude and false prophet – a chef whose career was made with the speed of a cheaply built tower block rising out of the ground – in a rush to tick the boxes of whatever social movement of the moment they felt they ought to be covering.

Earlier that same year, in 2022, a Jimmy misattributed my work, again. I honestly would have preferred to never think or write about them again, but here we are! This time I was forced to witness a chef being given a major award for plagiarising my cooking, with a copy of a dish I created inside an emu eggshell in 2016. It was a painful and humiliating feeling. I hated myself for being there, my face a vivid display of discomfort. Of course, I would never stand up and make a scene, so I just grinned and bore it, nervously playing with my glass as I sat at a table right in front of the stage.

Although I think the whole situation is lame, much of the responsibility rests with Jimmy, which is why I'm writing this. These critics are part of the same organisation that is handing out the award and writing the review – which, in their own words, lists copies of three of my dishes as well as other practices from our dining room, all unacknowledged. This shows how poor Jimmy's research is. My copied dishes had been published before; I've cooked them all over the world. I should be mad, but I'm just embarrassed and frustrated. The chef receiving the award had dined at Attica eight months earlier.

For clarification, I don't think that I should have received that award. But it was a missed opportunity to give some sun to someone who truly deserved it, of which there were many at that ceremony. (Our cooking and service practices have been copied and not acknowledged from as far back as the first year of Attica, and my way of dealing with this is to continuously come up with new ideas, which are then copied, so in a paradoxical way the plagiarism of Attica has propelled it further forward – which, upon reflection, is hilarious.)

Outside of hip-hop, many music writers often hear the echoes of history in the work of new music and write about those influences. As part of my creative practice, I've always publicly attributed the source of my inspirations for dishes. It doesn't diminish me for a second, quite the opposite: I benefit from the positive feelings of telling someone else's story to our guests through our food, especially if that person hasn't had my privileges.

As I've discussed, the incredible food of Thailand has influenced the way I season our dishes at Attica. Burru (a Dhurga word for kangaroo) is used on our menu, and the grilling of the meat follows ancient traditions of the Budawang people cooking food over fire, whose permission I sought before using their cooking techniques and language. There have been dishes inspired by fabulous meals at legendary Melbourne restaurants, restaurants that helped build the path that Attica walks on and helps to repave. I'm honoured by these influences. These, and hundreds of others, tell the story of where we are and how we got here, and add a richness that we couldn't achieve alone. If someone wanted to use our dishes and acknowledge them, I'd be so honoured.

The point is that all restaurant cooking is influenced by other cooking, from the top to the bottom, or the bottom to the top. Some of it is more obvious, like a French bistro in Los Angeles, which is clearly influenced by food and techniques from France, than say an ambitious restaurant, producing knock-offs of another creative restaurant's dishes that are nonetheless identifiable by those with the knowledge.

Of course, that was not the first time Jimmy's organisation got it wrong. Pre-social media, they caused an international maelstrom when they handed out multiple awards to a young chef whose entire menu was composed of rip-offs, down to minute details like the serving plates, and whose life imploded in the ensuing fallout. The furore began not because of journalists understanding the plagiarism and calling it out, but because another restaurant owner did. This chef should never have been given that platform. I ate at their restaurant twice in a year and was sceptical. The first visit they were cooking refined, elegant classical food; eight months later it was avant-garde, and they had seemingly evolved a whole new language in cuisine. At the time I was slowly struggling along with the development of my own menu, influenced by my significant mentors and my early experiments, and I simply didn't believe it was possible for someone to develop as quickly as this chef had. Turns out it wasn't, because none of the dishes were theirs. The whole sad episode could have been avoided, but Jimmy's employers got over-excited, and in their rush to be the first to publish the story and to dish out awards, they didn't ask the necessary questions.

Over the years, many a Jimmy has displayed a lack of knowledge that has been jarring, but I cannot point this out to them. I've tried, and it comes off as sour grapes or professional jealousy. They are a sensitive bunch. One little bit of criticism directed their way, and they freak out, whereas chefs have to learn how to deal with criticism from day one. That's because, for them, the stakes are so low, while the inverse is true for restaurants. Unfortunately, Jimmy doesn't understand how to properly attribute work – but they should, because this work takes a huge sacrifice of time and money, and to 'borrow' it is a large competitive advantage that should be written about. The money I invest in the development of dishes at Attica each year is in the hundreds of thousands, but at the beginning it was next to nothing.

Jimmy's silence exacerbates and supports industry-wide plagiarism practices. If a chef is not being honest about their inspirations, then it's up to the writer to inform the reader. This is an area where journalists could actually help, by recognising and researching influences. Isn't the principled questioning of everything a fundamental part of being a journalist? As far as I'm concerned, a food writer's baseline qualification should be knowing what's up, not just in the beats of the city that they write about, but in cities and countries all around the world. If I can know, then they can know; after all, writing for a living is meant to be a profession.

Warren G, fellow BBQ fan and G-Funk pioneer, says, 'And when I barbecue, I put on a lot of jazz and smooth music to help me with my cookin'. Cause when the music is right, that means you cookin' right and the food comes out right.' Amen to that, Warren. Warren G and Nate Dogg's huge mid-90s hit song 'Regulate' was founded on a sampled riff from Michael McDonald's song

'I Keep Forgettin''. To gain permission to use the sample, it had to be cleared by Michael McDonald first, who stood to benefit financially if the song did well. Imagine the royalty earnings if the same laws applied in the restaurant world! Not only would untrammelled plagiarism stop, but so too might cultural appropriation, especially the largely unacknowledged cooking that dominant cultures appropriate from minority cultures. As Warren puts it, '[Michael McDonald] was cool with it, 'cause he got paid twice.' Unlike a musician who can benefit from a hit song forever, chefs from creative kitchens cannot. We must perpetually come up with new stuff, and that effort should be supported and defended by the Jimmys who claim to be the industry's biggest supporters.

DEFINITION OF A CHEF, FROM A CHEF TO A CHEF

'Being a chef is really the ultimate team sport.'
Matt Boyle

My mentality at Attica has been based on the philosophy that no one is coming to save you, so you'd best get on with the business of saving yourself. If the definition of business is problems, then I needed to come up with something to resolve two problems at once, with no increase in staff or investment.

Problem 1: We had no customers.

Problem 2. We had no ability to develop new dishes because we were a kitchen staff of two or three and spent all our time running, and so could scarcely prepare the day's menu, let alone try a new dish.

My answer to these problems came in the form of a Tuesday-night menu I named Chef's Table. I set the price low partly as an enticement and partly as a mea culpa. Due to the highly experimental nature of the menu, the bargain was not always a bargain – it was a *Mad Max* landscape of ideas, like the time I cut a 44-gallon drum in half to fashion a homemade wood grill in the courtyard to cook in front of our guests. This seemed like a brilliant idea...until the wind got up and blew smoke into the dining room and ash over the fish all service long. I pretended that's how I wanted it.

Although this was revolutionary for Attica in the long term, laying the groundwork for our now well-known approach of constant evolution, there were nights where the cooking was so bad we'd desperately try to change dishes mid-service.

Here's the original menu blurb from 2007:

'Welcome to Attica,

'Chef's Table was born out of a desire to progress faster with the development of our cuisine, throw caution to the wind and offer guests more variety at a reasonable price. The menu is a living, breathing thing that evolves week to week. I work on it during the weekend and let the seasons dictate what they may in terms of ingredients; many of the dishes are inspired by memories of my childhood in rural New Zealand and by sights of nature and life that I discover on my drive to work from my home on the Bellarine Peninsula. Some dishes are just inspired by common sense and beautiful produce.

'The team and I arrive each Tuesday morning to begin the day's preparations; we gather around a bench and discuss how we will go about forming these new ideas and thoughts into something cohesive as a menu.

'None of the dishes have been cooked before...'

It was on one of these early nights that I had cast my eye out to the dining room and got the biggest shock of my young life – a man who appeared to be the identical twin of Michel Roux was about to sit down at a table. It couldn't actually be him, I thought to myself. What the hell would he be doing here? At this restaurant, that no one knows or cares about? Hadn't someone told him this place sucked? Should I tell him it's not too late to go somewhere else?

When he sat down, I realised that Michel wasn't a doppelganger. He was indeed the French-born chef and restaurateur who, in the 1980s, alongside his brother Albert, had opened two of the world's greatest restaurants – Le Gavroche, in London, and The Waterside Inn, on the banks of the River Thames in Bray. Their book *The Roux Brothers on Patisserie* is, to this day, one of the most important cookbooks I own. My surprise quickly turned to fear, because Michel was renowned for his classic French cuisine and here I was, at 28 years old, turning out a menu of pure gobbledygook, rebelling against hundreds of years of French culinary tradition.

Even worse, on this particular night, I had duck on the menu. LE CANARD! Although I'd put my money on Chinese chefs being the first and true masters of cooking duck, by this point, the French might as well have invented fancy duck cookery, adding pomp and ceremony to proceedings. In the 1800s a French dude named Mechenet invented an elaborate duck press to squeeze the last of the flavour from the bird's bones for diners tableside.

I was convinced that Michel would find my cooking deplorable, and that this was about to be a deeply humiliating experience for us both. But there was no way out, and no time to change a thing. In a blur, we cooked and served Michel Roux five courses.

Before I knew it, Michel was standing in front of me at the pass. I could hardly speak. He thanked me for a 'lovely meal' and then went on a tirade of sorts about a 'terrible meal' he'd had the night before in Melbourne. I could make out that it had been his birthday that night, that he'd ordered two bottles of vintage wine, only to have the chef 'ruin the wine with his dreadful cooking, an insult to the ingredients'. He spoke about how he couldn't get the bitter taste of the 'terrible' sauce out of his mouth, some kind of burnt soy-sauce glaze. He was really upset about it.

It was obvious that he passionately loved restaurants, and was struggling to understand why they had served him such food. Michel then turned back to praise the meal I had cooked him, which was, 'thankfully, nothing at all like the dreadful meal from last night'. It was a candid and honest conversation. I said goodbye and thanked him for coming, and I thought I'd never hear from him again.

A couple of months later, a handwritten letter arrived in the mail. It was from Michel. I had thought he would dislike my creative approach because it was so different to his classical sensibilities, but instead he wrote some of the most empowering lines anyone has ever said to me. He wrote that he was disappointed we didn't live closer together, because if we did, he would visit me often 'to understand better how your brain works, and to get to know you as a friend'.

The letter was graceful and generous; I cried as I read it. The previous years had been so hard and I was in such a bad place, and yet this busy and important man had taken the time to write to me, a nobody. I clutched that letter for years afterwards, and read it whenever I needed a boost. Sadly, Michel passed away in 2020 and I never had the opportunity to tell him how life-changing his words had been. That letter was a lesson in so many things, but one line that stuck with me was, 'You should never change who you are as a chef.'

Rolling, cooking, humming, buzzing. All fired up and fired up. A fistful of stinking rose. Fanatically transmuting raw materials into gold. Direct to a fault, out of necessity, baby. You'd never fucking wonder. The look that says it all, terrified or terrifying. Jammed at the axis of high and low, and the ebb and flow between the vassalage of requests and fuck the world and all the fucking fucks in it. Right from our milkcrate seats. Flashpoint hidden behind a grind of the teeth. That's goddamn right. Bravado skins insecurity: D– for math, absconding reality or new to *here*. A false martinet, obedient and disobedient. Crunching up through the gears of service, relentlessly tearing towards the finish. After the stage is packed down, the drop is steep. Bill Callahan's 'Riding for the Feeling'. The fragrance of fat and fire. Enter the quiet, still night.

At ten years of age, as I nervously set foot in a professional kitchen for the first time, I became aware of one thing: chefs were 100 per cent fucking committed to what they were doing. Even in the most misguided of kitchens, despite whatever extracurricular activities were taking place, it was still an undeniable fact. Shit will be cooked. Amen. This stood very much in stark contrast to what almost *everyone* else seemed to be doing and getting done. When regular folks enter professional kitchens they soon realise something is happening that makes it quite different from other workplaces.

It's all about time. Chefs are committed to time in a way that very few people are – our fidelity is to the minutes and seconds, and to the tiny measurements in between. Time is *everything*. With the exception of perhaps lawyers billing clients, no other vocation is as obsessed with time. I know what you are thinking – surely a Formula One racing driver, a musician, a surgeon, a teacher, these people must be just as focused on time as a chef. Absolutely, but only for fixed periods and usually not in such a sustained way. High-level performers who visit Attica often comment on this difference – that the chefs are performing nightly for up to six hours at a stretch. Not many performers do five nights a week, for decades on end.

Chefs are committed to time from the moment they set foot in the kitchen and begin their shift. In a professionally run kitchen, no one is fucking around. The dishwasher is first to be fired up, the food deliveries arrive thick and fast, to be urgently and carefully packed away, the 40-litre batches of stock have been simmering through the night and must be strained and cooled, any slow-cooked meats and vegetables must be quickly put on to cook. The start of the kitchen day is like a vintage car on a winter morning, coughing, spluttering, fighting with itself to start and warm up. What's not well understood about the kitchen is that from the moment the fluorescent tubes flicker on, and the bug-zapper crackles into life, the clock is ticking, and the preparation can be more intense than the service. Cooking for a living is like a marathon runner who runs a four-hour sprint to arrive at the starting banner, then runs the marathon.

Time is *everything* to a chef. In case you think this might only apply to ambitious restaurant chefs, it absolutely doesn't. The breakfast you enjoyed at your local cafe this morning? If it was good quality and promptly served, then that chef is a master of time management. Breakfast is one of the most difficult in the cannon of kitchen shifts, the-five-jobs-at-once throwdown between the cook's bench, stove and docket printer aligns with the pentatonic rhythm of Hendrix's ripping guitar and foot on wah-wah pedal across 'All Along the Watchtower'. The best early cooking shifts are on the intoxicating edge of a total loss of control. But then, suddenly, like Jimi's solo, when it appears as if the situation will go into overdrive, the cook brings the whole service cleanly back together on the plate. When the breakfast crush hits, there is no way outta here. Want to know what it truly feels like to get fucked over? Volunteer for a busy solo weekend breakfast shift. At worst, you'll suffer from mild

PTSD, and at best you'll have a little extra pep in your step for the next day or two.

When you are totally committed to something and used to everyone else around you setting the same exacting standard, the lack of commitment you experience in the outside world can be excruciating. That relatability is why chefs become so close. The intensity of the work we do bonds us in a way that I find exceptionally beautiful. If a new cook is struggling, in good kitchens, the others will jump in and lift them, like worker ants building the colony. This mentality is born from a genuine love for one another that is forged in the finest of kitchen relationships; we would do ANYTHING for each other. From my perch, this is one of the single biggest factors in explaining why chefs are drawn to *the life*: in kitchens you can find your family, your clan. The kitchen is that rare place where it doesn't matter what school you went to, what your qualifications are or where you come from. Judgement is left at the door. In the kitchen all that matters is what you will do, not what you've done.

People who work in kitchens can be relied upon. The gang of painters who paint Attica twice annually is managed by ex-chefs, and they paint our dining room as if their lives depended on it. They move with an alacrity learnt in kitchens and apply it to painting. They continue to work as they talk, as they eat; they are never not working. They are painters, and although they haven't picked up a knife professionally for a decade, they are chefs. Once a chef, always a chef.

I look around our kitchen at all the earnest faces. They are so deeply keen to get it right. It's a wonderful thing; there's an alert energy running through the air. Not a single one of them wants to take a backwards step. Each one has carefully sharpened their knives, laid out their tools, folded their tea towels, set their board straight, tied their apron tight and tweezers (although I don't dig them) slung over the tops of their aprons, in preparation for the day ahead. Readiness and discipline personified. In a well-run kitchen, there are few distractions from the task at hand. But what is it, this high-definition focus? What makes chefs some of the most ready and reliable professionals on the planet?

In part, it is environmental: because of the complexity and labour-intensiveness, the volume of the menu items being made, and the deadlines set to serve those items, chefs don't focus on being focused. Every day, from beginning to end, is a mad hustle. The immensity of the workload automatically brings with it a razor-sharp focus, like a Leica lens on wildlife. The environment, a kitchen team's mentality, and the tasks at hand, naturally clear a cloudy mind. Much of the work in kitchens could be seen as mind-numbing, but not to us — chefs have a natural habit of turning monotonous tasks into a sort of quest, breaking down this work and reframing it as something fun. An admirable way of being, in a time where there's a high price placed on doing work that looks 'glam'. There is no cheat-code for chefs. You've just got to put in the time. A quick walk around the kitchens of Attica on any given day will produce the sight of small groups of chefs happily working on repetitive tasks, like the arduous shelling of thirty kilos of tiny peas, as if it were the most fun a person could have in the world.

In every successful chef I've known, more than any other trait, resilience is the most constant attribute. In kitchens, resilience is taught young and is connected to the threat of constant and present failure. To chefs, failure is not the Silicon Valley catch-cry needed to motivate us; a chef's professional life is a constant state of fluid failure. During a rampaging service, it's not if we'll fail, it's by how much and will anyone fucking notice? It's completely and utterly normal. It's so constant that chefs themselves probably don't even fully understand it. Chefs pick themselves up and return the next day to try again, building their resilience, and almost without exception they will do it better.

When the food preparations are complete, there is a quiet just before the storm of service that we call 'set up'. We fill the void with loud music, like an elite sports team building themselves up in the locker room before running out onto the pitch. If our guests had a window into the last hour of a restaurant before the doors open, they would not see the illusion of calm that we create nightly, but a scene that is halfway between Tokyo's Shibuya crossing, a rammed nightclub, and parents with screaming young children trying to pack their bags before a long trip — the whole thing being narrated by a rapper's hype man.

On exceptional nights, the glide of a (near) perfect restaurant service is like the feeling of hammering in row upon row of nails. Each one perfectly straight, the metal slipping like silk through the grain. The perfectly weighted final blow of the hammer driving the nail head ever so slightly beneath the surface, without leaving a mark. The call of the food order, the return call of 'Yes, Chef' — the first blow of the hammer. The precise countersinking of the nail head — the impeccable dish placed on the table at the appropriate time, with flowing repetition. These are the nights we all live for. The rhythm of hammers and nails and dockets and dishes.

Chefs are the grand masters of getting shit done. One study, admittedly a small-scale one, suggests that office workers are only genuinely productive for some three hours of their workday. The rest of their time is spent reading news websites, checking social media, chatting with co-workers about non-work-related subjects, searching for new jobs, making calls to friends or partners, and the list goes on. Shit like this would cause chefs to go into anaphylactic shock. Not only is this lack of productivity unnatural to chefs, it's practically impossible to imagine — people are relying on us. Those office workers need their lunch within fifteen minutes of their order, right? Those who kill time rely on those who don't for their meal.

In kitchens, there is absolutely nowhere to hide. Slacking off? That's not a fucking thing. I'd estimate the productivity levels of the chefs in our kitchen to be 99 per cent. Want something done? Give the task to a chef. Any chef. From street cleaning to the sourcing of some impossible-to-find thing, to the organisation of a large-scale event, give it to a chef and, balls in the air, they'll figure it out. Chefs are multifarious problem solvers, and chances are they won't complain as they do it.

Cooking for a living is an honest and honourable way of spending one's time, in the personal and dedicated service of others' hedonism. It is an argument for the underrated pleasures of manual labour in a modern world seeking to mechanise *everything*. Go to hell, AI, you might start writing all the cookbooks, and you'd be welcome to them. But AI, please, no promises of 'recipe hacks'. If I want something 'hacked', I'll talk to my butcher about it. And besides, why would anyone want a less-good version of a good recipe in the first place?

An aside: Moley. That ridiculous cooking robot that has its sights set on replacing commercial kitchens, but instead makes lumpy bolognese with a metal fish slice...facepalm. Which is what you fucking well get when you choose a TV chef to train your robot. I watched your promo video, Moley, and saw you scraping metal on metal and barely cooking your soffritto. Get your shit together. Moley, I hope you read this. The whole point of this damn book is so there will be less lumpy bolognese in the world, and for half a million dollars, there you are, unleashing your wave of extremist lumpy-mince populism.

The relationship between the chef and eater is intimate. Besides sex, making food for another person is the closest agreement two humans can have. Meditate on this: a chef makes a dish for you, sculpting raw materials with their hands, labouring with full focus as they cook them, and then presenting this food to you. And you bite it, you chew it, swallow it. You put that food from our hands and mind inside your body. Chef as courtesan, puppet master and voyeur, patron as submissive pleasure-seeker, restaurant as a den of iniquity. It's a freaky level of cognitive dissonance. Perhaps if we started contemplating the level of intimacy involved, we wouldn't eat food unless we made it ourselves, but humans have a natural appetite for risk-taking with food, barely an ounce of it rational. (Cut to me in a Japanese forest accidentally eating raw bear.) Luckily, chefs know what's going on. That's how the fuck we all got here in the first place. We put our faith in chefs.

Here's my rant, a call to chefs and waiters with integrity and heart: we must protect our culture and our independence; we must value our expert knowledge. Unless we can do this, we'll stay pinned down in the past. We must stand up to the vultures who have never spent a day working in a kitchen, or on a dining-room floor, and yet are so entitled that they own restaurants, and seek to benefit and steal off our backs. They take and take and take from the culture we built, to commodify and homogenise it and run their enormous fake restaurants. Raiding other cultures the world over, like Christopher Columbus, to build their banal 'concepts'. To hell with that – fuck those people. Hospitality workers must become the conscience of restaurant culture. There is not one single restaurant in this vast world that I respect that isn't owned by a restaurateur who was once, or still is, a chef or a waiter.

And to you good people reading this book, you have so much power. By choosing where you dine, you alone can change the face of our industry and the future of restaurant workers. Here is my message to you: support the real pleasure-makers, the experts who toil to provide you with these memorable times in restaurants. Support all of us by only frequenting restaurants independently owned by hospitality workers. That is how the wheel will turn.

STAFF SPEECHES

Yas is fidgeting with a piece of paper, holding it with his arms extended in front of him, moving it in and out like a person who suffers from short-sightedness. Nervously, he says, 'Sorry for my poor English.' Someone calls out in a kind voice, 'You got this, Yas.' I say, 'Your English is great, man; way better than my Japanese!'

Yas lifts his shoulders, takes a deep breath and begins: 'Hello, my name is Yas. I come from Japan and, from the time I was a little child, I fell in love with cooking Italian food.' Yas describes coming to Attica for dinner with his partner as 'life-changing'. He says, 'I never knew cooking or service could be like that. Even when I went to the bathroom and passed the kitchen everyone seemed so happy, and they all smiled at me and said a big hello.' Yas recalls every single person who was working the night he dined. 'I left Attica that night knowing this was the place that I really wanted to work at.'

I steal a quick look at the team: all faces are on Yas; he has their complete attention, absorbed in the moment, and he begins to sense it. Yas says, 'So I sent an email and I waited. Two weeks go by, no response. So I send another one, no response. So I send another one. In total I sent seven emails, and still no response.'

The room erupts into laughter, except for the senior kitchen staff in charge of responding to job applications, who shake their heads through red faces. Everyone is in hysterics, and it feels good to laugh. Our Eat the Problem lasagne is coming onto the menu tonight, and we are under the pump. But Yas isn't done: 'I even sent Chef Ben a DM on Instagram, but still no response!'

The room roars. Yas says he turned up twice at our back gate and talked to kitchen staff who told him to write again, mentioning that he'd eaten here. Finally, after writing again, Yas tells us he got his response, a paid trial shift and, following that, a full-time job offer. 'I was so happy,' he says. Then he grows quieter. He tells us that he didn't really believe that he was good enough for the job. Softly, he says, 'Every day is a struggle because I don't feel good enough, but I know that the difficult feeling is a positive one because I know that each day I'm getting better, and you are all so good at teaching me, very patient and kind. I like the feeling of struggling. Thank you for taking care of me. To be here with you is my dream come true.'

The entire team cheers Yas, like in that final scene in *Top Gun 2* when Maverick and Rooster crash-land their jet onto the deck of a ship. We ask questions and I tell Yas that I had almost the exact same experience when I was 21, dining at the Roxburgh Bistro in Wellington, New Zealand. I was so blown away by the cooking and the connection of the staff that it made me feel sad I didn't have that in my life. After desperately trying to land a job there for six months, it was life-changing when I eventually got one. I congratulate him on his resilience.

This is Yas's very first Staff Speech. It happened in early 2023. Three days later, I wrote this. Yas's speech is one of hundreds that have taken place at Attica weekly since 2010.

In every restaurant I have worked in, there were two distinct teams: the kitchen team, commonly known as the back of house; and the waitstaff and sommelier teams, commonly known as the front of house. It was often said that there was one team, one dream, but really there wasn't; there was always two separate teams, and at times it felt as if those teams were working against each other, rather than for each other. The friction and factions existed because the teams do two wildly different jobs, in different spaces, where different attributes, skills and personalities are required.

While not a hard-and-fast rule, chefs can be introverted and still succeed, but to be a successful waiter it helps to be an extrovert. Being a front-of-house person involves talking to people all day, accommodating other people's needs, constantly being hospitable and making sure the guests are happy. This requires a person who is able to expend a large amount of social energy on a daily basis. Generally, in the back of house during service, a chef's main social interaction is replying with a loud YES when an order is called away, without so much as a lift of the head from the task at hand.

Add in a pugnacious and historic distrust of the other team, the imbalance of how tips are shared and roles valued, and occasionally, when the burden became too much to handle and mistakes were being made, tensions between these two groups came to a head in fiery circumstances.

Let's say you have two people. One works in the bar, in the front of the restaurant. The other works out the back of the building, in the pastry kitchen. These two people almost never come into contact with each other. There is no need for them to; they are working for the same company but independently. Then service kicks off and the pressure begins to build. All of a sudden, a mistake is made – like a plate crashing to the floor, or a miscommunication – and these two strangers are thrust into the same intense environment.

One or both of them lose their cool and say something harsh. When a person loses control of their emotions, they lose control of the situation. And the situation, whatever it is, requires constant focused attention to resolve.

More than a decade ago, I noticed that this was happening at Attica, and I wanted to find a way to tackle this problem that was so ingrained in the industry. Unless I could, I knew that we as a group, and as individuals, would never reach our potential. Attica would never be truly high-performance if we didn't fully respect each other.

It is harder to feel empathy for someone who you don't know. How many times have you sworn at a stranger in a car for some trivial grievance? Now imagine that as you went to swear at that same person, you recognised them as someone you knew. Would you still swear at them? I know I wouldn't, because I would be more aware of their experience. That's empathy.

Understanding this, I began to work on a plan to solve our problem. I knew that if I could build a mechanism to bring the team closer, we would have more outcomes like the second scenario above. I also remembered the way I had been made to feel at some of the jobs I had worked before – places that made me feel like I was just a number.

In those places, it felt as if my hopes, dreams, experiences, ideas, my very personhood, were inconsequential. The feeling ate away at me until I saw a chance to address its source.

Because I knew empathy was a key tenet of great hospitality, and I knew it to be a major contributing factor in human happiness for both giver and receiver, with one initiative I wondered if I could help our team improve in four areas.

1. **Build empathy.** Through listening to a person's story and respectfully asking questions, allow our people to put themselves in a colleague's shoes. To try and understand where they come from, a little of what they have experienced in their life, and what their passions are. With this knowledge, we can make a connection and get to know each other better.

2. **Give individuals a voice within the team.** My feeling was that I needed to allow each member of our team to say who they really were, beyond their ability to make a perfect consommé or mirror-polish a piece of cutlery. I wanted to offer each individual a safe space where they could express themselves through storytelling, without judgement.

3. **Increase the performance of Attica.** My theory was that if we could build empathy for each other, then the benefits of that empathy would naturally flow to our guests. And our staff would enjoy the increased overall happiness that connectedness provides.

4. **Build social skills and confidence through public speaking.** Taking the time to lock down your thoughts on a subject before speaking is a sure-fire way of developing emotional intelligence by looking inwards. Nailing a thoughtful speech and receiving recognition for it provides a foundation for more confident future communications. It provides positive reflection, too: *They like what I said; I feel good.*

After thinking all this through, I decided that we would invest time weekly to give our staff a voice. I called the initiative Staff Speeches. There would be no rules on what they talked about, no expectations or direction. The choice of subject and content would be entirely up to the individual.

The concept is very simple – we have a roster, and every single member of the team has a place on it. Every Wednesday, at 4pm, an individual has the opportunity to give a speech to the rest of the group. Our staff take the privilege of speaking in front of their peers really seriously, and a lot of preparation goes into the speeches. Our whole team gathers in a semi-circle in front of the speaker and, for thirty minutes, whoever is speaking has the floor, and the complete and undivided attention of the group. It is the speaker's time to shine, their time to share their hopes, dreams and aspirations, their struggles or their passions. If they feel comfortable doing so, it is their time to show vulnerability, knowing they will only receive love in return.

In these speeches we have heard stories of heartbreak, stories of joy, stories of overcoming. Through sharing and listening, connections can be made in the most unlikely of places. The empathy generated teaches us that, as humans, we have much more in common with each other than the things we imagine will drive us apart.

Although I never intended for it to happen, Staff Speeches became a forum for some staff to share really personal stories. Most speeches are light or funny, but about once a year somebody will share an intense personal hardship. These speeches have brought the team closer than ever, allowing people to feel seen and understood on their terms.

I will never forget the day someone shared the story of their family attempting to defect from one country to another because of persecution. In their matter-of-fact way, they told us that only one family member survived the attempt. Tears streamed down my face – but not theirs.

A female team member told their story of being sexually harassed in restaurant kitchens. She told us that this was the first workplace she felt safe in. I know her bravery meant so much to the sensitive young men in the room, to hear how it can be for women. I also believe it was important for the other women in the room to see the men listening intently, as it was an experience sadly familiar to almost all of them.

The day a team member revealed that they suffered from schizophrenia was a big one. Hearing how hard they tried to keep it together, but sometimes there were days that were just so much more difficult than others, gave us all a new sense of understanding and helped us support them. We have all had to pull ourselves up to this level, but some of us have had to pull even harder just to be here.

A team member told me that sharing their story of a childhood filled with domestic violence was a huge relief. Their speech detailed how cooking had become a form of therapy and had helped them move forward in their life. I thought about the power of hospitality, as a welcoming place, a haven, and reflected upon the people I have met along the road who found a supportive 'family' in restaurants.

Each of these stories, and many more, were stories of overcoming. On every occasion, it felt like a deep privilege to hear them. I have also shared some of the more challenging times in my own life, so I know what it feels like to be that vulnerable in front of your colleagues. (I'd also like to point out that this is not a counselling session, nor are any of us qualified to offer counselling, and if a person asks for help, or our managers think someone needs support, we speak to them privately about options for providing what they need.)

The harder moments might be the ones that stand out in memory, but really there are so many more joyful moments, like the way everyone roots for someone delivering their first speech when English is not their first language. Extra attention is paid to every word, the team willing them on, applauding loudly and telling them afterwards how great their speech was; their smile afterwards says everything. Sometimes the connectedness comes not from what was said, but from the effort made by the person who is saying it – it is a courageous thing to put yourself out there like that.

I don't know if it will come across as tender, awkward or just plain embarrassing, but this is probably where I should admit that I have cried more during Staff Speeches – giving or listening – than at any other times in my life. It's so common that I think my team might be disappointed if I somehow managed to hold it together for once.

Some of the lightest times at Attica have also been during Staff Speeches. Matt Boyle repeatedly uses his speeches to declare his deep love for Richmond Football Club. Footy trivia sweepstakes, with prizes, have formed more than one of his many speeches. Given the different nationalities in our group, and the fact that many don't yet have a footy team, Matty uses the sweepstakes as thinly veiled enticements to ensure any 'stragglers' sign up to support Richmond. Occasionally someone falls through the cracks and becomes a Carlton supporter – Matt's worst nightmare.

Once, one of the kitchen staff said not a single word during his speech, but instead whipped out a classical guitar and began playing Bach. He had kept his musical cards close to his chest and no one had any idea he could play. We were blown away, and he beamed with pride, knowing he had gotten one over us.

Dom Robinson, Attica's head sommelier, gave one of his talks on his former life as a professional jazz drummer. He studied at the prestigious Sydney Conservatorium of Music, and on his last gig before hanging up his sticks played on tour with Zambian rapper, singer and songwriter Sampa The Great. Dom spoke about how he worked at a wine shop for a summer, began to fall in love with wine, and then landed a job at Attica, his first in a restaurant. Across seven years he studied hard, applied his understanding of musical excellence to wine, and worked his way up to the top. It was a fascinating story about the detours Dom had taken in his life, on the way to finding his true passion.

A team member recently finished up at Attica after four years and, during their final week, gave their last Staff Speech. As they spoke, I reflected on how much they had grown. It was like listening to a different person speaking – they were now vibrant and self-assured. They had undergone a transformation. I cried because I would miss them, but also because right before me I was witnessing the cumulative power of massive personal growth in a once-shy, quiet person who had overcome a rough earlier start in life. All they needed was the right environment, where they felt heard, valued and respected. Combined with their own determination, they ran with it and had become a confident leader. I could not have been more proud of them, and was grateful for the opportunity to tell them so.

As a child and a young adult, I hated speaking in front of other people. I was very quiet, and suffered from watery-eye syndrome whenever I was nervous. When I entered high school and had to speak in front of the class, my eyes would water and everyone thought I was crying. I was often mocked for it.

Later, when I was working at Government House as a sous chef, I encountered Dame Silvia Cartwright. An incredible woman, she had been New Zealand's first female High Court judge before being appointed governor-general in 2001 – at a time when all of the most powerful political and legal positions in the country were held by women. As in her earlier career, Dame Silvia broke with convention in her new role: she was publicly outspoken on important issues, whereas past governor-generals had stayed silent. In private, she was always respectful and kind towards her staff. We had very much been treated like servants under her predecessor, a self-important, sexist and rude man who raided the wine cellar for his last hurrah. Dame Silvia could not have been more different. An empathetic person of the people, with not a hint of snobbery about her, she had never forgotten her humble beginnings. My favourite memory of that time was of her taking the staff for drives in her new convertible – to the chagrin of the poor on-site police, who had no warning of these impromptu departures and had to scramble after us with a security detail.

As part of my role at Government House, I had to give a speech about being a chef to 200 high-school students. The speech lasted twenty minutes, and every second was torture. The teenagers weren't the slightest bit interested in becoming chefs. A few actually fell asleep. Their boredom wasn't helped by my stilted, robotic delivery. Teenagers can always smell fear.

I carried those failures across many years, right up until 2010, when I was due to give my first major speech at a conference. I had two months to prepare, and no idea where to start, so I googled 'how to make a successful speech'. The one piece of advice I took away from that research still rings true today: only speak about subjects you are an expert on. If you talk about things you aren't knowledgeable about, the audience will sense your uncertainty and you will lose them.

It's a total privilege to have an audience listen to you in the first place, so I would never disrespect them by orating on a subject I'm not really familiar with. Determined not to repeat my earlier failings, I wrote a speech about my cooking and practised it in front of the mirror hundreds of times, virtually committing it to memory. This time, in Madrid, in front of 1400 people, I finally nailed it. What a feeling.

I've been in love with speech-making ever since, and it was my hard-won understanding of public speaking as a way of building social confidence that led me to implement the practice at Attica.

There are two times in the week that I will never book something. One is Sundays, my sacred family day. The other is Wednesday afternoons at 4pm – Staff Speech time. This time is for my other 'family', and it breaks my heart to miss a single one. For thirteen years now, we've pulled our chairs together. Publicly, our cooking and service has been recognised, but Staff Speeches are a central part of the spirit I'd privately like Attica to be remembered for. If you take a closer look at any successful organisation, you'll notice that there are things they do differently that contribute to their success. Staff Speeches have been a fundamental part of our success, and are an ongoing reminder that kindness is the older sibling of performance.

EVOLVE OR DIE

The layers of my early years are still with me now, rippling around unseen – the way eels travel across land – shaping and influencing the decisions I make today. There's the independence and the questioning of rules that comes from the isolation of farming in the back country. Out in the great silence, you make things up as you go along. My mother and father just got on with it every day, and as hard as things were at times, I can't remember ever hearing them complain. Then there's skateboarding.

While it's not particularly known as a back-country sport, I was fortunate to cut my skateboarding teeth in 1988, on the only piece of concrete for miles around, at Whareorino Primary School, where my mother was the teacher, principal and only staff member. There was a grand total of seven students, two of whom were my sisters, Tess and Tamie. While I've never been a great skater, the sense of solitary freedom that four polyurethane wheels and a deck of plywood provided was significant. Skateboarding offered me self-expression, creativity and pain. Unlike team sports, there was no wrong way to skate, nor any risk of getting into trouble with a coach.

The mysterious physics of my very first ollie – a trick where the rider jumps into the air, their board following their feet – is still one of my favourite feelings to this day. Learning the move required commitment and patience. Over and over and over again I would try, until it began to feel natural. Nobody was watching, there was no one to show off to. The gratification I felt from learning to ollie came purely from my experience and the satisfaction of it for its own sake. I just wanted to learn how to do it well. Ollies, like signatures, come in all shapes and sizes; no two people ollie in quite the same way.

In some respects, learning how to ollie is the same as learning how to run a restaurant. With skateboarding, you have to learn on a stationary board first, before you progress to rolling up to a kerb at speed, popping an ollie, landing smoothly onto the footpath and rolling away. With a restaurant, you need an absolute minimum of a decade dedicated to learning and experiencing all the different aspects of running a restaurant, before opening one of your own. If you try to cheat and roll up to the kerb before you are ready, the pain will be significant – for both the skateboarder and the restaurateur.

It might appear from the outside that I've always been nailing ollies at Attica. I really haven't. I've spent more time undoing the bad habits I've learnt, and owning the mistakes I've made, than I have enjoying the successes. I've hit the kerb so many times I've lost count. Problems in business are daily, constant and forever. Problems in both life and business are often viewed negatively, but I'd like to say here, for the record, that problems should be normalised and viewed in a more positive light. Problems are just things that happen and that need to be addressed and worked through. The skater doesn't think, *Oh my god, I have to ride over this rough section of pavement, how terrible.* The skater thinks, *How can I ollie over this rough section as quickly and stylishly as possible?'* If the skater falls and bloodies their knee, they pick themselves up, analyse what went wrong and improve their technique, then the next time they work out how to clear that rough section better.

One comment I hear quite a bit is: 'Well, it must be really easy for you. You are Attica, after all.' But what the people saying this so easily forget is that for several years from 2005, Attica was a restaurant that only a tiny number of people knew about, and those who did knew about it for the wrong reasons. It was an absolutely terrible restaurant. When it comes to restaurants people vote with their bums, and if early Attica was to be judged by that metric, it was a complete failure. On a great many nights, there were few to no bums on seats. Through many desperate years of trial, error and hardship, gradually more and more people began to support our restaurant. I learnt that adaptability is one of the most important values in a business. Perhaps because change is one of our priorities, it makes what we do seem more effortless than it actually is.

My plan was never to be on the list of the World's 50 Best Restaurants. That's because when judged through a business-oriented prism, some of the world's greatest restaurants are some of the world's most terrible businesses. My goal at Attica was not to be one of the best restaurants in the world, but one of the best small businesses in the world. There is an important distinction. I did not want to repeat the mistakes of the past.

With that in mind, here's my 'Evolve or Die' list of some dos and don'ts for modern restaurants. All are things we apply to Attica, with varying degrees of success.

Don'ts

1. Don't be a mother-fucking arsehole.
2. Don't underpay staff.
3. Don't allow negative attitudes to fester.

4. Don't be racist, sexist, homophobic, transphobic, bigoted, ableist, etc. There's no place for it. Educate yourself and your team.

5. Don't neglect to say hello, how are you? To everyone, every single day.

6. Don't allow knock-off drinks.

7. Don't buy into the myth that drug and alcohol abuse has amplified anyone's career.

8. Don't forget that change begins from the top, but when supported will grow anywhere.

9. Don't repeat your own history. Just because it happened to you, doesn't mean it should happen to others.

10. Don't acknowledge criticism from someone you wouldn't seek advice from.

11. Don't forget that a restaurant can perform at an elite level and still be a lovely place to work.

12. Don't fuck the planet.

13. Don't focus solely on profits. You'll miss the 'wealth' that an equitable restaurant provides.

14. Don't get a business partner. Risk your own cash, make your own decisions.

15. Don't accept 'Can I have a chat?' emails from staff on the last day of the week, which then sit unresolved for a couple of days across an anxious weekend. Instead, encourage more direct means of communication, so that any issues are dealt with quickly and respectfully.

16. Don't use cocaine and then demand natural wine and organic vegetables for your dinner.

17. Don't forget that monotony is a part of crafting anything handmade.

18. Don't treat employees like numbers. Learn their names.

19. Don't feel overwhelmed by problems and give up before you've started. Chip away at them, one at a time. You'll get there.

20. Don't think that major cultural change requires money. Effort is free.

21. Don't overshare business or personal anxieties with staff. Employees are not mules.

22. Don't punish people for their creative mistakes.

23. Don't call people out. Call people in and have an honest and principled conversation.

24. Don't lose sight of the fact that no one is perfect.

25. Don't charge your staff to dine at their place of work. Understanding the dining experience from the other side needs to be part of their training.

26. Don't let team members leave the restaurant by themselves late at night.

27. Don't ignore that there's a solution to nearly every problem. Go get 'em!

28. Don't forget that it's not all about you.

Dos

1. Do apologise sincerely if you have been a mother-fucking arsehole.

2. Do be considerate of others with your ambition. You are not a tortured genius.

3. Do serve a nourishing, interesting, free staff meal, made from the same standard of produce that you serve your guests.

4. Do question the point of things. Just because you can do something doesn't mean you should. Balancing 500 baby peas on top of a piece of fish is some dumb-arse shit.

5. Do keep the ship steady: the highs should never be too high, or the lows too low.

6. Do acknowledge that if you don't introduce a 'no knock-off drinks' rule, the staff may, from time to time, hold an exuberant human drag race on the main street of Ripponlea.

7. Do enter every staff member's birthday in your diary and be the first to wish them a happy birthday. (Thanks, Kylie!)

8. Do train your managers in mental-health first aid. Being a manager is a tricky job.

9. Do take sexism seriously. There's no room for it.

10. Do share tips evenly between every member of the team. (But not the owners!)

11. Do lead by example. Your demands without your actions won't change a fucking thing.

12. Do pay your suppliers the day you get their produce. Suppliers are not banks.

13. Do allow for flexibility with rosters, or suffer high staff turnover like a goddamn fool.

14. Do promote inclusiveness by getting as many people as possible involved in the creative aspects of the restaurant.

15. Do understand that truly ethical businesses must be profitable, otherwise they can't look after the people they are tasked with caring for, including me and my family.

16. Do allow your successes to be enjoyed as a team. Success, of any kind, is not endless. If you are moving so quickly that you never celebrate anything, you might miss it when it's gone.

17. Do know that you can't enjoy the successes you've had if they're built on someone else's misery.

18. Do be willing to admit ignorance. No person is an expert on everything.

19. Do allow team members to discover their passions at work. We are prepping them for their futures, right?

20. Do make the difficult decisions, especially if you think it's in everyone's best interests.

21. Do state the obvious, time and time and time again.

22. Do acknowledge that not all paths here have been the same. Some people have had to work so much harder just to get to the same place.

23. Do share any particularly soul-crushing tasks with the whole team. Solitary monotony is a killer.

24. Do take the time to meet your team's loved ones when they dine in the restaurant. Look 'em in the eyes and tell them how special you think their person is.

25. Do take gender diversity seriously and make a strict pay-parity rule. It's not the 1950s, people.

26. Do understand that outside criticism of your change often comes from other people's fears.

27. Do know that while everyone would like restaurants to be absolutely perfect, perfection is a myth. Keep on trying.

28. Do know that we are all flawed. Try not to take it personally. Most people really are trying to do their best. The rest are mother-fucking arseholes.

29. Do understand that these ideas require constant attention and re-evaluation. Re-read #28.

This is part of our blueprint for a restaurant. You are absolutely welcome to copy it. While there are a few non-negotiables in the lists above, I'd suggest you use them as inspiration to draw up your own blueprint. Analyse your values and create a plan that fits the way you'd like to run a restaurant – a restaurant that, if you get really lucky, might just be around for the long term.

People often tend to focus on one thing. Some think that sustainability is all about being a zero-waste restaurant. Some think it's about using the whole animal. Others believe that organics is the way to go. The reality is that these are all tenets of sustainability, but none of them alone makes for a sustainable restaurant. Most often, the treatment of humans is not even mentioned in the conversation. The only way to be more sustainable is to take a holistic approach, to apply the principle of not-fucking-shit-up to all things – humans and the planet.

In 2015, as a first-time restaurant owner, I began to look outside of the hospitality industry for inspiration to do better. A company called Patagonia kept coming back to me. It seemed like an organisation that was really trying to take responsibility for itself. It frequently advocated for the environment and its employees, and it seemed genuine – motivated by a different kind of mission than the profit-at-all-costs one I was used to hearing about. Its founder, Yvon Chouinard, a self-described 'reluctant businessman', presented an ethical way of doing business that seemed achievable and wasn't hamstrung by pretending he had all the answers. He was measuring his company's success in unusual ways. One of those measurements, which I really took notice of, was that in 2012 Patagonia became the first Californian company to become a certified B Corporation. What appealed to me about B Corps was that, as Patagonia seemed to be saying, *It's easy to look good, it's harder to be good – but don't take our word for it, we've got this certification.* On the day he signed up his company to the initiative, Chouinard stated, 'Patagonia is trying to build a company that could last 100 years.'

By 2018 I was becoming increasingly frustrated with the status quo – the meaningless merry-go-round of awards and fake sustainability initiatives that made 'success' feel flimsy. Fake sustainability is rife within restaurants (and in the business community more broadly), and the responsibility to do better rests with restaurateurs and chefs. But at the point in history where our planet needs us to care about the consequences of our actions more than ever, Jimmy stays silent. If a critic's job is to critique, then why do food critics flatly refuse to point out unsustainable ingredients on restaurant menus when they write reviews? Jimmy is just as much of the problem as the restaurateurs and chefs themselves – all are complicit in the continued damage being done to the environment.

As I write this, getting a good review or winning an award has absolutely nothing to do with taking responsibility for the collateral damage a restaurant does to the planet. Every restaurant does damage – it's a question of how much. There are no totally sustainable restaurants, they're all on a sliding scale, but that doesn't mean we all shouldn't be playing our part. It's madness to me that there are ZERO criteria in a restaurant review for a judgement on sustainability. Only quality matters. But what quality? Quality of life? Quality of the decisions we make that will affect our future?

A restaurant can win an award serving endangered species without their reprehensible practice being questioned. Take a bow, chefs serving beluga caviar from the critically endangered wild beluga sturgeon (extinct in the Adriatic Sea) and other threatened species of fish worldwide. Take a bow, reviewers writing about the deliciousness of dishes made with animals at risk of extinction. A Jimmy recently gave a restaurant an award after mildly complaining in their review that they didn't like eating the critically endangered fish the restaurant served. Why the fuck did you do it then? What is wrong with you? If you suffered from coeliac disease, you wouldn't eat products containing gluten just because they were on a menu. Was it because you couldn't resist a little spoonful of extinction? So decadent and delicious, right? Just part of the job, hey? How about you flip the script and mark restaurants down for inexcusably serving such foods? Change is not going to come from you 'wish(ing) sustainability were higher on the list of priorities for this (and other) restaurants'. Stop sitting on the sidelines, and actively encourage sustainability by demoting restaurants who deliberately and wilfully hurt the planet. Some chefs are apparently perfectly happy to continue cooking with unsustainable ingredients when the planet is in the grip of a biodiversity crisis. You are a professional eater; start acting like one. Refuse these foods every time you dine, and write about the unsustainable foods you encounter on menus. It would be an appropriate use of your guillotine and privilege.

Amid all this insanity, a major restaurant award for sustainability does exist, and I was asked to nominate Attica for it, but declined for years. To win it, all I would need to do is fill in a form saying how great I'm doing with sustainability! There would be no on-site visit, and no verification to back up any claims I might make. It's just greenwashing. The deceitfulness of awards such as this are damaging to the planet, and to businesses doing their best to make a real and honest attempt to improve their sustainability. With so much 'winning' going on, where are all the Jimmys when we really need them to inform the public, so that when you eat out, you can make a truly informed decision to choose to give your hard-earned money to restaurants that are sacrificing a chunk of their profit margins by trying to do the right thing? The deliberate underpayment of staff, the use of unsustainable foods and other shady practices confer a massive competitive advantage, both financially and creatively, over those of us who choose to do our best to ensure that there will be viable food ecosystems and equitable workplace environments for future generations.

The guides, the Jimmys and the award systems, as well as journalists and the media more broadly, need to think long and hard about their priorities, because what they claim they value is not coming through with any sincerity in their actions.

Against this background, I began to think about trying something different. The more I learnt about B Lab, the not-for-profit organisation that believes 'business could lead the way towards a new, stakeholder-driven model' and that certifies B Corporations, the more I began to feel this could be a good fit for Attica.

Certified B Corporations are companies that have gained a designation through strict verification by B Lab. These businesses meet high standards of performance on environmental and social fronts, and on transparency and accountability through demonstrated actions.

In short, a B Corp is a company that has taken a look at the organisational nitty-gritty of capitalism, and used the tools and policies that B Lab provides to counter it, moving the traditional profit-at-all-costs model of business towards something that seeks to address some of society's biggest challenges. It's about understanding that the world of business is bigger than just the needs of an individual, and that a business can and should work towards social change. B Lab helps companies balance 'profit with purpose'.

In 2021, after procrastinating for years, Kylie and I finally began the process of certifying Attica as a B Corp. It was time to make a fresh start, to move past the meaningless hype machine and focus our time and energy on something with real structure.

At the time of writing, there are only 22 restaurants worldwide with B Corp certification, and since B Lab opened in Australia in 2013, only one other restaurant has gained certification. At first, we weren't sure that we would actually be able to get certified – but our close friend Fleur Studd had recently gone through the complex process with her outstanding company, Market Lane Coffee, so she helped advise us on the 360-degree assessment of our business that B Lab would make.

During the certification process, we wrote Attica's first mission statement:

To holistically take care of ALL THINGS to the best of our ability, our people, our community, and our environment, and to have as much joy as possible while doing it.

I did say that I was giving up on awards, but I didn't say I was giving up my competitive spirit. The difference is that now it's pointed into the future – so we'll have a future. In early 2024, with Kylie doing the majority of the hard work, Attica became a certified B Corporation.

To me, change represents fun. There's nothing I find more exciting than analysing something and conceiving how it could be different. For chef-restaurant owners like me, creativity needs to be found not only in the dishes we create, but within every aspect of the businesses we own. I try to take an outsider's approach, mixed with a bit of innocence and my best intentions. I always try to make decisions with a long-term view, because the restaurant industry is my profession, and I think that restaurants are some of the most imaginative, creative and vibrant businesses in our society. When I make changes at the restaurant I own, I think about how these decisions affect our team, but also about the teams that members of our team will one day run themselves. I have a responsibility to contribute to a better restaurant industry in the future. Throwing my hands up and saying something like, 'the system is broken, I can't fix it' is irresponsible and reckless.

The working hours I've endured throughout my career are longer than any other person I know – other than my chef friends, of course. Many years ago, when I turned forty, I calculated that I had already worked around the same number of hours across my life as a person retiring at age 65. I felt those 25 extra years' worth of work in my bones, and in my pockets – 25 years of labour for which I hadn't been paid. Rather than being bitter about it, though, I decided that, when I became an owner, the buck stopped with me. Instead of looking for someone to blame, I looked at what I could change. I could teach my staff not to accept what I had once accepted. I could teach them not to do that to someone else in their own business, either.

The change since then has been monumental. There is nothing for a business to fear from teaching workers about their rights. It amuses me now to think of how Kylie and I would have to 'police' new team members, who would turn up hours before their shift. We'd watch them arrive on the office security camera and gently say, 'We appreciate your commitment, but there is no need to be here now. Please go do something else and return to work at your start time.' Chefs have been so conditioned to long hours that initially it proved a difficult habit to break. The benefits are obvious, though – a happier, more balanced person performs at a higher level than someone who is run-down.

The overworking of staff is not a practice that benefits anyone. It's obvious that it hurts the employees, but really it hurts a business just as much. Is it any wonder there's a staffing shortage in the hospitality industry globally, with the pay and conditions that restaurant owners have historically laid out for their workers?

Go out and be good motherfuckers.

NO NEGATIVE ATTITUDE

I used to be a truly terrible manager. I had no people-management skills whatsoever. I didn't know the first thing about how to correctly hire staff, or how to provide direct and honest feedback to them. I had no idea how to build and maintain a positive and healthy workplace culture. By the late 2000s, I had built a small team, based mainly on technical skills. The restaurant had been surviving on its creative output alone, and when that team began to devour itself, I did what I had always done – I shrank away from the impending situation, failing everyone involved. During that time I fell into a circumstantial depression. For eight months I went missing, consumed by what I perceived to be the insurmountable problems of Attica's near-bankruptcy, the collapse of my relationship with the owner, and the grind of hundred-hour weeks and a four-hour daily commute. All these things led to a disconnection from my young family, and an inability to deal with conflict and lead the team. For fear of being seen as weak, or as damaged goods, I didn't tell a soul about my problems. I internalised them, believing I was the only person who was going through something like this. I began to ask myself if all of it was actually worth it, and came close to handing in my resignation and applying for a job as a catering assistant.

At the lowest point in my depression, I had an appointment with a kind supplier of ours, Jason Jurie, to visit a mussel farm. He was meant to pick me up early that morning, but I struggled to get out of bed; had it not been for the fact that Jason was taking time away from his family while he was on holiday, I would have cancelled. Together we drove to Portarlington Harbour, where we met Lance Wiffen, a mussel farmer with a weathered and kind face, who had farmed and fished Port Phillip Bay for thirty years. Gently, Lance began to talk about his life in simple and honest terms – the extremes of the weather, overcoming the impact of overfishing, the effects of climate change on wild mussel spat populations, and his deep passion for the mussels he produced. In the boat's cabin, Lance cooked some just-harvested mussels in a microwave, and when I told him they were the best I'd ever eaten, he gave me a look of complete and utter disbelief. It was a wonderful moment – no one had ever thought to recognise his excellence and tell him straight to his face. There are few greater privileges than telling another truly deserving human how incredible their work is.

Lance's talk turned to family, and he told me that, at 55 years old, he'd got a second chance. Although he had adult children from his first marriage, he had remarried and had an infant son. He described the joy of truly experiencing parenthood, as if for the first time. He told me that one of his greatest regrets the first time around was that he had been so busy keeping his business afloat he'd practically missed the childhoods of his first three children. He said he'd never make that mistake again. Although we had only met two hours earlier, and he knew next to nothing about my life, he looked me in the eyes and said, 'I will never be able to get that time back.'

Those words were the first thing that cut through the hopelessness I'd been feeling for months. I reflected on how similar our paths were, and I recognised that it wasn't too late to change the trajectory of mine. Looking back on it now, this was a defining moment in my life – it was the moment when I realised I could change.

Across the next few months, I began to resolve the issues I was facing, one by one. I started coaching Kobe's basketball team. I regularly went mountain biking with Ella. I repaired the relationships I valued, and let go of the ones that weren't healthy. I began to exercise more and eat better. The grey clouds parted, just a little at first. A small ray of light burst through, and then another, until eventually the sun began to shine once more. I'll never forget what it felt like to realise that I was going to be ok. I returned to work with a new attitude. I analysed the conditions that had caused my depression in the first place, and resolved to put protections in place that meant I would never end up back there.

Due to my lack of strong leadership, I had allowed a cancerous negativity to grow at Attica. When I 'returned', I dealt with it swiftly. I learnt how deeply it had been affecting everyone in the team, and I knew that the buck stopped with me. Really, I alone had the responsibility to correct the direction of the culture. Trying not to overcomplicate things in life is a core philosophy of mine, so I made a simple new rule: No Negative Attitude.

It means just that – no disrespectful behaviour, no sulking, no being rude, no talking back, no laziness, no dropping of the shoulders and no selfishness. Central to my new understanding was this fact: negativity is contagious.

Whenever I am interviewing a potential new staff member, I let the manager who I'm conducting the interview with ask the more structured interview questions: 'What was your worst moment?' 'What was your best moment?' 'What would your last employer say about you?' Then I ask questions about their life, their family and what their passions are. I see my role as being to disarm them. I don't ask any technical questions about their skill set. I give them a rundown on some of the things that Attica represents – excellence, independence, community, creativity, and deep care for each other and our guests. If an interview is going well, and it seems like the applicant could be a good fit for our team, I say: 'I really only have one rule here and it's called No Negative Attitude.' I am careful to define exactly what No Negative Attitude is and isn't. It isn't about a person feeling down because they have been bullied, yelled at, or subjected to harassment of any kind. I tell the applicant that while we have a strong and positive culture, if any of these things ever happen to them, they are to go straight to their manager, Kylie or myself. It's important to make this point crystal-clear, because getting down when you have been treated poorly is *not* negative attitude.

And in case you think I'm some kind of eternal optimist, glossing over everything – a Ted Lasso type, a character so positive his positivity is toxic, forcing himself and others to bury and suppress the difficult emotions and the ups and downs we all face, I'm far from it. While generally I'm a positive person, and Attica as an environment is a place where being yourself is encouraged, we take the issues our team go through seriously. This is about an attempt to reduce genuine toxic negativity, which in my experience is a killer if left unchecked.

After this clarification, I look them directly in the eyes and ask, 'So if you are successful in getting this job, can you agree to this rule?' If the answer is yes, then I say, 'Excellent, I will remember that we had this conversation, and please keep in mind that, at the first sign of negative attitude, we will sit down and I will remind you of your obligation and promise to me, yourself and the team.'

The commitment is important, because we are hiring first and foremost for character. While I do believe that a person's character can evolve and improve over time, it's harder to teach than the skill of finely chopping an onion or pouring a glass of wine beautifully. Someone who commits daily to being a positive, hard-working force in the workplace has good character.

Over time, this simple rule revolutionised the culture at Attica and took the restaurant to completely new heights of performance. It transformed it into a joyful place to work, where everyone strives together for the same shared goal – to get better every single day, in any way we can. The key is the point at which the team member commits to no negativity, verbally and with eye contact. This uncommon directness doesn't allow for any wiggle room, and the overwhelming majority of staff keep their promise. Experience has taught me that, when managing a team of forty, it is impossible to completely eliminate negativity, but destructive negativity has decreased massively. When it does occasionally raise its ugly head, it becomes much easier to have a respectful conversation about it, ask if that person is ok, and get them headed in the right direction.

In my mind, negativity equals selfishness. The truly negative mindset puts its own needs ahead of everyone else's every single time, pulling others down. Negativity in its many forms often stems from unhappiness. I have learnt that I am responsible for my own happiness. If I don't like the job that I am doing and it's getting me down, then it's up to me to find a different one. If a strained relationship is making me depressed, then it's up to me to either try to improve it, accept it, or end it. I cannot change anyone else, but I can change myself. In a fair, kind and equal environment, I'm 100 per cent responsible for working on my positive mental health. I have an obligation to seek help, so it doesn't negatively affect those around me.

My friend Mariam Issa, who was born in Somalia and raised in East Africa, has overcome more hardships than just about anyone

I've met. Mariam arrived in Australia as a refugee and smashed through a host of obstructions, including race, culture and gender, to become one of the most positive community leaders I know. Mariam once said a very profound thing when we were discussing negativity. Describing someone very negative who had strolled into her garden, she told me with a laugh, 'Ben, people who are negative are really putting their backs into it; it's a full-time job being negative, and they are absolutely committed and serious about it.' I laughed out loud at the sharpness of the observation. I would point to Mariam as the epitome of resilience, and a reason why there are few excuses for negativity. Due to her life's circumstances, if anyone had cause to be negative it would be Mariam – and yet, in sharp contrast to those experiences, she is extraordinarily positive. If a person who has been dealt one of the harshest hands in life can pick themselves up each day and not wallow in self-pity, then what excuse do the rest of us have?

But a rule in and of itself is not enough. Neither is a demand. You have to actually provide an infrastructure for a positive culture first, then give people the support to grow, encourage and protect it. If you are the leader of that culture, then you must live what you ask. Every time I ask for No Negative Attitude from my team, I am also recommitting to it myself. To avoid negative thinking is hard work, and it requires real presence of mind to keep it at bay. I have a responsibility to keep myself in peak mental fitness, so I can bring the energy required to support our team. On the days that I can't do that, I make sure not one of them knows the difference, and I make sure I do something for myself outside of Attica to fill my cup, like going for a bike ride along the coast, a hike in the bush, or throwing on a great record at home and listening to it super-loud before heading to the restaurant. As a leader, I plan and choose when to share my imperfections, so it doesn't negatively affect the team's daily work lives. We all sit somewhere on the spectrum of glass half-full or glass half-empty, which is to say that we all have negativity within us to a degree. That's completely normal. But we also all have the chance to know this: negativity robs a person of the ability to receive the maximum potential from every opportunity.

Because of No Negative Attitude, staff going through a hard personal time have found Attica a sanctuary. It has been a place where they have been able to focus on something positive, sometimes a welcome distraction. This has applied to me, too. Many years ago, when I was going through divorce, one of the hardest times of my life, I would come to work and see everyone smiling and feel the positivity, and I knew that I couldn't put my problems onto those happy faces. They lifted me immensely. It was a refuge where I had to focus on being positive, not on anything negative that was going on in my life.

THIS ONE TIME, AT
ATTICA SUMMER CAMP

Words that no person should ever say: we are on a family exercise walk in Chadstone Shopping Centre. On this locked-down Sunday morning it's a ghost town. We stroll past closed shop after closed shop, until we approach Gucci – which is open and, astonishingly, has no queue, and not a single customer. Its masked sales assistants stand alert, like sentries guarding the palace. Very odd. In Australia, Gucci always has long queues to get in, a cringy phenomenon. Ella tells me to pick up the pace and I snap back to reality. The five of us march on, eager to get our steps per minute up. After a five-kilometre circuit, lapping both levels of the mall, we take a left and arrive outside Kmart.

More words no person should ever say: Kmart is full and has a queue of 150 people waiting to get in.

The world has flipped. In this moment, I am witnessing everything I need to know about the state of business in Australia in the winter of 2020. Attica is at the Gucci end of the scale, and, well, we need to be at the Kmart end of the scale. There is no time for business plans, what I must do is right here in front of me. A plan begins to form.

I dream of happier times, of summer coming. I want to build something uplifting and fun. I want to have a damn good time while I do it. Fuck this lockdown shit. They might be necessary, but they are breaking my spirit.

I dream of the smell of cut grass and ice-cold lager, car rides out of the city, the wind in your hair, heading with anticipation towards your destination, a restaurant called Attica Summer Camp, with its stop-you-in-your-tracks, sunset-over-the-ranges views, its killer playlist of upbeat tunes, a menu of succulent grilled meats, cunning Hasselback potatoes skewered on a rotisserie and – the pièce de résistance – a dessert trolley of pure insanity. Did I mention there would be Friesling (frozen Riesling slushie)? It goes without saying. An air freshener for your car with a cute tree logo? Those will be available as you exit through the gift shop. All at the most reasonable prices possible.

We enlist our winemaker mate and local legend Mac Forbes to help us find a vacant restaurant site in the country. Due to wealthy international investors buying up wineries and then not knowing how to run the restaurants attached to them, there is no shortage. After an exhaustive search, we settle on an old, run-down winery in a near-deserted corner of the Yarra Valley.

In what could be considered one giant leap backwards for mankind, the winery restaurant had formally been a grill-your-own steak restaurant, where you chose your raw steak and salad from a hexagonal salad bar and then grilled your steak to your preferred doneness on a hexagonal grill in a hexagonal room. In the centre of the room an enormous hexagonal extractor fan hung from the ceiling, every bit the replica of Apollo 11's command module. This trippy prism of DIY steak had closed three years before and was now mothballed. (Could it have been because customers want restaurants to perform their traditional role of cooking the food for them? Customers these days! Outrageous!)

There was nothing we could use except a working cool room, but the site had a certain something – the right vibe and a massive covered outdoor dining room, also hexagonal, with a beautiful view that, for the times, was just perfect. I knew it from the moment we set foot in the place, despite it being the least-resourced site from any angle of infrastructural usefulness. I could smell fun, I could see the potential. It had to be here.

We signed a five-month lease, and then the battle of all battles began with the local council, who from the outset seemed completely determined to work against us. Although the site had been a licensed restaurant just three years before, the council had somehow lost their documentation to support this fact and so, without a planning permit, they stood in our way to apply for a liquor licence. And without liquor sales, there would be no business and, horror upon horror, no Friesling. It is a known rule, and a matter of etiquette, that you cannot open an uplifting summer restaurant without Friesling! It just isn't done.

After email upon email of painful communication with the council, and at their insistence, we hired a liquor licensing 'expert' and paid him $2500 to tell us to walk away. He said that no matter how hard we tried, the council would stand in the way of our liquor licence application. He told us that if we proceeded, we'd 'die out there'. It felt as if we had hiked into the middle of a vast desert without water (or Friesling) and were now lost. By this point, we'd sunk about $30,000 into the project in design work and permits, a massive amount of money to us at any stage, but particularly in this lean time. After months of stonewalling by the council we had no option but to cancel the lease. If you know anything about me by now, you'll understand how painfully hard it was to face the fact that we had to quit before we'd even started. I come from a long line of back-country folk who have the strongest possible dislike for being beaten by bureaucracy. Against the odds, stories of getting one over on 'the man' lie at the heart of bonfire storytelling in my family. I felt as if I'd let my lineage down, and the thought of how disappointed my council-bamboozling uncles and aunties would be in me was depressing.

To commiserate, Kylie and I met up with Mac for some drinks in Healesville, a wine town close to the restaurant site. At the renowned Four Pillars gin distillery, the three of us sat with shoulders slumped over our gin and tonics. I was mentally preparing myself to go on *Today Tonight* and throw the council under the bus when Cam Mackenzie, Yarra Valley royalty and Four Pillars co-founder, approached us to introduce himself. Cam had heard through the grapevine that we were opening close by, and he was really pumped about it. I had to deflate him by saying we'd just cancelled the lease. Cam, a former professional athlete who represented Australia in the men's 4 × 400-metre relay at the 1996 Atlanta Olympics, was not having a bar of it. He became incredibly animated, saying, 'No fucking way, MATE! That is complete and utter bullshit. You are trying to save your business in this extraordinary time, and EVERYONE should be working together.'

Cam recognised the importance of our decision to open in the area, the number of jobs it would create (sixty). Not to mention the tens of thousands of people who would visit the Yarra Valley to dine at Summer Camp, and the attention it would bring to an area often overlooked in favour of the more glam beach-going wine region of the Mornington Peninsula. He asked/demanded, 'Can you hold off announcing this for the weekend? Give me 48 hours and I'll try and sort these dickheads out.' Although I thought it was hopeless, Cam wouldn't relent, and I said, 'Sure, knock yourself out.'

What ensued was unlike anything I have experienced. Cam, who is far more politically connected than I am, fired off a series of scathing missives to the powers that be, detailing the injustice of our situation. Within 24 hours I'd had a call from a government official, saying how disappointed they were that we had been put through this, and could we send them all the documentation we had, so they could see what was possible. I emailed everything we had to them and the next evening, as I walked on the beach with my family, I received a call from an unknown number. It was good news. 'Mr Shewry, we've reviewed your documents, everything is in order, and we don't require anything from the council and will issue you a temporary emergency liquor licence. Have a nice night.'

I got off the phone, overcome with emotion, and burst into tears. Kobe, Ella, Ruby and Kylie looked concerned. Through hiccups, I hugged them with tears of relief. Writing this, I feel as if that night on the beach should have been more like some victorious scene out of *Rocky*, where I triumphantly raised a fist in the air, but the challenges were only just beginning, and anyone who has dealt with the nonsensical and combative rules of local councils, whether it be at their private home or business, knows how difficult and deflating it can be.

But I'd like to just say, though: YO, CAM MACKENZIE! YOU ARE A FUCKING LEGEND AND IF IT WERE NOT FOR YOUR DEEP KINDNESS TO A STRANGER, WE PROBABLY WOULD HAVE LOST OUR BUSINESS.

Dreams are fabulous. Realities are dreams in action. The reality was that, initially, no one except Kylie, Mac and our architect, Iva, thought my idea was any good – but I have an ability to shield what I know I must do from outside noise. Generally, people are threatened by change, and would often prefer it if everything remained comfortably the same. I was determined to escape the ambitious-restaurant prison I'd built for myself and do something new. After we had started a T-shirt company, a pottery studio, a bake shop, a meal delivery service, an online dance party, a takeaway shop, a soup kitchen, an online store and numerous other side hustles, and after opening and closing Attica as a restaurant several times within eight months, Summer Camp was the move I hoped would generate the extra income for us to survive long-term. And while I thrive in the chaos of change, I also fundamentally believe that legacy should never hold a creative entity back; it should be seen as the reward that it is – the capacity for continuous reinvention.

I was working by myself at the Attica Summer Camp site for the first two months of the build. It was an exceptionally lonely time. I have overseen a dozen renovations of Attica over the past decade and there has been a moment in each of them where the builders or my family had left, or I was working alone to complete the job, unsure if I would finish it before the opening date. These have been the most bereft and desolate times of my life. At Summer Camp I worked from an enormous to-do list and Iva's design. I built the main kitchen and the massive service bar, renovated the outdated toilets and constructed the colourful outdoor Friesling station, which was inspired by 1960s stripy beach umbrellas. Then there was an undercover outdoor grill kitchen to house our two massive charcoal rotisseries and, lastly, the landscaping.

The nature of builds is that as they unfold, more and more jobs are uncovered, and the to-do list grows bigger and bigger. I began to feel as if I was adrift in the middle of a job ocean, treading water with no land in site. I'd be lying if I didn't tell you that I had a good amount of self-doubt through this period, and it was mixed in with a surprising amount of anger, too. Some days I felt as if I was fuelled by it, but instead of Rage Against the Machine, I was raging with the machines: mitre saws, hammer drills and concrete grinders. The anger came from the situation I had been forced into, and by the lack of support I had at this time. Back in Melbourne, Attica was bleeding money at unprecedented levels. The lockdown had ended, but because of government restrictions, the number of customers we could serve had been reduced by 60 per cent. We were losing $70,000 a week. We found ourselves in a sort of no-man's-land where takeaway no longer worked because customers wanted to return to restaurants, but at the same time we were unable to serve enough of those people at Attica to survive. Summer Camp was the outdoor-dining race to generate another income stream to support Attica.

Rightly or wrongly, I carried the weight of the world on my shoulders, as if I alone had been tasked to save the business. I had friends call to try and talk me out of it. I was living in the country, howling at the moon, doing the kind of reckless solitary work a person does when they are by themselves and under the pump. I was sleeping above the kitchen, in a windowless room inside a swelter-ing uninsulated shed, with emergency lighting providing 24-hour daylight that I couldn't turn off, on a cheap airbed on the floor that had a habit of deflating in the middle of the night.

I soon realised that I am not a solitary person. I love to build things with other humans. Every time a person visited, I was uplifted. Our head pastry chef at the time, Rosemary Andrews, was the first person to join me on-site to waterblast pavers, paint things and scrub everything – menial tasks that many people would have turned up their noses at. Not Rosemary, though; she is one of the hardest workers I've ever known, and her arriving on-site, along with some local builders, gave me a huge lift. Soon Kylie and our Summer Camp restaurant manager, Lyndal Taylor, joined us too. Lyndal was an Attica veteran, and with her sense of just, compassionate hospitality and deep care, was the perfect person to lead the service – a moral authority for our young team. She is one of the finest people I have ever employed.

Shortly after, we took on George Wintle as Summer Camp sous chef – he had to make the snap decision to drop everything, pack his bags and drive through the night to escape a New South Wales border lockdown. If he didn't make it over to Victoria in time, he would have been stuck on the other side and missed the whole thing. Attica head sommelier Dom Robinson was regularly on-site to sort out the wine program, but more importantly to tune the Friesling machine. All of a sudden we had a team, and things began to happen.

Because Attica has always been DIY central, and I am only one man, I've often asked our managers and team to pitch in to help complete projects outside the scope of their day jobs. Together we've built all sorts of things, and I've found the experience brings me closer to the individuals involved. It teaches them practical life skills and gets shit done. Summer Camp was no exception. We were trying to build a new restaurant from the ground up in ten weeks. We intended to open in January and we called in every favour we could from our community of friends and collaborators to complete the restaurant. Grafting and building things is so much more fulfilling than being given things or buying them.

Kylie was appalled by how long it seemed to be taking me to install the sound system. She was vexed by my inability to correctly calculate how much speaker cable we required. I kept running out, and twice she made a three-hour round-trip to purchase more. In my defence, restaurants with bad sound are atrocious, so I gently reminded her that her sacrifice was appreciated and worth it. As it turns out, with modern technology, a small budget, and a bit of thought, you can build a system with killer sound. So, restaurants, there's no excuses. There's categorically nothing more irritating than sitting down at a table and being subjected to poor-quality sound. It can ruin all the hard work going into the cooking and service. If you can't be bothered installing at least a half-decent stereo, then the solution is simple – don't play music.

To back up my strong opinion, I decided that the sound system at Summer Camp had better be kick-ass, so I spent 1000 hours (Kylie's estimate) installing the system with hundreds of metres of copper speaker cable, giving myself the cheesy online moniker: 1800CABLEGOD. I purchased twelve Dynaudio bookshelf speakers and one hell of a grunty amplifier to power it all. Once I had routed all the cables and hooked it up, I couldn't get the damn thing to work, prompting another cry for help – this time to the lovely husband of our team member Amy, who works in AV and saved the day. It takes an army to build a camp.

A favourite team memory of the Attica Summer Camp playlist (take a listen on Spotify) was whenever Briggs's powerhouse of a track 'Bad Apples' would come on, always at a higher volume than the rest of the playlist. This always seemed to happen in the late afternoon when the restaurant was dead quiet, except for one poor table of four unsuspecting 75-year-olds, who, as they heard Adam's lyrics 'What the fuck are you staring for?' spluttered and coughed through their smoked king salmon and dill.

In many ways, the team we built at Attica Summer Camp was the greatest team we've ever assembled. I say that with utmost respect for all the incredibly talented, skilled, experienced and high-level teams we've built at Attica across the years. But because this restaurant wasn't Attica, and because the location was in the country, and because there was a staffing shortage, we basically employed anyone who wanted a job. That meant lots of first-time hospitality workers, veterans who wanted a new start, and many people who had not previously worked at the standard we set. I'd describe the bunch of us as the most ragtag group of hospitality workers ever assembled. There was no time for proper training, nor the building of systems – and I didn't even have time to write the menu until two days before we opened! It was complete and utter chaos. We were perfectly imperfect.

I recall the first day we opened, for friends and family only: 120 people descended upon us, like a pack of seagulls on a hot chip (our hand-cut chips were taken as seriously as our stereo), and we went down like the steaming pile of shit we were. As the first-course orders flew in, I hadn't shown anyone how to plate anything, and I was on the entrée section by myself getting annihilated while the kitchen staff, through no fault of their own, had to stand back and watch. A few friends wandered into the kitchen from the dining room and tried to say hello but quickly retreated as they saw the shitstorm that was unfolding. Mercifully, they couldn't complain because they weren't paying!

The first two weeks were very rough, but we got good quickly. I found it deeply inspiring to watch all of these different people take their opportunities and run with them. I marvelled at their ability to pull this project together – there was no avoiding how difficult it was. Soon we were cooking for up to 485 people on Saturdays and Sundays, and the restaurant was flying. Unexpectedly, a review came out in the *New York Times*, online and in print, the rarest occurrence for an Australian restaurant, let alone one that was only in operation for five months. I stood in front of the team that day and said, 'Do you know what you've done?' – which caused confused looks. 'Do you realise that the vast majority of people in the world work their entire lives and never get their work recognised in a positive way by this publication? Do you realise what you have done?

Can you comprehend how massive this is? This is all YOU, every single one of you. This is ALL you. I have never felt more proud of a group of people. We have come from the lowest point but now you should be standing proud, and I hope you see yourselves the way I see you, you fucking rule!' I will never forget the happy looks on all the different faces.

Our wild bunch, front of house and back of house, working together as one, no job above or beneath anyone. The camaraderie was electrifying. There are so many stories about people lifting themselves up that I could probably fill a book with them: things like watching chefs run from their stations to clean up under a customer's table whose children, no doubt influenced by Jackson Pollock, had splattered food all over the floor. Or chefs who would stand in the bar cheerfully polishing cutlery. Or the way the pastry section would jump on the deep-fryer to cook the chips, as if there was nothing more important to do in the world. Or watching Kylie and Lyndal, both of whom suffer from chronic arachnophobia, save each other from the endless stream of spiders that called Summer Camp home. Front of house would bring endless icy drinks to the team enduring the scorching heat of the grill station. It became a competition to make another person a coffee before they made one for you. It was a powerful lesson to see all the divisions that exist in restaurants being smashed to pieces, and instead everyone dedicating their service to one another. Humans are so much greater when we can find ways to work together than when we define our roles and defend our territories.

One of the greatest stories of my life happened at Summer Camp, and the best part of this tale is that it's not really mine. I wasn't even there.

The property didn't have a town supply of water and instead operated off some very old concrete water tanks that were down a hill, about 50 metres away from the restaurant. On our biggest ever day, a Sunday with 600 guests booked for lunch and dinner, the restaurant suddenly ran out of water. Completely and utterly out of water. This happened just as our first 120 guests walked into the dining room at 11am.

No water means this: no water for guests on the tables, no water to wash the glassware in the bar, no water to cook with, no water to wash dishes with and, desperately, no water to flush toilets with. No water is worse than no electricity or gas – both situations Attica has worked through many times. No water is a catastrophe of the most distinguished proportions. If I had been there that day, I would have closed the restaurant. I was at home taking care of my three children, oblivious of the chaos about to unfold – which, like all great stories, is best told as an oral history:

George: I remember being on the pass, expediting, and Kylie came up to me and was like…

Kylie: Hey, I think we need to change the water tanks over. There's no more water. The water is not working.

George: I remember walking down to the tanks and pressing the button to flip them over. I love whenever I can help to fix a problem. I remember walking back up feeling so good, like, *I just fixed this problem.* Someone said, 'Nah, still not working.' I thought, *Oh my god*, and I ran back down and got on the ladder and checked all the tanks. All empty. I'd never felt so scared. I didn't know it, but the tank had cracked, and we'd lost all our water. I gathered six kitchen staff with cars and was like, 'Go to Woolworths now and every bottle of water you can see, buy it.'

Jo was real keen to go to Woolworths, because she would always have a smoke as she drove.

(When Drusilla Ratnam joined the Summer Camp team, she was working at a sandwich shop and had never waited a table before, but she had been gently guided by Lyndal and Kylie.)

Dru: My role at Summer Camp was essentially just polishing glasses, polishing cutlery and checking the toilets. I could hear people running around, screaming, 'Boil the ice, boil the ice.' I was like, *Oh, what's going on?* All I could think about was how am I going to polish all this cutlery. I remember freaking out. I remember being passed a bucket and someone saying, 'Hey, Dru, the toilets aren't flushing. You know what you need to do? After every single person that goes to the toilet, just go in there with a bucket of water and pour it down the toilet.' And I remember being like, *This is great, this is restaurant life.*

Because I'd never worked in restaurants, I was like, *This is what must happen. This is it. The peak of my career.* And it was hot, and we had that big function coming up. And every person that went to the toilet, and I'm not even joking, would come up to me like, 'Hey, just letting you know the water's out,' and I'd say, surprised, 'Thank you for letting me know.' Then I'd dive in there and pour the water down the toilet. They would ask, 'How do I wash my hands?' and I'd say, 'Well, we've got hand sanitiser.' I was like how *do they* wash their hands? Yeah, that was wild.

But then the water would just keep appearing in the bucket, and I was like, they must be boiling the ice. I feel like people just kind of accepted it at a point; they were like, *Aw, we are in the country, why not, water runs out.* I remember my breaking point, though. I think I held up pretty well, considering I'm quite an emotional being. I went into the toilet and there was just blood everywhere. And I was like, *Holy crap! Shit, what is this?* There was blood on the seat, there was blood on the floor, and I was like, *These are adults, why is there blood? Why me?* And there was no water to wipe it, so I had to get every cleaning chemical I could think of, layer up on gloves, and everyone was running around headless, and I was dealing with this blood. But I got through it.

George: I remember calling the water tanker and they said, 'We are three hours away,' and I was like: 'IT NEEDS TO BE QUICKER. PLEASE, I BEG OF YOU!' I remember taking the Summer Camp banner down, so the truck could get to the tanks. The banner read, 'This one time, at Attica Summer Camp' – which, reliving this story now, feels appropriate. I accidentally unthreaded it completely. Ben let me know the next day how hard it was to put it back. Kylie gave the truck driver a huge plate of cake and he was stoked.

Dru: Everyone just went into action mode. Kylie and Lyndal just kept such calm heads towards us, all these twenty-year-old front-of-house kids who knew nothing. If Kylie hadn't been so calm and level-headed with us, regardless of if she was dying on the inside, I don't think anyone would have been able to soldier on and deal with the situation.

Kylie: Closing was never an option. It wasn't even discussed.

George: I think Summer Camp was the most fun, and the best team I have ever worked with. In other restaurants when something like this happened, I probably would have been like, *Oh sweet, we'll close, I might get to go home early.* But this was the first time that it didn't even cross my mind. Everyone had a common mindset that it didn't feel like a job; you just wanted to be part of the greater good. It didn't matter what the issue was. Everyone just jumped on, front of house or back of house.

(George Wintle became a sous chef at Attica.)

Ben: When I pulled into the car park at 5pm, to work the function we had booked that night, the sight of a water tanker blocking the driveway told me something must have gone wrong. There were MOUNTAINS of dishes in the pot wash and bar areas, and frantically washing them was the most exhausted but happy team I've seen. Everyone told me the story, their own experience of it, and I couldn't believe it. I was speechless. The way they told it was beautiful, too, like they had got one over on 'Dad'. I was in awe of them. I went around and shook everyone's hand and looked them in the eyes and told them how fucking awesome I thought they were. They saved more than $70,000 in revenue that day, but the money wasn't what moved me, because their actions represented so much more than that. You couldn't pay people to do what they did. It represented a decade of work building teams, learning from leadership mistakes, doing better, believing in the magic of having faith, trusting that people are good and will do the right thing and, when treated fairly, will bend over backwards for you. This team put themselves through the wringer for me that day, but it would be arrogant of me to think it was me alone they did it for – they each did it for themselves and for the team. It was leagues above what I would ever ask of them. And, fuck me, they could not have been more proud of their efforts. Knowing smiles. This was the reverse of the day of the *New York Times* review when I asked them, 'Do you know what you have done?' Their faces said: 'Do *you* know what we have done?'

Dru: I always tell people this. Summer Camp was a whirlwind but the funnest time of my life. And I don't think I'll ever get that fun back. I remember driving home at the end of that day, and I was so tired I had to drive with all the windows down, like just blasting music but with a huge smile on my face. I was shocked at myself for not crying. It was such a hard day, and I was exhausted. My muscles hurt, but I was like, *Wow, I loved that, I felt alive, that was so fun.*

(Dru is now a professional waiter and supervisor at Attica.)

THOSE BLOODY BIMBULLAS

Budjaan flies through the forest, darting between the spotted gum, mountain ash and fragrant myrtles. In Dhurga, Uncle Noel Butler says, 'Hello, Budjaan'. He then turns to me and says, 'Rain will come Thursday.' It's less of a statement and more of a breath. Two days later, on Thursday, the rain comes.

We are guided up Gulaga, the Yuin people's mother mountain. We've been told it will be difficult, but brother Dwayne Bannon-Harrison holds my hand, the way his grandfather once held his. On the journey he says softly, 'I'm honouring that old man.' At the summit we look down at the distant coastline and it hits me suddenly, in the heart, the head and the gut. All I can manage is, 'It's undeniable.' Sculpted into the coast far below is the black duck, the totem of the Yuin Nation.

Later our boat pulls up to the dock on a twilight river of melted lead. Three large pelicans stand over us, looking sideways, as if to say, 'We aren't really watching you two.' Uncle Bruce Pascoe greets them and as he dispatches our catch, he apologises for the life taken:

'Sorry, Buda.' The pelicans wait patiently as Uncle Bruce says, 'Some for us, some for them, and some for the earth.'

On Budawang Country, bimbullas (wild blood cockles) sit in the silt and brackish water of the inlet. Knee deep, Uncle Noel and I are hunting for enough for a feed. It's not my first time around bimbullas, but my first taste a year earlier had not gone well. Post-harvest, I'd been left to my own devices with them, and in the kitchen at Attica I had cooked them the way a chef would typically cook a mussel or a clam. I placed them in a hot saucepan for a quick steam with a tight-fitting lid, until the shells had just begun to open, then ten seconds more. Matt and I had eaten one of the molluscs each and, for a pair of whitefellas, they had been confronting. Gruesome is the sight of a mollusc that oozes blood. These were full of haemo-globin, slightly metallic from iodine and as chewy as a beef tendon. *These are not for me,* I'd thought to myself.

Earlier that day Uncle Noel had happily declared, 'We are going to have a big seafood cook-up tonight. We'll go and gather some mutton fish (abalone), some oysters, some prawns and some bim-bullas.' 'Sounds wonderful, Uncle,' I said. Although I'd never be so disrespectful out loud, I glanced at Kylie and Trish Butler and thought, *Not those bloody bimbullas again!*

Uncle is showing me how to find them. 'Use your feet as a radar, Ben. You can feel their shell under your toes.'

Like the harvest of pāua in New Zealand, first you see none, then you see them everywhere – but in the case of bimbullas, it's first you feel none, then you feel dozens. Their shells are thick and old, prehistoric-looking. Uncle and I gather enough for the night's feast. In the water, Uncle says, 'When we were children, these were our food. We'd be starving but the bimbullas would always nourish us. My brothers and I would walk hours from our home to gather them.'

Uncle's story echoes that of his cousin, Uncle Bruce, from further south. 'After the Great Depression, forced off their lands around Mallacoota, to live on the islands and headlands of the Wallagaraugh River, without the offer of work, and starving, our people survived off bimbullas and mutton fish.'

The stars race across the great big old sky, the silhouettes of undressing trees echoing the music of the forest, our voices interrupting the gentle crackle as the fire dies down. Uncle Noel says, 'You see that, that's the embers we are looking for to cook bimbullas and oysters. That's why we've used spotted gum; it burns down to large coals. You must always select the right wood to cook the right food.'

The night before, as Uncle had cooked a whole mullet, he told me a story of the food of his people. 'We only fish for mullet when the bloodwood tree is flowering. That's when the mullet is fat. But we don't use that tree for the fire because it burns to embers, not ash. For ash, we use acacia wood.'

Eventually the fire died down and Uncle placed the mullet – its guts, scales, its everything intact – in the centre of a slight indentation in the ground, and buried the big fish in ash. Landscape entombed in landscape. 'Ben, if we'd used spotted gum there would be too many embers, and it would burn the flesh before the fish was fully cooked.'

Uncle is a fire man and had started the fire earlier using his fire-sticks. He rolled the mullet over in the ash. One and a half hours later it was cooked. He carefully lifted the gnarly, grey fish from its shallow grave and laid it out on a bed of anise myrtle, the heat of the fish against the fragrant leaves perfuming the night air with menthol and spice. Uncle peeled the skin from one side of the fish, taking it from tail to gill in one piece, and removing all traces of ash and scales to reveal glistening, moist white flesh. We devoured it, pulling at the flesh with our hands. It was perfectly cooked, remarkable, ingenious.

In my thirty-odd years of cooking, I'd never seen nor heard of such a technique, and it made me think of the massive amount of time the rest of us waste preparing fish. Any amateur fisherman will tell you that it takes as much time to scale, gut and fillet the fish as it does to catch it. Uncle's respect and connectedness to the animal was humbling. It made my knowledge feel superficial and pretentious, the use of my time misguided.

Finally, Uncle is happy with the embers for the shellfish BBQ. He places the bimbullas over the embers, alongside the other seafood. Standing around the fire, we eat as each of them are ready: first the briny prawns, a just-caught bounce of texture, heads and all. As the oyster shells pop open from the heat to reveal steamed-in-their-own-juices righteousness, we rip off their tops, heads tilting back as we feast, like birds swallowing fish. Kylie has oyster juice on her chin; her eyes shimmer.

Throughout all of this, the bimbullas have been cooking silently. Ten minutes go by, and I'm beginning to think, *Uncle Noel is really cooking those bimbullas*. At fifteen minutes, I'm getting a little nervous and starting to wonder if Uncle has forgotten about them. At twenty minutes, the chef in me desperately wants to remove them from the grill, but I know my place, and I don't say a word or move a muscle. By twenty-five minutes, I think to myself, *Uncle Noel is cooking the shit out of those bimbullas*. At thirty-five minutes, the bimbullas are moribund and gnarled, with black scars from the fire. Uncle announces, 'I think the bimbullas are ready.'

Uncle excitedly passes us a couple straight from the grill. For a moment I juggle the hot shell in my hands, studying the bimbulla's prune-like form. With respect to Uncle, it does not look appetising at all. I pop it in my mouth, and I'm smacked in the face with the profundity of the moment and how little I know. Through its long, smoky grilling it has been completely transformed. It is tender, utterly delicious and nothing like my clumsy attempt to cook bimbullas at Attica. Now I realise my unavoidable mistake: I did not have the cultural context of this food. I hadn't even considered that I'd cooked them wrongly.

Budawang culinary technique was not developed over hundreds of years, like most of western food culture, but many thousands of years. The shell middens around Country are evidence, but I'd been ignorant to the most obvious fact – the living, intimate knowledge of Country, and how best to cook the foods that come from it.

Years later, I shared my first, unsuccessful attempt at cooking bimbullas with Uncle Noel, and he roared with laughter. 'That's Blackfella knowledge,' he said. Every inch of his beautiful face was animated, the age lines a map of his life, beaming with his huge smile.

I experience this time and time again, cooking and talking on Country with Elders and young leaders who are passionate about their food. Over the years I will come to see this continent more clearly. For the first time it will begin to make sense to me. And I'll feel more at home than ever before. The story has always been here, but I was slow to realise it.

The question that I've been asked hundreds of times is: 'What is our national cuisine?' All along, the answer was simple and right there in front of us, tugging at our hearts, unacknowledged, wilfully ignored. Although I shouldn't have to, I'll say it here for the record: Australian food is the food of Aboriginal and Torres Strait Islander peoples. From saltwater people to freshwater people to the islands of Zenadh Kes (Torres Strait), across the hundreds of nations and language groups, it is the ancient living cooking of this country. It is the real 'Australian cuisine'; it is vibrant, vital, distinctive, ingenious, and as regional as romanticised Italy. It is unimaginably more interconnected and sustainable than any other cooking on our planet. It is our guide for the future.

We are a nation stuck between the ignorance of our past and an unimagined future in front of us. But the arm is always outstretched to those who show respect. There's a willingness and generosity, a sense of belonging at last, a kindness as immense as the vast landscape – and this comes after everything that has been said and done to First Nations peoples. It is hard to understand the spirit that remains in the face of it: the innocence, the openness. Goodness, it has made me feel small, like a speck of sand in the desert.

Uncle Noel said to me, as together we cooked a dinner of his foods at Attica: 'I'd really love to see our food being used by all Australians, these superior-quality, natural foods of place. For the improved health and welfare for all people, and for Minga (Mother earth) and Gadu (ocean). To especially help Aboriginal people, but to move forward as one, with our knowledge and our hope to benefit everybody.'

EPILOGUE

I wrote this book in steamy indoor swimming pools, on trams, trains and planes, courtside at basketball games, in airport lounges, hotel lobbies, food courts, cafes and bistros, in a rented house beneath a misty mountain, on the pass at Attica and in the restaurant dining room. But most of my writing time was spent at the dining table at home, coffee cup in hand, headphones on and music blasting, from 5.30am to 9am every day for the past two years. My kids and Kylie have told me that I am a most 'animated writer', witnessing me at different times rocking in my chair, sometimes swearing, occasionally muttering, then singing, often laughing, and sporadically crying into the keyboard. Any stolen moment was useful, and some of the most explosive writing was done in the confines of an economy airplane seat. There is something about not having quite enough time that focuses a person – that's my takeaway from a full-time job as a chef overlaid with my part-time job as a writer.

Recipes are the most direct and honest form of writing that exists. I've applied a little bit of that mustard to this book. There are similarities between the development and writing of recipes, and the forming of an idea for a chapter and the building of that chapter. Both start off with an excess of ideas, which are then honed and refined through testing, nurturing and love. Whether that be one of many elements that make up the recipe for a dish, or multiple paragraphs within chapters: a completed manuscript is but a menu.

As I wrote, a painting by Raymond Pettibon kept appearing in my online feed. In this painting Pettibon, who created early album covers for Black Flag and Sonic Youth, depicts a man frowning, forehead wrinkled, his pointer finger and hand covering his mouth as if concentrating on something that troubles him. To the left of the painting is handwritten: 'I see before me words you should not have written.' My first interaction with this painting felt somewhat ominous, causing me to nervously laugh out loud. The second and third times it popped up, it appeared that Mr Pettibon was attempting to send me a message.

I did not heed his advice. Perhaps I have penned many words I *should not have written*. As if intending to add to my concern, my development editor, Jaclyn Crupi, remarked that 'you write like a man who has nothing and everything to lose'.

My rationale for this approach is that I try not to experience my life as the central focus of everything. By that I mean that I don't view the machinery of life as being so immense and overwhelming that I can't stop at some point, survey the landscape, realise my own moral culpability and do something about it. I refuse to accept that I am a mere puppet in a show. Yesterday at Attica, during a torrential downpour, a dead bird blocked a drain and the dining room began to flood. It would have continued to flood if I hadn't scaled the ladder to the roof, put my hand down the downpipe, and pulled out that rotting carcass. There are times when it is necessary to get rid of your own decay.

I adore writing, and it was one of the only subjects I felt good about in high school, thanks to the encouragement of a great teacher, Mrs Meads. Despite this, putting some of these stories down on the page has not been easy emotionally. The writing depressed me at different moments, especially the handling of others' traumatic stories. Writers have a great responsibility when they share another person's story. And to truly share some of these stories, I had to put myself in their shoes, in an attempt to feel what they must have felt. Occasionally, I found it hard to leave. But writing a book is an epic adventure, with massive highs and lows, and I spoke about it with other writers, learnt that this wasn't so unusual, and that it was vital to write with truth.

Right now, given the serious issues they face, restaurants are easy targets. There are some who hope that ambitious restaurants will dissolve completely. Every year since my first at Attica in 2005, I've read a different version of the old 'fine dining is dead' line. It's a ridiculous thought to hold. Within every group of humans in history there have been people who wanted more. That will never change, and it's not wrong if it's thoughtful. The point of ambitious restaurants is that the change that comes from the best of them has a useful purpose for the future. Eventually, these purposes make their way into the broader culture.

It would be a shame to pretend that it's only restaurants that are facing these shared societal issues – it's all of business. I recall the doping scandals of the 2000s in cycling, where the media and sports fans piled on as if cycling were the only professional sport affected. Since then, cycling has done more than any other sport to improve, and is now perhaps the cleanest in the world, but it is still judged unfairly by its past. Cycling didn't change its culture overnight, so there needs to be some grace extended to the restaurants who are improving, and a little support given to those that have changed, because I can envision a future where the hospitality industry outgrows its past to become one of the most ethical around. It's for the people who share this vision and who will lead us into that future that I write this book.

One of the things I've kept returning to, throughout the years spent working on this book, is that many of the issues facing humanity are deeply entrenched, simply by a lack of imagination. Ultimately, this book is about using imagination and creativity to solve problems. It's also about the search for the meaning in everything. And really this book is not about food; it is about an acute dislike of bullshit.

WITH THANKS

I owe a debt of gratitude to the people below. Thank you all for your honesty when I was being ridiculous, and for your encouragement when I wasn't being ridiculous enough.

To Kylie, my best friend, wife and partner in all things. Without you as the central figure in my life, I never would have written this book; I simply would not have had the courage. You willingly share the risks I have taken. You allowed me to share your pain, and private details from our life together, without reservation. I adore you for your commitment to self-improvement, unselfishness, courage, intellect, sharp wit and absolute love for me and our family. You make every moment better, and I would not want to do any of this without you.

To Kobe, for inspiring me with your dedication to the things you love. For being a much more self-aware, considerate and kind man than I was at your age.

To Ella, for your luminous mind. I know you will be one of the first to read this. For your support and unwavering love, and your jokes at my expense.

To Ruby, for your deep kindness to everyone you meet, for your love of food and adventure (and Frankie and Yuki!). But especially for the way you always see the best in the world.

To my mother, Kaye. Your determination not to pass on trauma to your children is a breathtaking quality that very few possess. Now, as an adult with children of my own, I am so inspired and grateful to you. If I have a backbone, it is because of you. Without your example of honesty and inspiration in my life, I never would have had the courage to write these things. I know at times they have scared you, and for that I'm sorry, but really it's your fault for being the courageous person you are!

To my father, Rob, for showing me that a man can be gentle, emotionally connected and strong. For being the kind of dad who prioritised time spent with his family, rather than down at the pub with his mates. For showing me that creating art is one of the best forms of communication. For demonstrating that it is ok to cry. For always being the finest example of a deeply kind and loving husband, father and friend.

To my sister Tess, your contribution to this book is significant. Thank you for punching holes in my theories, for always having my back with every piece of advice. For the love, intelligence, sensitivity and honesty behind every suggestion. Few people know me better.

Thank you for being my reader, Tess.

To my sister Tamie, one of the themes in this book is resilience and overcoming adversity, and I'd like you to know how much strength and inspiration I take from your life. I am so proud of you.

There's an irony in the fact that, during a time when I was writing critically about food journalists, I became very close friends with a journalist and editor of a newspaper, one of the most admired in this country. As that well-worn cliché goes, it's more about the journey than the destination. The gift of this journey is a new friendship that

I know will be lifelong. We write letters to each other several times a week, sharing the beauty and, on occasion, the pain of our lives. It's a way of making sense of it all. To Erik Jensen, my dear pen pal, your contribution has been immense and more than I could ever ask from a person. Thank you for being my reader.

To Jaclyn Crupi, my development editor. For your belief in this book from the outset. And for not running away when I started crying as I read you those first words. For crying alongside me at nearly every meeting. Thank you for your passion and smarts, and for holding my hand.

To Jane Willson, my publisher. If you hadn't hit me up to write another book, I don't think this book would have ever come to life. Thank you for believing in and supporting this book, even when you didn't really know what it would be. For trusting in my process and letting this book be exactly what I wanted it to be, even when I didn't really know what it would be! I wouldn't have wanted to do this with anyone else.

To Justin Wolfers, only a sensitive, thoughtful person could take on the structural edit of this book. Thank you for being that person, and for graciously accepting the many things I wouldn't allow to be changed, because you have the self-confidence to understand that an author's voice is critical to a book's honesty. This is a better book because of your gentle hand.

To Alison Cowan, to have an absolute expert editing this book who understands the dual worlds of food and words so sharply has been one of the great pleasures of this project. I'm indebted to you.

To Paul Kremer and Rebecca Stewart, for allowing me to use the stunning artwork that graces the book's cover, I am so honoured and proud. And for the friendship that is a result of this project. Thank you so much.

I'd like to thank every single person who has worked at Attica over the past nineteen years. I'm really sorry I can't acknowledge each of you by name, but I want you to know that I'm grateful to you. Especially those who put their heart and soul into making the restaurant what it is, I'm deeply indebted to you. But also, the small number of people who it didn't work out for, I took lessons from that too and wish you the best.

To the hospitality industry, and to every person who has ever cooked or served me a great meal, you warm my heart, you nourish me, both physically and psychologically. I hope you know you matter, that your work is important. I appreciate you. Thank you.

With special thanks to the following people and organisations:

Adam Briggs
Al Parton
Alon White
Andrew McConnell
Andri and Chris Staddon
Anna and Morry Schwartz
Australian Marine Conservation Society (AMCS)
Brian McGinn
Bruce Dunlevie
Cam MacKenzie
Colin Page and Sue Wheelhouse
DabsMyla
Dom Robinson
Drusilla Ratnam
Dwayne Bannon-Harrison
Eddie Walton
Fabian Sfameni
Fleur Studd, official recipe taster

Gary McBean
George Wintle
Hamish Blake and Zoë Foster Blake
Hugh van Cuylenberg
Jacinda Ardern
James Snelleman
Jane Kennedy
Jane Lopes
Jane Morrow, Sue Bobbermein, Daniel New, Megan Pigott,
    Ashleigh Jordan, Eleanor O'Connor, Mary-Jane House,
    Matt Hoy and the entire Murdoch books team – from editorial,
    marketing, design and sales
Jane Tewson
Jason Chong
Jo Barrett
John Shewry
John Wardle
Johnny Abegg
Kevin McSteen
Kyran Wheatley
Lennox Hastie
Lisa Donovan
Mac Forbes
Mariam Issa
Mark and Helen Limacher, mentors and flat-out legends
Matt Boyle
Matty Matheson
Max Veenhuyzen
Michael Kane
Murrundindi
Myf Warhust

Patagonia
Paul Sullivan
Reko Rennie
Rhys Nicholson
Ryan Shelton
Sharon Winsor
Simon Bell (aka Bolognese Luke Skywalker), official recipe tester
Simon Gerrans
'Solid citizens' Ira Kaplan, Georgia Hubley and James McNew,
    of Yo La Tengo
Stephanie McGee, GoodFish Program Manager, AMCS
Tara Wilkinson and John Garnaut
Tim Bartley
Tony Hawk
Trish Nelson
Uncle Bruce Pascoe
Uncle Noel and Trish Butler
Uncle Tracy, Uncle Mark, Uncle Kerry and Auntie Claire
Vincent Jaillette
Will Horton
Zan Rowe

PLAYLISTS

Uses for Obsession

Every moment of inspiration, every word written, every fear and every dream was put down on the page to music. This is the soundtrack to this book. I made it as I wrote, and it follows highs and lows of a person's life – perfectly imperfect. Please shuffle.

Attica Summer Camp

A comin-outta-the-tunnel-into-the-light playlist, designed for the good times. Casual festivities, car rides with the homies, or smoked New Zealand king salmon with dill feasts, I got you here – go ahead and shuffle.

Attica Dining Room

The ultimate dinner party playlist, if your dinner party happens to be at our restaurant. Built following my 1-in-10 playlist philosophy, where listeners connect to the occasional pop song I've thrown in. We all belong. Please shuffle.